GIVE YOUR ADD TEEN A CHANCE

A Guide for Parents of Teenagers with Attention Deficit Disorder

LYNN WEISS, PHD

P.O. Box 35007, Colorado Springs, Colorado 80935

OUR GUARANTEE TO YOU

We believe so strongly in the message of our books that we are making this quality guarantee to you. If for any reason you are disappointed with the content of this book, return the title page to us with your name and address and we will refund to you the list price of the book. To help us serve you better, please briefly describe why you were disappointed. Mail your refund request to: PiñonPress, P.O. Box 35002, Colorado Springs, CO 80935.

Cover illustration: Celia Johnson/The Stock Illustration
Source

All illustrations in this book are composites of real situations,
and any resemblance to people living or dead is coincidental.

Weiss, Lynn.
   Give your ADD teen a chance : a guide for parents of
   teenagers with attention deficit disorder / Lynn Weiss.
      p. cm.
      ISBN 08910-99778
      1. Attention-deficit disorder in adolescence—Popular
   works.
   I. Title.
   RJ506.H9W4455   1996
   616.85'89'00835—dc20

Library of Congress Catalog Card Number: 96-8057

Printed in the United States of America

2 3 4 5 6 7 8 9 10 11 12 / 05 04 03 02 01 00

CONTENTS

Give Your ADD Teen a Chance
is dedicated to my son, Mendel,
as he enters adulthood.
He provided me with a reason to become involved
with ADD in the first place.
He taught me much of what I know
about living and guiding a young person
through the teen years when ADD is a part of his life.
Finally, Mendel serves as a model
for the hope that ADD can be lived with,
coped with, and turned into an asset.
I feel thankful that Mendel is in my life.

ACKNOWLEDGMENTS

Thanks to all the teens who have shared their lives with me. By being themselves they have taught me to honor and respect our youth and to learn much of what is important for them to grow into adulthood as responsible, capable people who can live up to their potential.

Growing up with my sons gave me a firsthand opportunity to see just how fine young people can be. Thanks to Mendel for letting me share aspects of his story. He's a real winner who weathered ADD and growing up. And thanks to Aaron for helping us gain insight into the many ways that youth mature.

Without the expertise, guidance, and special talents of my outliner and editor, Janis Dworkis, the orderliness of this book would be compromised. As someone with ADD, I know the value of working with an organized person. Thanks, Janis.

My gratitude includes thanks to the Comma Queen, Mary Schultz, my copy editor. In addition, her expertise as a school counselor provided us with the opportunity to share of experiences with teens. She, too, treasures the youth with whom she worked. Thanks, Mary, for being who you are.

My agent, Mary Kelly, continues to believe in my work and endeavors tirelessly to provide me with opportunities to share what I know and believe in. Thanks, Mary.

I am pleased to work with my new Piñon editor, Traci Mullins. Your attitude, Traci, and obvious delight in what you do makes gathering the details of publishing palatable. Thanks.

Finally, thanks to all my friends for their enthusiasm and support during the writing of this book, including Wendy Richardson, Jo Schaefer, and Debbie Sager. Thanks, friends.

꧁ ⚬⚬ ꧂

CHAPTER ONE

ADD IS SOMETHING YOU ARE

A Unique Style of Brain Wiring

I'll never forget Carrie Curtis. I was in Oklahoma City, in a blustery storm in the middle of winter, walking toward the lecture hall where I would soon be speaking about ADD in teenagers. Somewhat disheveled, Carrie rushed up to me and said with an urgent tone that she needed to speak with me. I reached my arm around her and pulled both of us inside the building as she started to tell me her story.

Carrie told me about her thirteen-year-old daughter and her fifteen-year-old son, both ADD. As her words tumbled out, I could feel her desperation.

"I'm so scared for Sissy," she said. "She's sweet and kind, but she gets yelled at a lot at school because she never gets there with her homework, even if she's done it at home. After school she just goes to her room and stares at her books. They rarely get read. And Jake, he's mad. He hates school and talks about quitting. I'm afraid of what he'll do. He's not dumb. But he's never done very well. And he's always had a big mouth. Yesterday he told his teacher off. His teacher had embarrassed him in front of the whole class, telling him he could have done better if he'd just tried harder."

Carrie said her son had come home and told her about the incident. He said that something just snapped inside him. He went right up to that teacher and told her she didn't know how to teach and that he was sick and tired of someone criticizing kids who are doing the best they can. Jake told the teacher he was through trying to do his best in school. He said nothing seemed to help anyway.

"I don't want my kids to fail. I try to help them, but nothing works. I've tried everything. No one has been able to help me. Please tell me what I can do." She continued without waiting for an answer, "I feel awful. All I've done for years now is talk to the school and try to help my kids feel okay about themselves. They're wonderful kids. I love them. But I can't seem to fix things. They both have had such a hard time. I hurt for them. I'm afraid things will never, ever, get any better. And I don't know how much longer I can hang on."

While Carrie was talking, my mind raced, my stomach churned, and I felt tears welling up in my eyes. For a minute all I could do was reach out and hug her, saying, "I know, I know."

Carrie's story sounded all too familiar. I remembered my own fears and desperation at times as I reared an ADD child. I also recalled my own feelings as an ADD child—feelings of frustration and failure. And I remembered the many, many people like Carrie who had come to me over the years with the same basic story.

I took Carrie's hand and said, "Come on. Sit down. I'll try to help you and the others in the audience figure out steps you can take to help your ADD teens. I'll share what I've learned. The reason I can do this now is because things are okay for me and my family. There *is* hope. When I was in your shoes, I needed someone to tell me what I'm telling you. I couldn't feel it for myself then. So I do know what you're going through."

When I started speaking at the lecture that night, I said, "Those of you who are here because you are the parents of a young person who is ADD need to know that your story is the story of everyone else in this room—and it's my story, too. We're all in this together. We'll help one another, and together we'll make our way through to a successful outcome.

"I am ADD. And I've made it. My son is ADD. And he's making it. Many of you are ADD, and you can make it. And the young people here who are ADD can make it, too.

"I know you've had a rough time in many cases. I also know that you have many wonderful talents and gifts. You are smart. And you can learn how to use your natural skills to feel good about yourself and make this world a better place. There's not a person here tonight who is a failure or a throwaway. So just get that through your head.

"Now, let's start with what this ADD stuff is really all about and what in the world you can do with it."

As I spoke these beginning words, I saw parents' anxious expressions soften a bit with the hope that maybe someone really understood and could help them find some answers. And I saw interest on the previously blank faces of the teenagers who had been dragged to a meeting they feared would just make them feel bad—an all-too-familiar feeling. Young people who felt hopeless, angry, depressed, and inadequate began to respond to the glimmer of hope they were offered.

By the end of the evening I knew that, although I would leave Oklahoma City the next morning, these people would remain to help one another—both emotionally and practically—to correct situations that should never have been a problem in the first place.

JOIN ME AT THE KITCHEN TABLE

If you and I were to sit down at your kitchen table to talk one-on-one, chances are your story would be similar to Carrie's and to mine. Because we've lived through many of the same experiences, we would understand one another quickly. I know a lot about what you feel, because I've felt the same way.

I know these things, not just because I've spent more than thirty years as a psychotherapist, the last ten specializing in ADD in teens and adults, but because my son is ADD, and I am too. I know what it's like from your perspective as the parent of a teen with ADD, and I know what it's like from the teen's perspective.

11

I know that to really understand the whole ADD picture, you must know this: *ADD is a neurobiochemical style of brain wiring with which a person is born.*

Think about the implications of that statement. No matter what your neighbors think, ADD is not an excuse you use to explain your child's behavior. No matter what your own parents say, ADD is not a fad that you fall back on when you're too tired to deal with your children. And no matter what your friends say, ADD is not the description of every child who is active and requires energy from a teacher.

Think about it again: ADD is a neurobiochemical style of brain wiring. Your children can't change their brain wiring any more than you can change yours, no matter how many times they are told to "just try harder" in school.

And ADD appears to be genetic. That means that one or both of your child's parents are likely to be ADD. Because of this, many of us who are the parent of an ADD teen are more familiar with ADD than we might suspect. And we have our own personal difficulties and issues to deal with.

This may mean that even if you haven't been diagnosed with ADD, learning what your child is going through might remind you of many trials and tribulations you have suffered over the course of your own life. This can make it difficult for you to confront your child's struggles. But the first thing both of you need to realize is that ADD isn't something you *have*. Nor is it something that's wrong with you. Instead, it's something you *are*. It is simply the way in which your brain is "wired."

Undiagnosed, an ADD person doesn't realize why it's so hard for him to fit into a culture and educational system primarily designed and run by people who are not ADD. Most of us who are ADD are not interested in building systems that control others. Neither are we interested in administrating anything. We tend to be the dreamers, the ones who express from our hearts, do things spontaneously, and, in some instances, conscientiously work within a structure that fits us. Being extremely sensitive, we are empathetic, sometimes wearing our hearts on our sleeves.

Also, we use a lot of energy to fend off the intrusions of a world that tries to make us what we're not.

The label ADD (Attention Deficit *Disorder*) needs to be changed because ADD is not a *disorder*, it is a *difference*. Those people who are not wired like us are also different—different from us. But they are not labeled.

It will take time until differences are truly understood, rather than judged. Meanwhile, you must still be content with raising your ADD teen to survive, to manage, and to excel in a system that often doesn't understand her. You, too, might find the going tough because of your own ADD issues.

If you are ADD, you may have just begun to figure out that ADD explains some of the issues you have always dealt with. If you know you are ADD, then chances are you probably figured that out as an adult. I, like you, realized only a short while ago that ADD is the reason for many of the difficulties I have had in my life. Knowing this about ourselves helps us to empathize with our children, even though we might simultaneously be dealing with our own struggles to overcome some of the effects of being ADD.

If you are not ADD, you might find this whole discussion confusing, or you might not understand that the way you've been used to doing things is not the *only* way to accomplish tasks and reach goals. You may have exhausted yourself, spending a lot of time trying to get your ADD child to be something different from what she is, going against her natural grain. As both of you struggled, your frustration level probably rose. You might have felt as if you were "at the end of your rope."

In any case, all is not lost. We're going to use this book to sort the whole story out.

MY STORY

For most of my professional life I had no idea what ADD is—much less that I was and still am ADD.

In a way that was good, because I expected the same out of myself that I expected out of everyone else. But it was definitely not good in the sense that I used a great amount of energy over-achieving and working, just to keep up. Until recently, there wasn't much time left for me to just "live" or enjoy a good quality of life.

I want to tell you my story so that you will see some of the struggles that face an ADD person and how well things can go when that person finds a good "fit" between professional skills and work style.

I was always a very sensitive and introspective person. I knew I looked at things differently from the majority of people around me. I even solved problems in a unique way. Because I didn't live in an environment that respected or valued those differences, I learned very early to hide them.

I worked hard at school to become the professional I was told I should become. I wanted to help people, and for some time I wanted to be a doctor. But I couldn't figure out how to memorize the information I needed to remember in order to get the grades for acceptance into medical school. And I wasn't able to read well enough to get high enough test scores on the required medical school entrance exams.

Nevertheless, my drive to help others, and myself, remained. When I flunked out of science and math courses at an undergraduate level it forced me to the counseling center. I took tests to reveal where my interests and aptitudes lay, and I found that the fields of sociology and psychology were compatible with my interests. But psychology is also based on a lot of linear learning and memory work. Although I instantly understood the principles of clinical psychology and counseling, and even figured many of them out myself before I was taught about them, I wasn't able to manage experimental psychology. So I majored in sociology, thinking that I might be able to help people out that way. But I was far too sensitive for social work, at least in those days.

After graduation I worked for a while as an artist and employment interviewer before returning to school to earn my master's degree in anthropology — the best training to work with people I've ever received. Though I didn't know it then, my study of sociology and anthropology was the first "open door" that highlighted the relative differences between people. It showed me the effects that cultural beliefs have on learning. In fact, it provided the groundwork for me to understand ADD almost three decades later.

As I was finishing my courses in anthropology, the National Institute of Mental Health decided to offer three fellowships to study clinical mental health techniques at the University of Washington Medical School's Department of Psychiatry. I received one of those fellowships. That's when I discovered that I was smart. How did I figure that out? Because the whole training program was a hands-on clinically based learning opportunity. It was the best way in the world for me to learn. My mind buzzed happily, active and alert for the first time ever in school.

Instead of fighting to stay awake in class and feeling frustrated and depressed because I had to work so hard, I breezed through two wonderful years of clinical training. From there I began to work in the community mental health movement of the 1960s and, again, I found I was very effective and somehow "automatically" knew what to do.

Then followed more than thirty years' work as a psychotherapist, marriage-and-family counselor, play therapist, teacher, and educational and mental health consultant. In the early 1970s, I completed my doctoral studies through the University of Santa Barbara, a primarily hands-on program.

For seven years, my work included hosting a radio talk show in Dallas, Texas. Three hours a day, five days a week, I talked and answered questions of callers who wanted to know how to make their lives better. I also worked as a television commentator and was interviewed myself on many radio and TV shows.

All of this came easily for me.

It was through my experience on talk radio that I began my work of addressing ADD in adults. Thanks to callers who responded by the score to comments I made on the show about ADD, I recognized a huge need that demanded attention. And I have been attempting to help meet that need ever since.

MY SON'S STORY

My son was in fourth grade when I realized he was ADD. That was when his teacher said, in a scolding voice, "He could do it if he'd just pay attention."

This comment followed six years of pain and frustration for my son and me that began with his first preschool reading-readiness program. From that moment on his life had been hell. I watched this enthusiastic, very bright, active little boy begin a path of suffering that I was unprepared at the time to deal with.

By fourth grade I realized he was ADD and dyslexic, and I took over. I became an advocate for him. I made it my goal to find out all I could about what made him tick and what could be done to utilize the wonderful skills and talents he possessed.

In those days, we were taught that ADD would disappear at puberty. But puberty came and went and my son's ADD certainly did not. By that time I had learned to trust my own observations and intuition more than anything I could read in a book or hear from any expert. So I continued to deal with my son's ADD—thank goodness! With the help of a wonderful tutor who ran interference, we demanded a school conference. At that conference—which I will *never* forget—I ran into an administrator who had no idea at all how children learn or that they learn in many different ways; a counselor who summed up my son's entire problem with, "His self-esteem is low"; and his previous teacher who continued to say, "He's lazy. He doesn't pay attention."

Luckily for me and my son, one more person was present at that conference—a newly hired fifth-grade teacher who listened and cared. He said he'd like to work with my son. He wasn't put off by hyperactivity, restlessness, impulsivity, or a kid who was depressed and felt like a failure.

For two years during fifth and sixth grades this man resurrected my son's hopes that maybe he could actually learn "something" in school. (Now, as my son prepares to graduate from college, this teacher is one of only three people from my son's twelve years of public school whom he plans to visit. My son says he wants him to see "how good he's turned out.")

By middle school we began working with medication for my son. In retrospect I wish we'd begun sooner. The medication helped him a lot with his behavior and attentiveness. As he later said, "Mom, I always knew what to do. I even wanted to do it. But I couldn't get myself to do it." That's ADD!

Also, by middle school I had become a lot more aware about how an ADD person learns. I positioned myself between my son and the school, parceling out work at a rate and level he could manage. And I told the school what I was doing.

At first I told them he could only do thirty to forty-five minutes of homework a night; I wouldn't allow any more. As he grew older, I lengthened that time. There was no point in expecting a child who had been "in prison" all day to come home and do more of the same kind of work that wasn't really helping him to learn in the first place.

I spent time reading his work to him and verbally providing him information. I helped him write papers so he had a model to follow. Slowly he took over more and more of the writing until he could do the whole paper for himself.

I made sure he developed extracurricular activities. It turned out to be football that kept him alive, even in college, until he found a career that motivated him to do the paperwork and other types of learning that are very difficult for him.

In the world outside of libraries, desks, papers, and pencils, my son shines. Initially he learned to manage his behavior with the help of medication. Impulse and temper control became habits. He found ways to protect his hypersensitivity to avoid getting into trouble. He learned to organize by systems that work for him. He learned to study in ways he could manage. All of this took many years.

Now, on the threshold of college graduation, he knows who he is, what he likes, and he feels good about himself. He has a career direction, good friends, and knows how to network. He's successful—just as he was always meant to be.

DISCOVERING MY OWN ADD

It wasn't until my son was in college and I had spent seven or eight years intensely involved with ADD in adults that I realized I am ADD—very ADD. Up until that time I truly believed I should *easily* have been able to accomplish the things I did, despite the high cost. I also felt I could have experienced different outcomes from my failures if I had just worked harder.

I am an example of an overachieving, incredibly disciplined person who worked very, very hard to do everything I did. In fact, I worked so hard that I lost touch completely with the fun-loving, creative part of myself that is the natural me. I mention this because the incidence of ADD is much higher than is generally thought, but it's often camouflaged by overachievement or misdiagnosed as depression, anxiety, or mood disorders, chemical-dependency problems or other addictions, oppositional and defiant behavior, and many other "mental health" and behavioral problems. In reality, these conditions and problems are frequently the result of ADD that the person has not yet learned to accommodate and deal with in a healthy manner.

Knowing that I am ADD has helped me to acknowledge the problems I've faced throughout my life. I know more now than I ever did before about ADD by studying myself and clients in my clinical practice.

I can relate to you and what you might be facing in yourself. I also know that many of the difficulties I faced with my son during adolescence are similar to what you have faced.

YOUR GOALS AND CHOICES AS A PARENT

You make choices every day of every year that directly involve the raising of your child. These choices are based on the goals you want to achieve as a parent in relation to your child. By adolescence your teen must have a say if you are to achieve long-term goals that are in his or her best interest.

As a parent, you decide how to use your time and energy and

how to steer your teen to use his time and energy. You also make choices about how the two of you will relate to one another. And one of the first things you must realize is that *parenting is not about forcing*. It's about *guiding* and *enjoying* your teen—not about being in control all the time.

I, like you, was constantly making such choices. One that especially stands out in my mind had to do with my son's style of learning and his need to feel successful. It was really about his ADD.

Every night when he brought his schoolwork home, he had to decide how much time he would spend studying. To make that decision, I first sat down with him and asked how much time he wanted to spend on his schoolwork. On occasion we talked about the kind of grades he wanted and how much time he would need to study to accomplish that goal. Other times we discussed his interests and how much time he wanted to commit to them. Sometimes we talked about his future: college, jobs, hopes, dreams. We talked about how he felt, how hard it would be for him to study, and what he needed to feel really good about himself.

Then I sat down to think about what *I* needed to feel successful as a parent. I thought about what I wanted for my son and how I viewed his talents and interests. I concluded that whatever the decision, it had to reflect what was best for my *son* rather than what I needed in order to look like a good parent. I also decided that my job was to give him information and leave the decisions up to him.

I knew that the most important goal for every teenager is to feel good about himself and have a way to utilize his talents and develop his interests.

My son and I talked. I shared my thinking and he shared his. He decided on a moderate amount of time for homework and studying. That amount was not enough to yield A's or even B's in many cases, but it was enough to keep him in school. It was enough to give him time for activities he liked. In the long run I have no doubt that his decision was right.

Now, at the end of his college education and with the

developmental maturity that years have brought, my son wants to get A's. He's not always able to achieve them, but he sees the importance of making good grades. He's come through with a desire to learn, though books are still not his best or favorite way to gain information. But he tolerates them. He is truly in command of himself and has the ability to make choices that are in his best interest.

GOALS FOR YOU TO SET

Because of my experience I want to help you reach your goals. They may be similar to mine or they may be different. That doesn't matter. The process stays the same. As the parent, you are the one who sets the goals for yourself and for what you want to see reflected in your family.

Remember: A teen is a state of mind and a level of development. It is a time of transition from childhood to independent adulthood. That means that your job and your goals, if they are to be successful, must reflect the normal requirements of that stage of life.

You want to work yourself out of the job of caring for your child's everyday needs. You want him to learn to do that and more for himself. When you are successful in helping him learn to fend for himself, your job as a parent will have shifted. Then you and your child can walk parallel paths as two responsible people who like and respect each other. You still have a relationship with your child, but it's not based on dependency; it's based on mutual respect and caring.

My goal for this book is to help you discover ways to be a wise guide during these changing years. I want to help you understand the needs of your growing child and find his assets and strengths while compensating for the liabilities and weaknesses that ADD brings. I want you to know that you do not walk this path alone.

Most important, I want you to walk away with a feeling of hope—glad that your teen is who he is.

❧——❧

CHAPTER TWO

WHAT IT'S LIKE TO BE THE PARENT OF AN ADD TEEN
Validating Your Emotions and Needs

Richard is exhausted after staying up late to help his thirteen-year-old son, Michael, finish a Scout project. Michael wanted to join the troop his best friend was in, but since then, it's been nothing but struggle.

Richard has a feeling he and his son are "flunking" Scouts. There's something they just don't understand about getting all the pieces together. Michael wants to do the projects, but there always seems to be something left unfinished. Richard tries to help Michael with the timing, but somehow it never comes together completely. Richard sees the other Scouts completing their projects, but he has no idea how they do it.

Michael's family has known about his ADD since he was in third grade. When Michael was younger, Richard was able to help him, but each year it's become more difficult. Since Michael started junior high, both father and son feel frustrated and overwhelmed. Richard feels he's letting his son down. There's something he ought to be able to teach Michael—something he knows other dads can do—but he can't figure out what it is.

Michael is starting to complain that he wants out of Scouts— *after* Richard and his wife spent money on the uniform and project supplies. Richard vacillates between saying, "Oh, well. It's been a learning experience," and feeling deeply worried that

Michael will never amount to anything because of his disorganization. One day he scolds Michael, the next he wants to cry for his son. He doesn't know whether to push Michael and try to make him finish the year or tell him it's okay to quit.

Richard feels terribly guilty because he hasn't been able to give his son the key to success—stick-to-itiveness. When he shares his frustration with other dads, they nod their heads and say, "My son complains, too, but he can do it when he puts his mind to it." Richard knows it doesn't work that way in his family. And he feels responsible.

LaTrell, at age sixteen, was a beautiful young woman with a spectacular figure. I saw her as an adult, and she and her parents related the following story.

LaTrell had always struggled in school; outside of school she seemed smart enough. No one realized that her problems stemmed primarily from ADD. Her parents noticed her self-esteem deteriorating, especially after she could no longer be a member of drill team after flunking algebra and barely passing French.

The one thing LaTrell always talked about was modeling. From the time she turned twelve she had pored over fashion magazines, spent lots of time in the mall trying on clothes, and created amazing "looks" with her accessorized wardrobe. At first, her parents thought her interest would pass, but it didn't. So, at sixteen, her parents decided to let her take modeling lessons.

Because LaTrell daydreamed a lot and didn't pay much attention to what was going on around her, she and her parents agreed she would wait a year before getting her driver's license. That meant someone had to drive her to modeling class. LaTrell's mom had as much trouble getting ready on time as she did, but together they managed to make it to most of the classes.

When LaTrell began to get modeling jobs, it was another story. The unpredictable schedule and the need to keep up with make-up and accessories seemed more than either LaTrell or her mom could manage. LaTrell's mom felt frustrated, got angry, and finally threw up her hands. She was as upset with herself as she was with LaTrell, and she felt panicked that her daughter's last hope for success was going down the drain.

Zack's parents thought they had it made during his teen years. He did very well in school, focused exceptionally well on his class work, took tests well, and generally excelled—until he got out of college. Then, at twenty-one, Zack fell apart. He couldn't figure out how to get a job. He didn't know what he wanted to do and finally went back to graduate school. Again he did exceptionally well and his professors thought he was wonderful.

As long as Zack was in a structured environment—such as school—he did well. But his parents came to realize he had little ability to "go with the flow." His social skills were limited, and he could only deal with one person at a time. Zack was hyperfocused, resulting from a form of ADD that is less well known than the hyperactive forms. (See chapter 4.)

Because of his parent's worries, Zack finally agreed to be evaluated. What they found is that although Zack is technically no longer a teenager, he is still functioning much as a teen, trying to learn how to stand on his own two feet independent of his parents. With this information his parents vacillate between thinking they should cut all financial support so he'll have to face the "cold, cruel world" and feeling that perhaps he truly cannot figure out how to negotiate the many-faceted requirements of everyday life. They don't know where to turn.

Do the feelings of these three sets of parents sound familiar? As a parent of an ADD child myself, I know they do. You are not alone. For each of these stories, there are thousands more like them.

The good news is that most of these ADD teens do make it in life. Families come to realize that although their teens may have taken longer to find a niche, they do reach adulthood and take on responsibility or at least accomplish it with proper recognition of ADD and training to remove the obstacles to successful living.

The one exception are those teens who do not have enough hope, support, or direction to stay healthy. Drugs, alcohol, and addiction take a toll as many teens self-medicate to avoid their pain.

Many of these teens manage to escape long-term problems, but some don't. Some begin a cycle of involvement with the criminal-justice system, primarily because of drug and alcohol problems and impulsivity. Teens who are ADD are in no way more prone than other teens to become serious criminals, but far too many end up in jail or prison because of thoughtless acts and drug and alcohol involvement.

I'm saying this right up front because I know it's on your mind. As parents of ADD teens we have all prayed, "Keep my child out of trouble." No one wants his or her teen to end up in prison or with a chemical addiction.

Some parents have poor habits themselves and model behavior that directly leads their teens into inappropriate ways of problem solving. But most parents, including you, do try. The fact that you're reading this book means you are trying to understand your teen and how best to help him or her.

Sometimes there are too many factors working against a teen, with too little information available to the parents to make knowledgeable choices. For that reason, I want to be sure you have as much information as possible to help you guide your teen to responsible adulthood.

YOUR EMOTIONAL ROLLER COASTER

One thing is for sure; emotions tend to run high in ADD families. That's true whether you are *also* ADD and haven't managed to solve many of the same problems confronting your teen, or whether you are *not* ADD and have great difficulty understanding your child.

One minute things seem okay. The next, all hell breaks loose.

One day your teen studies productively for a test and receives a good grade, and you feel as if a physical weight has been lifted from you. You relax and stop worrying for a few hours. Maybe you curl up and read a magazine or treat yourself to a long bath. The next day you discover a crumpled detention slip on the floor by your teen's bed, under some library books he said he'd return. That familiar ache in your chest and stomach grabs you so quickly it almost takes your breath away.

It feels like you're on a roller coaster that has suddenly dropped after a long climb. You are not alone with those highs and lows. Just knowing this can bring a certain measure of comfort. Let's look at some of your emotions.

Frustration

Frustration runs rampant in families with ADD. But as you learn more about ADD, frustration will decrease. Until that time, the behaviors and problems associated with ADD are often defined as laziness, inadequacy, or lack of motivation. Parents of ADD teens get frustrated because they feel those are not really the issues.

If you think things are bad now for those with ADD, they were much worse a few years ago when the experts told parents that ADD went away at puberty. That expectation caused parents tremendous frustration. If ADD was supposed to go away at puberty, what was the matter with their teen? Those parents who recognized on their own that their child's ADD had not gone away felt tremendous frustration with the professional establishment who didn't agree with or believe them.

I'm sure you've already run into your share of difficulties with your child's school. You may even have had problems at the preschool age if your child is hyperactive and impulsive. But now that adolescence is upon you, I bet your frustration level has risen drastically.

Our culture perpetuates the idea that teens ought to act like self-controlled, responsible adults. Since teens are not adults, and far from that maturity level in some cases, there's a built-in frustration factor when parenting a child through this period.

ADD teens tend to take even longer than their peers to grow into maturity in certain areas. Unfortunately, those areas tend to relate to schoolwork, organizational skills, and behavior control — areas significantly affected by ADD. Consequently, the expectations our society has for all teens are even more unrealistic for ADD teens. That becomes a major source of frustration for parents.

Don't forget the possibility that your own level of sensitivity is high and you react intensely to your teen and her difficulties.

After all, ADD is genetic and there is great likelihood that you, too, are ADD. In that case your teen may serve as a painful reminder of all the difficulties you experienced at that age and have not been able to solve to this day. What a setup for frustration!

I know you want *so* badly for your teen to be successful, and it may seem that the harder you try the worse things get. It's very frustrating to feel you can't control what's happening around you. In a way, that frustration measures how much you want for your teen and how inadequate you feel to make that happen.

Of course this is an issue during the teen years whether or not your child deals with ADD. Your frustration is normal, and your inability to do much about your situation is normal. But there are many things you can do to help your teen — and that's what we'll be discussing throughout this book.

Anger
Anger lies right next to frustration — and I mean anger *at* your teen. Feelings of helplessness and fear lead to anger because anger is a cover-up emotion, a shield that protects us from what we don't want to feel — helpless, hopeless, frustrated, and fearful.

When you deal with threats to one of the most valuable people in your life, your teen, you are going to feel the most challenged. It's common to strike out at the person for whom you are afraid. Because you want the best for your teen, you are likely to want him to somehow fix the situation. And when that doesn't happen, you feel angry. Your whole emotional system becomes energized toward solving the problem at hand.

Your anger is partly based on the myth that your teen could fix his situation if he would just try hard enough. But the truth is, if your teen could fix his situation, he would have done it long ago.

You may also be angry at yourself, fearing that you've somehow failed and that *you* could have done something to fix your teen's situation if *you* had just tried harder. When you're hurting from this kind of self-blame, it's fairly normal to yell at your child or make unrealistic demands such as, "You *will* bring your grades up this semester." Threats usually accompany this kind of demand, such as, "If you don't, you're grounded for the rest of the year."

Even as you're acting out this anger, I'm sure you realize there's a more positive and productive way to deal with it. That awareness also brings a sense of frustration.

If you are ADD but have not recognized it, you may be particularly susceptible to feeling angry because you still have your own difficulties to understood before you can think about ironing them out. If you do realize you are ADD, you are more likely to have compassion for your teen and be easier on yourself. It's one of the benefits of recognizing how you are wired.

Guilt

You might as well realize that guilt stalks every parent at some time, whether or not your children are ADD. Guilt is even more prevalent when ADD is a part of your life. You probably feel guilty about your reactions to your teen—for being angry at him, for saying things that are better left unsaid, and for making threats that are a sign of frustration but useless to help your teen. You may also feel guilty about what you think you should have been able to do or not do to help your teen avoid his current problems.

There are two kinds of guilt—burdensome guilt and realistic guilt. If you've been taught you *should* be able to do something, and you believe you should be able to do it, then you'll feel guilty if you don't achieve it. If you react in ways you've been taught you should *not* react, you will feel guilty. Both situations create burdensome guilt. In reality, you can only do what you are capable of doing.

On the other hand, if you do not exercise the control you want to exercise and are capable of exercising, you will feel legitimate guilt. That kind of guilt reminds you to be true to yourself.

Much of the guilt suffered by parents of ADD teens is burdensome guilt. As you learn your limits and your teen's limits, you have to dismiss this form of guilt by giving yourself and your teen permission to be who and what you are naturally and normally. When you give yourself the benefit of acceptance, many of your guilty feelings will disappear.

Feelings of Inadequacy

Feelings of inadequacy haunt most parents of ADD teens. Sometimes it's because we can't get our teen to do something we think she should do or want her to do. But many times it's a reflection of our deep feelings of inadequacy that come from our own difficulties with ADD. Even very successful adults who are ADD feel this inner gnawing of inadequacy reflected in such comments as, "People will find out I'm a fraud" and "I feel like a fake who will be found out." Is it any wonder that feeling inadequate as a parent falls right in line?

Abject Helplessness

Abject helplessness is likely to hit you from time to time when you don't have any idea what else you can do to help your child. In the dark of the night, after you've exhausted all your resources, when you're tired and alone, you may sink into this frightening, depressing state of mind. Though it will change in time, it is truly an awful feeling.

When it hits you, your best action is to do absolutely nothing in relation to your child. Take care of *yourself* until it passes. Although the feeling is related to your child, it is a sign that *you* are in need of nurturing. Later, you can seek advice from others who are farther down the road. Then you will not feel so alone and helpless.

Fear and Grief

Fear that verges on terror is probably one of the worst emotions you can experience. If this happens, ask yourself, *What are my worst fears about my child?* Be honest. What do you fear most about your child's future?

Like most parents of ADD children, you have deep fears that you probably have never shared with anyone about the way your child's life will turn out. You are not crazy, and your child's future is not hopeless. You need to know that all parents of all children have these fears from time to time. As the parent of an ADD teen, you are likely to face them more often.

The two most basic fears are that your child will not live up to his potential or be able to fulfill his potential and that your child won't make it in life.

You've recognized your teen's potential since she was a toddler. But for years you may have watched that potential become compromised as she was forced to spend much of her time trying to do things that didn't come easily and didn't fit her natural bent. So it's not unusual that you would conclude that your teen's potential is in jeopardy.

As you watch her peers win honors, take responsibility, and prepare for life after high school, your worst fears may look like reality when she can't seem to keep up. You may anguish over your inability to figure out how to help or get your teen to work up to her potential. That's because it's difficult to tell the difference between a *loss* of potential and a *delay in reaching* potential. But remember this—delays are many, losses are few. I've seen it time after time.

The journey through your fears about lost potential will be shaped somewhat by your experiences. If you have ADD and have "made it" in life, you will have done so at considerable cost. You may find yourself mourning your own losses. It's been an "expensive" trip paid for with lost freedom as you did work that was too hard. Often you paid with the loss of your true nature, which you had to suppress to make it in the non-ADD world.

If you haven't made it, according to your criteria, you will also mourn, this time for your *own* lost potential.

In either case, you don't want this for your child. We would rather go through loss and pain ourselves than have our children be forced to face these feelings.

Even if you or your child are getting by and making it, it's likely you have lost intellectual potential. Most people with ADD are much brighter than they can demonstrate by traditional schooling and job demands. Because we learn in alternative ways that are not measured by commonly used tests, we don't *appear* as bright. Yet some of the most brilliant people I've known are ADD. You have to get to know them more deeply in order to realize it.

The second fear is that your child won't make it in life. Are you afraid your child will end up in jail or as a street person? When you're thinking rationally, you probably laugh at this. But down deep in your heart it's not unusual to have such thoughts from time to time.

It's always best to state your fears openly to another adult, not to your teen. You are not alone in having these fears. Most of us have them, myself included. Yet we rarely mention them to anyone, perhaps for fear we will turn them into reality.

Not so. Most people with ADD are amazingly resilient and eternally optimistic. That doesn't mean we are never hurt and, at times, painfully depressed and feeling hopeless, but we usually recover and try again.

YOUR RELATIONSHIPS WITH OTHERS

Your Marriage

Your marriage, current or previous, cannot help but reflect the presence of an ADD child. And even though you may not have realized it, at least one of your child's birth parents is ADD because ADD is a form of brain wiring that is passed on genetically.

With one or both parents dealing with his or her own ADD, stresses such as temperamental differences, exaggerated mood swings, disorganization, impulsivity, and extreme sensitivity impact everyday family life. An ADD household has a whole lot more activity and emotion than a non-ADD home—and that has its good side as well as its bad.

Couples who work together to support and guide their ADD child provide a wonderful environment for that child's growth. However, individual spouses can see the situation from a different viewpoint. If you alone are understanding and supportive of your child, while your spouse is critical or judgmental, saying, "He just needs to try harder," then you carry the stress of dealing with ADD as well as the need to protect your child against your spouse's input.

You may even go too easy on your ADD child to counter-balance what your spouse does. That's not good for your child either. And it's devastating for your relationship with your spouse. Love can fly out the window pretty quickly with this kind of stress.

If you are a single parent, you may carry the whole burden of raising your ADD child. Are you tired most of the time? Do you feel as if you alone are trying to help your ADD child survive? Most probably. With no one to turn to when you need to make a decision, do the best you can, keep your intent clear, and seek outside input from a friend, confidant, or mentor.

Your Other Children
Other children in the family are affected by the ADD child. One young man told me he wished he'd known his brother was ADD, because he would have been nicer to him when they lived together as children. In an ADD family there's a tendency for the ADD child to get a lot of attention, not necessarily for positive reasons. Be careful that you don't forget the needs of your non-ADD child or children.

On the other hand, it's easy for families to label the children—one is "good" and the other is "bad."

Separate your child's *behavior* from his *self*. You may not like what your child does at a particular stage, but you can still love him. Help your ADD child weather the tough times with firm but loving limits. Let him know what you expect. Meanwhile, see that the other children get a share of your attention.

Another common experience for parents involves the birth order of their children. If your ADD child is not your firstborn, you might have thought you had it all together. Then along comes this child who challenges your most fondly held beliefs. You probably thought your first child was "good" because you were such a "good" parent. Well, you probably were, but that's not the whole story. Our children come into this world with different temperaments and talents, and they experience their own unique pathways.

For starters, your ADD baby may have been colicky and finicky from the very first. It's not uncommon to have difficulty

31

comforting an ADD child. Right away your parent/child bonding gets compromised. And oh how bad it feels to think there's something wrong with your parenting skills!

Please don't judge yourself too harshly. You did what you could, and you learned what worked and what didn't. That's what you can rely on. Remember, each child is a unique individual.

People Outside Your Nuclear Family
Though you may have come to understand ADD, chances are your extended family, friends, and neighbors have not. Within the warmth of your four walls you can come to a workable solution as an ADD family. But the minute you venture into the world, you may as well prepare yourself to be criticized, pressured, and stressed.

Perhaps you discover that friends or neighbors don't really want you to visit because your child is "too wild." This can leave you feeling depressed and rejected. Your child might not notice that your family hasn't been invited back to so-and-so's house. But you notice, and that sense of alienation compounds the hurt you're already dealing with.

YOUR NEEDS

Let's look at *your* needs for just a minute. I don't want you to discount your child, but you must care for yourself before you can effectively meet the needs of your ADD child. Just as you are advised to put an oxygen mask over your face before attending to a child in case of an airplane emergency, you must care for your own needs before you can be there 100 percent for your child.

So what are your needs? First and foremost, you need support and information. It's devastating to feel that you're alone without anyone who understands what you're facing. That sense of helplessness compromises your ability to be patient and supportive of your child. Even without ADD, life is too complicated to go it alone. When you add ADD to the mix, I advise you to call for reinforcements.

You need support and understanding, so don't be afraid to ask family and friends to help you out. Don't be a martyr by trying to do everything yourself. Our children are everybody's business. Find a mentor who's been down the path you are now traveling. He or she will truly know what you are facing and be able to empathize with you.

Next, get informed. Information gives you power to know what to do, when to do it, and why you are doing it. Again, seek out mentors who know tried-and-true ways to make life with ADD better—even enjoyable.

A support group is one of the best sources for meeting your needs. Most communities have at least one support group for parents of ADD children. That's where you'll find people who truly understand what you're going through. Sometimes you'll find educators or counselors who share your interest and are willing to provide the support and information you need. And don't forget a friend or neighbor whose ADD children are a little older than your own.

Learn to ask questions, show others what you need, and be a taker. Later, after you've walked your child and teen to adulthood, you can become the mentor. That will be your time to give back. For now, take! You've been giving and struggling for so many years. It's time to think about your needs for awhile. And that will help give you the energy you need to go on.

BUILDING A PARENT-CHILD TEAM

Your job as the parent of an ADD teen is to form a team with your child and be on his or her side. To do that, you probably need to erase a lot you have learned about what makes a good parent and a good child. Question your prior assumptions. Reevaluate your beliefs and adjust them to fit your situation.

Remember, no one did anything wrong to create ADD. No one is to blame. To a great extent the difficulties you are experiencing are simply a collision between some out-of-date cultural beliefs and the true nature of your child and, possibly, yourself.

There will be times when you feel alone and helpless. But please remember, you are never alone. There are many, many adults out there who have raised ADD children or are ADD themselves. We *do* know how you feel and what you're going through.

It's not easy, but together we can get a handle on ADD. You can learn to work through its difficulties and enjoy its benefits and take satisfaction in the process of watching your child grow successfully through the teen years to adulthood.

CHAPTER THREE

THIS CREATURE CALLED A TEEN
What All Parents Can Expect

Before we talk about your child as a teenager who is ADD, we need to peel back the ADD issues and take a look at the average teenager underneath. Quite often parents of ADD teens think that all the issues they face are related to ADD. That certainly is not true. So let's think about who your child is and who his peers are as he wanders through these teen years.

The first thing I want you to do is think about the word *teenager* for a moment. Okay, what are the first five words that come to mind? Were they *cooperative, achievement-oriented, thoughtful, respectful* and *responsible?* Probably not! Instead, you probably thought of words like *rebellious, lazy, thoughtless, disrespectful* or *irresponsible.* Or maybe you thought about how parenting a teen feels. Does just the thought make you feel tired, worried, frustrated, or even fearful? If so, you're not alone. We have about 24 million teenagers in the United States, and *all* their parents are tired and worried at one time or another, whether or not they've ever encountered ADD.

However, if you *expect* to feel tired and worried—or any other negative emotions—throughout your child's teenage years, you're setting yourself up for tough going. And the comments you hear from others aren't going to help. That's because teens have gotten a really bad rap in our culture. As soon as someone hears that your sweet child is about to become a teenager, you will probably hear comments such as, "Oh boy, you're in for it now!" or "Good luck! You're gonna' need it!"

The problem with this is that it sets you up to expect the worst. It's a well-known psychological outcome that if you assume the worst you tend to create the worst. The more afraid or controlling you are in relation to your son or daughter as you navigate the road through adolescence together, the rougher it is likely to be.

Though you certainly need to maintain your values and those limits that are most important to you, you and your teen will generally do a lot better if you can relax and "go with the flow" a bit. After all, the teen years are all about transition—the transition from childhood to adulthood, from dependence upon you to independence from you, from being controlled by you to being self-controlled.

None of these major transitions occurs overnight. In fact, it usually takes every single day from your child's thirteenth birthday to his twentieth, and then some, to successfully navigate all of these changes.

There was a time when our society was less complicated, and teens, whose lives were also less complicated, may have made these transitions more easily and quickly. The rules people lived by then were more rigid than they are today, and the roles each person followed were set. Whether that was a better situation than the one we have today is debatable. In any case, our teenagers have more choices today. Consequently, their road through adolescence is longer and rougher.

Because many adults were raised in simpler and more rigid times, and because a lot of parents don't know how to give their teens freedom within limits, many parents have a tendency to over-control their teens. When a healthy teen is over-controlled, he rebels. So, much of the teen's bad rap is created by the very people who talk about it. "I want you to do what I want you to do," they say to their teens. "And I want you to do it in the *way* I want you to do it. I also want you to do it *when* I want you to do it. That way, you'll arrive at the outcome I know is best for you."

The problem is, you can't raise a self-responsible teen with this approach. These parents have set up a system against which their teens will *have* to push and rebel. Yet when that rebellion occurs, these parents are shocked.

A DIFFERENT WAY TO LOOK AT TEENS

I look at the teen years differently. Perhaps what I have learned about teens will give you some needed perspective.

Adolescence is a time of transition and transformation. At the risk of sounding corny, I'd like to draw upon an analogy from nature. Butterflies spin a cocoon around their larva, their worm-like selves, withdrawing from the world. In time they reappear transformed into adult butterflies. So, too, our children at twelve or thirteen tend to withdraw to their room, shut the door, and isolate themselves with the companionship of peers, ignoring the adult world as much as possible.

Though it takes considerably longer for a person to transform into an adult than it takes a larva to transform into a butterfly, think about yourself. At a certain age, perhaps as late as twenty-five or thirty, you emerged — a self-aware, responsible adult.

All of us who are parents weren't always the way we are today. How did we get here? Think about what you've gone through to become the adult you are today. Don't talk yourself into believing you need to keep a firm grip on your child to save him from learning "the hard way," the way you had to learn about life. You can't do that. Each of us has to learn about life for ourselves. That's true of every generation. And that's what the teen years are about.

During thirty years as a mental health counselor I saw hundreds of families who demonstrated the principles I'm talking about. When parents tried to over-control their teens, trouble brewed and erupted. When parents developed a new attitude toward their parental role, the job became easier. They learned to guide and participate with their teens, not force and rule them.

If you want to develop this more relaxed relationship with your teen, the most important thing you must do, and the one thing that is nonnegotiable, is to model the behavior you want your teen to develop. Consider the values you hold dear and want to transfer to your children. Then select the most important ones—five or six may be plenty—about which you feel keenly. I'm talking about values such as being honest, caring for others as opposed to taking advantage of others, taking responsibility for work, and treating others with respect. You may have one or two more, but don't make the list too long.

The next issue is that your teen cannot instantly incorporate these values into his life, especially if *you* have not lived by these principles in the past. It will take the full time devoted to adolescence to accomplish this. You must be committed to these values, too. For example, if you want your child to become an honest adult, that doesn't just mean not stealing. It means that when someone calls and asks you to attend a meeting you're not interested in, you don't lie and say your mother-in-law is visiting.

Can you do a good job with an assignment you don't like? I can't. Or if I do, I resent it, and I don't get myself into that situation again. Yet our children must "take responsibility" to do things that are not of their choosing time after time, and they're supposed to do them with a good attitude, day after day after day. Most of us would have long since quit our jobs to find something that fits us better. But our teens can't quit.

Finally, how often are kids told to respect their elders? But you can't *command* respect. It's a free feeling that comes when the other person acts in a respectful way. By demanding respect from our teens when they don't feel it, we're teaching them to lie. This doesn't mean your teen is allowed to treat someone she doesn't respect in an ugly manner. That has to do with courtesy and your teen's ability to respect his own behavior, after the fact. But remember that you can't require your teen to *feel* respectful. Your best bet is to respect him and his needs. If he's been treated respectfully at home, chances are he will treat others with respect.

You need to have just a few nonnegotiable demands and limits that you expect your teen to live by. Then let loose of your teen to make the rest of his decisions on his own so he can learn about decision making and what to do with the outcome of those decisions. From your point of view the biggest conflict during these years is between your desire to protect your child, a job you've been doing for many years, and giving your teen the independence that could mean he makes mistakes, doesn't live up to potential for now, or gets hurt. Most of us really do want what's best for our children. It's only our methods we need to look at.

When we nag our teens to do their homework, ground them for coming in late, or scream at them because they didn't do their chores, we have to ask ourselves if our approach is helping to teach them what we want them to learn. Or are we just venting our own frustrations and fears?

All I'm asking you to do right now is look at your behavior as a parent and ask yourself whether you're being as effective as you can. Be sure your reactions are based on your own thoughtfulness, not on a myth that "the teen years are awful."

A TEEN'S UNIQUE TRANSITIONS

In many ways, parenting a teen is like parenting a toddler. Remember how your toddler would come over and hug your knees, then venture across the room, play for a minute, and come back for another hug? He was looking for independence, but he also needed the security of knowing you were there for him, no matter what.

A two-year-old struggles to separate from a parent for the very first time. And that two-year-old identifies herself by what she possesses — my mommy, my daddy, my doll. But much of the two-year-old's identity is tied to the approval she needs from her parents and other important people. Two-year-olds are great imitators. They do what those around them do and seek to be just like the important people on whom they depend.

A teenager's job is also to discover his own identity based on a newly emerging perspective of what he wants to be and what he feels himself to be inside. Less dependent now than at age two, the teen often goes to the other extreme in order to find an identity that is *not* dependent upon those who are closest to him.

Think about it. How could a teen come up with his own idiosyncratic identity if he only reflects what you want for him? Now he is strong enough to begin standing alone, separate from you. He'll become increasingly responsible and eventually have a clear identity as an adult. Like a toddler, your teen must "test his wings" then come back to get a hug or at least see that you are still there for him.

When your teen was a toddler, you spent time teaching him what was acceptable and what was not, and you spent time just accepting and playing with him as he was, picking and choosing your battles and not turning every issue into a struggle. Now, you must also choose your battles. If you don't, and you choose to turn every issue into a power struggle, you will find yourself fighting your way through the next several years.

That doesn't sound appealing to me. I don't think it would be very appealing to your teen either. So don't forget to have some fun and enjoy your teen during this transition.

Physical Development

Whether or not your teen is ADD, you will see an amazing transformation during this period. Girls tend to develop much faster than boys and may appear to be physically adult by age thirteen or fourteen. Some girls begin menstruating at age ten, and others, even girls who are physically mature in other ways, not until fourteen or fifteen. Because our society places a higher value on a petite body size, girls at this age often feel too big and clumsy and, often towering over the boys in their class, worry that they'll never find anyone to appreciate their physical attributes. Boys, on the other hand, worry that they'll never be tall enough because the girls outpace them in growth at the beginning of adolescence.

Adolescence is marked by so many body changes and rapid growth that the teen often wonders if he is the same person today that he was yesterday. Many teens have been teased about spending a lot of time looking in the mirror, but part of that behavior is an attempt to figure out who they are. *Am I the same person I was the first thirteen years of my life?* they wonder.

With puberty comes hormones, so you can expect mood changes that are physically based. As adults we still have problems with this, even after years of experience dealing with it. Do you recall what it was like when you weren't used to the effects of your hormones? And what about those aches and pains—"growing pains"— that would hit for a few months during major growth spurts. Then there's acne for some kids, a general embarrassment and apparently not the result of eating too much chocolate or poor hygiene, as was once thought.

Finally, these are the years that often make trips to the dentist a frequent habit, sometimes because of braces and sometimes because of teeth that didn't form perfectly and cavities that resist moderate dental hygiene.

Nagging our teens to avoid many of these problems rarely helps. Sensible care of the physical body along with consultation from a medical professional who is comfortable with teens will go a lot farther than expecting your teen to listen to you.

It's a good idea to start your teen on a medical connection that becomes his or her own. The doctor-patient relationship between your teen and his doctor needs to be private, with you standing on the sidelines to provide support—and pay the bills.

Cognitive Development
Incredible changes occur in the realm of cognitive development for all teens. Our ADD teens often demonstrate even broader-ranging changes than their non-ADD counterparts. The average teen becomes much less concrete in his thinking and is able to look at abstractions. Rather than focusing on one example of a principle, they begin to understand the overview.

A sixteen-year-old, for example, realizes not only why she needs to brush her teeth before bedtime but why she needs to brush each time she eats. It's no longer just something you've taught her to do. She can now generalize the principle. She realizes that if she eats chocolate in the middle of the afternoon it would be a good idea to brush, floss, or at least swish water in her mouth to avoid the continuing contact between the chocolate and her teeth.

Your teen can now use hypothetical reasoning based on logic, taking into account many variabilities. He will also be drawn to experimentation to see what works.

Teaching him by rote no longer works. "Do this lesson because I say so" or "because it's good for you" is not enough to get a teen to learn. But suggesting that your teen experience the principles—experiment to see if he gets the same results—is likely to be successful. He needs to find things out for himself.

Obviously, these cognitive changes do not all occur the minute your child hits thirteen. Rather, she will develop through her teen years and into her twenties. I've been amazed at how much broader the cognitive scope of many adolescents becomes as they move into their early twenties. They may even begin to enjoy learning if they haven't in the past. But, I must repeat, they will want to do it in their own way.

Many ADD teens make a cognitive jump in their early twenties and are much more ready to begin college at that point than they were at seventeen or eighteen. The brain circuitry simply matures, making learning and focusing easier. Add this to improved learning skills and your teen may be looking at success in school for the first time.

Social Development
Social relationships jump to an all-time high during adolescence, with peer relationships replacing relationships with parents and other adults. I've often said that during the junior high years, it would be a good idea to turn schools into social clubs and not begin teaching academics again until age fifteen. A lot of time is spent with behavior management during these years, trying to get young teens to focus on schoolwork. They are much more interested in discovering who is "going" with whom, what to wear to the dance, and how to make friends.

Cliques and clubs are also at an all-time high during the early teen years. Though often centered around an activity, more time will usually be spent socializing than "doing" the activity. Achievement will come at age fifteen and beyond.

Teens have a great need not to be different from whatever group they identify with. To be sure, young teens want to be different from adults, but not from one another. So you get "the jocks," "the cowboys," "the freaks," "the preppies," and whatever other group is popular in your area. All members of the group dress alike, act alike, and talk alike.

Later in high school, from about age fifteen or sixteen on, teens start to sense who they are as individuals and they begin to spend time with teens from other groups. Activity-centered groupings begin to form with participants displaying a wide range of differences. And as graduating seniors go off to college and work, they will be going their individual directions in most cases, although some small groups will want to stay together, perhaps even attend the same college.

From early adolescence to the end of the teen period, your child will change from someone who doesn't know much about how to make and keep friends to someone who knows a lot about same-sex friendships, best friends, casual relationships, and intimate friendships. That's a lot to learn in a few years.

Emotional Development

Your child will be changing right before your eyes from a little girl or boy to a fairly close approximation of a woman or man. This stretches even the most expansive imagination to wonder about how that process unfolds. That same stretching is happening to your teen emotionally. This is why emotions are expansive or erratic and just plain get out of control from time to time. (And, as discussed earlier, let's not forget the role of hormones in this.)

Every emotion possible will probably surface, including joy, fear, excitement, frustration, restlessness, impatience, depression, and anger. One minute your teen may be tender and compassionate toward a sick pet and the next scream irrationally at a brother or sister. Sometimes you will feel lucky to have such a wonderful teen, and at other times you will wonder whether you're living with a maniac.

Girls will tend to be more dramatic than boys, sometimes *so* dramatic that you'll wonder who you're living with. Boys are more likely to act out their emotions, roaring around in cars and whooping and hollering and pushing and shoving. There's nothing abnormal about any of this.

Adolescents need you to understand and listen without lecturing or trying to fix things. That's why they often choose each other to talk to, because so many adults shift into a problem-solving mode too quickly. Your teen may just want to complain or get something off her chest. It's not your job to fix it. You can ask, "Would you like me to help you?" But then abide by her answer. Don't try to get her to accept unwanted help, even if you think she needs it.

Teens need your care from a distance. They still like the nurturing support of good smells coming out of the kitchen, though they may not want to sit down at the dinner table to eat what you fix. Food will probably disappear from the top of the stove, ending up in their room. You'll know your cooking is appreciated, but don't expect your teen to say, "Gee, Mom, your dinner was great. You're sure a good cook." You might hear those words again when your teen is in her early twenties, so don't despair for the interim years when you're to be present but remain invisible.

Parenting a teen is a tough job when you're ignored most of the time only to be desperately called into action after your teen's way of doing something didn't work. *But that's what the experimentation of the teen years is all about.*

I know it can be extremely hard to be on the sidelines when you want to get out there on the field and do something or fix something or control something. Sure, you may have made a suggestion that probably would have worked, one your teen ignored or openly rejected, only to be asked to bail him out of a problem because he didn't follow your advice. Swallow your pride and help out. You don't need to lecture. Your teen can get the message by watching the outcome of the situation and won't tend to make the same mistake repeatedly.

If you rub it in you are only setting up an impossible situation, one in which your teen needs to continue to ignore your way of doing things because to do any differently would mean that you win, and he was wrong. No teen can tolerate that situation and keep a good level of self-esteem.

Self-esteem will tend to vary greatly during the teen years. A thirteen-year-old who is small for his age may have low self-esteem. A fifteen-year-old who is struggling to keep up in school may, too. A nineteen-year-old who hasn't been able to find a steady boyfriend may feel she will never have a relationship because she isn't "good" or pretty enough. Her self-esteem suffers.

Your job is to keep the faith for your son or daughter. Even though she can't openly agree with what you say, or maybe even feel it, your teen will remember that you continued to believe in her. Remind your teen that it takes time for some things in life to happen and that you know she will find the right mate or the right friends or the right job when the time is right.

TYPICAL TEEN PROBLEMS

These years can be a time of emotional upheaval and fear for many adults because their teens are taking over the reins of self-responsibility and will falter along the way. There are several problem areas that tend to affect perfectly normal teens in perfectly normal families.

Grades may suffer as your teen takes charge of his own learning in school. Experimentation with alcohol, drugs, smoking and, later, sex are likely to occur. As driving becomes a part of your teen's life, speeding tickets and other infractions happen. And then, forgetting to pay the tickets or show up in court may add to the problem. Staying out later than you want them to or allow, escaping through a bedroom window, failing to show up as planned at home or on a job, agreeing to do something then failing to do it, and ignoring responsibilities are all completely normal teen problems.

Your job as a parent is to choose your battles wisely. You need to be more of a teacher than a disciplinarian. Physical discipline and force doesn't work, but firm limits are important with issues that are dangerous and abusive to others or your teen. You can rise to the occasion, but you will need to use your head before you spout off. Be sure to get support for yourself so you are not in this alone.

SEEING THE WONDER OF THOSE YEARS

The teen years can be an exciting, expansive time of life. It certainly is the time when we change the most and come into our own identity. Our development during those years sets us on the path for the first part of our adult life.

Young people who are given support and feel at least moderately good about themselves are a wonderful sight to behold. You will watch your child grow, become able to have a discussion with you about interesting issues, and have opinions that are backed up with some experience. You may or may not agree with those opinions, but if you will listen, you'll find out that your teen has a reason for why he thinks the way he does.

You'll see your teen become very interested in some activities and develop a dislike of others. It will cease to be a time to try everything and become a time to further develop specific activities or interests that she likes. Some teens take longer to move into this aspect of self-knowledge, so don't be worried if your young teen hasn't arrived here yet.

If you could be the proverbial fly on the wall to observe your teen at school or in another activity, you would see a very social creature who acts quite differently than he does at home. During the early teen years, if you are the designated driver, and you don't say anything, the kids sometimes forget you're there. You will overhear some very interesting conversations. Later you may get feedback from sponsors of school activities and other adult friends. Keep your eyes open and you'll see a person evolving whom you probably won't see at home, but one you can be mighty proud of.

Spend more time looking for the good things your teen is developing rather than waiting for him to screw up. You and he will be justly rewarded when you do.

I know that parenting a teenager can be a scary, difficult task at times. I've been there. But I strongly recommend laughing more, looking for the good things that happen, and knowing that "this too shall pass."

One day your adult child will look back and treat you much like you treated him or her. It's a bit of an eye-opener. And it can be very rewarding when he looks at you warmly and suggests that maybe you ought to drive a little more carefully.

CHAPTER FOUR

෬ඁ—ඁ෬

THE ADD TEEN
Understanding Your Child's Unique Challenges

Your teenager and his non-ADD friends are more alike than they are different. The teenager we described in the previous chapter is probably familiar to you. That's because your child is going through a period of tremendous physical and emotional growth, just like every other teen.

But your teen is very different from his peers in some ways. The reason you're reading this book is because you either suspect or know that your teen has ADD. You've noticed that he doesn't seem to behave at school like his peers. He may have to work very hard to achieve what others seem to be able to do with relative ease. He is either easily distracted or he hyperfocuses on one thing at a time, unable to keep pace with his classmates. He has a difficult time completing tasks. And you've probably noticed these patterns of behavior since he was a young child.

Your daughter is not choosing to behave the way she does. She would like to be able to sit still and do what the teacher wants her to do. She would like to be able to make good grades. And she's felt that way since kindergarten. Now that she's in middle school or high school, she would like to be able to pay attention to a teacher's lecture all the way through class and take good notes. But she just can't seem to do it.

It's not your child's "fault" that she cannot do some of the things expected of her. Let me explain what's going on in your teenager's body if she has ADD, and you'll begin to understand why she behaves the way she does. And then we'll talk about how an ADD diagnosis is made and where you can go to get some help.

As I've said, ADD is a neurobiochemical style of brain wiring. Research continues to reveal the areas of the brain involved, and many advances in the understanding of ADD are expected in the coming decade.[1]

ADD affects the way your teenager can attend to a task, the ways in which she can express herself, and the ways in which she experiences her environment. ADD tends to be genetic, passed down from one generation to the next. And that means that either you have or your teen's other parent has some degree of ADD.

ADD—A LIFELONG CONDITION

ADD is not a temporary condition. If a person has ADD, he or she is born with it, lives with it, and dies with it. We used to believe ADD was outgrown at puberty. In fact, I was one of the parents who was told that my son would outgrow ADD. Instead, I noticed that his difficulties grew increasingly obvious around seventh grade—just when I had been told he would "grow out of it."

The attributes now known to be associated with ADD were once considered to be defects in moral character: laziness, lack of motivation, irresponsibility, rebellion. Professionals concentrated for years on working with children but failed to follow them through adulthood. The assumption was made that ADD went away. As I watched my son and the ADD people I worked with professionally, I began to realize the idea that ADD would just disappear was wishful thinking.

Today, the understanding that ADD is a lifelong condition is widely accepted in the professional community. Any controversy that remains is due to a lack of information and understanding by both laypeople and professionals who have not worked with ADD in adults.

Nothing about the physical cause of ADD changes throughout life. What does change is a person's ability to deal more effectively with his or her environment. As a person moves through the teenage years into adulthood, she has more power to make choices about her environment, especially if she believes in herself and is given the freedom to choose a type of work that fits her best, to decide how she will accomplish that work, and to pursue the goals she desires.

This is extremely important for you to understand. ADD is not your child's "fault"—and neither is it yours. Your child's inability to concentrate, to sit still, to avoid speaking out in class—those are not behaviors he or she has chosen to exhibit since kindergarten. Those are behaviors your child could not help but exhibit, because her brain is wired differently from other people's.

What produces conflict for the person with ADD and her family is not the ADD itself. The conflict, at least until a child's ADD is diagnosed, is that she spends her life as a square peg that her teachers, and probably her family, have tried over and over to fit into a round hole. Her inability to conform to the "round hole behaviors" society expects of her are not her fault. But once the condition is diagnosed, there are many ways to help your child attain a much closer fit between her abilities and society's expectations.

I know that ADD is, by definition, considered a disorder: Attention Deficit *Disorder*. But through my work, I have come to see it not as a disorder, but simply as a differently-wired way of doing things.

There seems to be a continuum of people all the way from those linear thinkers who are highly structured, intently focused, able to block out external stimuli, organized, and who even thrive on their attention to detail, to those analog thinkers who are hypersensitive to all stimuli, creative, always putting things together in new ways, and are more focused on the process or pattern of what is going on than the details involved in accomplishing the task. These are the two extremes of the continuum, with most people falling somewhere in between.

People who tend to be on the linear end of the scale are the ones who have tended to shape our institutions, administer

programs, do research, and define what is "normal" and "abnormal."
The people at the other end of the continuum are creative people who have trouble organizing their vision for others to see and follow. They are not the ones who defined the disorder called ADD. They don't tend to do the research or write the diagnostic manuals.

Creative, nonlinear people, such as your ADD teen, are not really disordered. They just have a different way of functioning. Unfortunately for them, our culture is designed on a linear model and is becoming more linear and detail-oriented all the time.

You are destined to failure if you think your job is to make your ADD teen into a linear thinker. If you try to mold her into someone she is not, you will erode her self-esteem and possibly keep her from fulfilling her own unique potential. Instead, the trick is to make her aware of her differences, help her learn enough linear skills to function well in our culture, and encourage her to use her strengths to her best advantage.

DIAGNOSING ADD

One of the difficulties families face when a member has ADD is that the condition is often undiagnosed or misdiagnosed. You may have been through months—or even years—of meetings with teachers and principals, discussions with your child about his behavior, and visits to the pediatrician.

Though not difficult to diagnose, few people are adequately trained to recognize ADD. There is no simple test for ADD—no blood test, no three-item questionnaire. And in many cases, ADD remains unrecognized. Popular diagnoses such as depression, bipolar disorder, conduct disorder and oppositional/defiant behavior, anxiety disorders, and addictions do not take into account the possible presence of ADD. Sometimes an incorrect diagnosis is made because the diagnostician is familiar with one of the other conditions and is used to treating it, and doesn't know about ADD in adults or how to treat it.

Luckily, there is an increasing number of knowledgeable professionals who can diagnose ADD in children, teens, or adults: counselors, social workers, marriage-and-family counselors, educational diagnosticians, psychologists, psychiatrists, and developmental and adolescent pediatricians. Those who are best at diagnosing ADD are often those who have a special interest in the condition because they, or a family member, have ADD.

Each of these professionals has his or her own manner of diagnosis. But no matter whom you work with, you should expect to receive a set of written recommendations for treatment in language you can clearly understand without a lot of medical jargon. It should also include a set of reasonable accommodations that will help the student in school.

As a psychotherapist, my most successful way to diagnose ADD is with an in-depth interview. I can ask all the questions I need to ask in order to determine whether or not ADD is present. The interview helps me sort out other potential conditions or situations that may be clouding the picture. And it lets me begin to develop a game plan to help the client—and his parents—best deal with his ADD and become a satisfied, successful individual.

Even though some professionals also use psychological testing, and some use a new and expensive computerized electroencephalograph for additional information, an in-depth interview is always the main diagnostic tool. If your teen does *not* have ADD, that fact will be highlighted by the interview.

When I do an ADD evaluation, I spend some time speaking with the teen alone, with the parents or guardians alone, and then with the adults and teen together. I try to get a written report from a teacher if the teen is still in high school.

My goal is to make the interview as relaxed as possible. I usually ask questions about family, education, and job history if the teen has any work experience. I also want to find out about the teen's personal life and relationships, family medical background, emotional make-up, and behavioral history. And I ask about any addictions.

I work to get beyond the surface of a situation. For example, if the teenager tells me he's had a problem completing homework assignments, I must go beyond that and find out *why* the assignments weren't completed. Did he even start the assignment? Did something get in the way of finishing it?

Suppose he says: "I didn't finish it because I got bored. Once I know how something works, I get bored and so I just decided it was too boring to finish." That gives me a lot of information because *deciding* to stop an activity is not an ADD response. So just knowing that he didn't complete the assignment would not have been enough information for me.

If I believe medicine should be part of the ADD treatment plan, or if I find that other organic problems or learning disabilities may be involved, then I refer the client to the appropriate professional.

There's a wide range of fees charged for ADD evaluations, so I suggest you shop around. If you have an ADD support group in your area, its members can suggest referrals. Some teachers and pediatricians keep a list of professionals who do ADD evaluations.

Once you contact someone about the possibility of an evaluation, be sure to ask lots of questions. You don't want to work with someone you're not comfortable questioning. After all, you've probably been dealing with this issue for years and you probably have more than a few questions you would like answered.

After a child or teen is diagnosed with ADD, the parent will often recognize symptoms of ADD in himself or herself. Remember that you, too, can turn to one of these professionals for diagnosis with your own ADD.

THREE FORMS OF ADD

During my years of psychotherapy, I identified three distinct forms of ADD: Outwardly Expressive, Inwardly Directed, and Highly Structured. A person may be primarily one type or the other, a combination of any two, or all of them. Understanding the specific form of your teen's ADD can take you one step closer to understanding why your teen does what he does and how you can best support and encourage his efforts. I have noticed that young children with ADD also fall into one of these three categories. But the differences between these forms of ADD become much more pronounced during the teen and adult years. Let me emphasize that these are my own categories. The person who diagnoses your teen's ADD might not break ADD into categories, or might use different ones.

All teens with ADD share a difficulty in starting and/or stopping an activity. I call this an "on/off switch" problem. But the specific way in which that problem translates into actions is how these three categories differ.

Outwardly Expressive ADD

Teens with Outwardly Expressive ADD seem to communicate so that everyone can hear their message, leaving little doubt as to how they feel or what they are doing. Their behavior is characterized by hyperactivity (physical and verbal), impulsivity, a low frustration threshold, a high level of risk taking, difficulty with long-term projects, little interest in details, lack of temper control, expressive moods, and an outgoing personality.

These teens can usually be successful in sales or entertainment or another career that requires quick responses and lots of energy. Outwardly Expressive ADD teens often make successful entrepreneurs.

One eighteen-year-old who is a child-care worker describes her Outwardly Expressive ADD like this: "Before I realized I had ADD, all I knew was that I acted a lot like the four-year-olds I work with. I always seemed louder than the other teachers, and my kids seemed to catch my enthusiasm and be the most exuberant at the center. I broke a lot of things, too. Somehow, I just bumped into things. But we sure do have a lot of fun. I love working with children. I have a reason, then, not to have to sit down all day or keep quiet. My parents want me to go to college or get a better-paying job. But I don't know if I could tolerate sitting still for that long. And I love what I'm doing!"

Inwardly Directed ADD

Teens with Inwardly Directed ADD "stuff" their feelings and inhibit their behavior. From the parents' point of view, they may not be quite as exhausting to be around as Outwardly Expressive ADD teens, but they can be equally as frustrating, because it's so difficult to get these teens to begin an activity that you think they need to accomplish.

Often "spacing out," teens with Inwardly Directed ADD may be underachievers, may overcommit themselves to activities, can be depressed, tend to spend a lot of time watching television or using a computer, have a difficult time completing assignments, and take on excessive self-blame. Though not hyperactive, they are restless. Daydreaming is a favorite pastime.

Teens with this form of ADD are often drawn to creative arts and crafts, inventiveness and mechanics, outdoor jobs, or teachers' helpers if they can make it through school. They usually prefer jobs that require teamwork as opposed to individual "high profile" talents.

Highly Structured ADD

Highly Structured ADD teens tend to worry. They are often perfectionists who are highly organized, have difficulty controlling their tempers, and difficulty resuming a task after an interruption. They may be underactive or compulsively active. They tend to be fairly rigid and controlling and have trouble cooperating with others.

This type of teen is drawn to highly structured jobs. The military, accounting, piloting aircraft, or any highly structured career attracts this type of person.

Teens with Highly Structured ADD tend to get "stuck" doing things. For example, a boy with this type of ADD might decide to play a computer game before starting his homework. But six hours later, at three o'clock in the morning, he might still be playing the computer game. Or maybe he fell asleep while he was playing and never did start his homework. When a teen with this type of ADD starts an activity, he tends to continue endlessly. The boy might really have *intended* to do his homework, but once he started playing the computer game, his mind never came back to the homework.

Different Forms of ADD, Different Behaviors

To see where your teen might fit into these patterns, let's look at how teens with each type of ADD might react to a request to complete a specific task. Let's say it's Saturday and you've told your teenage daughter that she can't go out with her friends until she cleans her room—everyone's favorite chore.

If your daughter has Outwardly Expressive ADD, she would probably throw her clothes and shoes in the closet, shove her school papers under the bed, and throw the bedspread diagonally across the bed. While she's doing all this, she'll be talking on the phone and complaining loudly to her friends about the terrible injustice you've just inflicted on her. In five minutes, she'll tell you she's done the job and is on her way out the door.

An inspection of her room reveals that "things" have been put out of sight but the contents of every drawer and closet look like a tornado has just hit. And she would never even think about vacuuming or dusting.

If your daughter has Inwardly Directed ADD, she would probably walk from one side of the room to the other, picking up piles of papers and clothes and putting them down again on the other side of the room. She might pick up a book and start reading but quickly gaze off into space, daydreaming. She would probably "get lost" in the process of cleaning and actually accomplish very little. She might attempt to dust or vacuum, but wouldn't be very successful at completing either task.

Her daydreaming about what she wants to do when she goes out stops her from completing the task at hand. Or maybe she starts redecorating her room. Even if she really tried, she probably wouldn't get much done. Eventually you might hear her whine, "I just can't do this."

A teen with Highly Structured ADD would probably focus on the details of cleaning the room, often overlooking the bigger picture. For example, she might start to fold her clothes very neatly but be sidetracked by the spot she found on her blouse. Then she would spend time getting the blouse pre-treated and ready to be washed. She might spend all morning washing her clothes and never think about the fact that her bed isn't made, her papers aren't put away, and the dishes from last night's snack are still on the dresser. If anyone complained that she was hogging the washing machine, she might lose her temper, complain that you were terribly unfair, and stomp out of the house.

Of course, not everyone falls neatly into just one of these categories. If your teen rarely "got into trouble" as a child and was a "good little boy," he might appear to have Inwardly Directed ADD. But maybe your child actually has Outwardly Expressive ADD and just hasn't given himself permission to express himself. He is inhibiting his natural manner and impulse. Or maybe he has characteristics from both groups.

Outwardly Expressive ADD is the form many people are familiar with. When they think of ADD, an image comes to mind of a child who can't sit still and is always getting into trouble. But that is only a part of ADD. And for some people, that's not part of the condition at all.

Knowing which form of ADD your teenager has will help you find the best treatment plan for him and will allow you to support him emotionally in the most effective way possible.

DIAGNOSIS: AS A CHILD OR A TEEN?

If your teenager was diagnosed with ADD as a child, you had an early opportunity to help him start learning to cope with his ADD. There's a vast difference between ADD children who are left to fend for themselves and those who know about their ADD early, are properly treated with medication when appropriate, and are provided with opportunities to learn to master skills needed to overcome the negative effects of ADD, such as temper control, organizational skills, successful study habits, and self-protection for their hypersensitive natures.

If your teenager was not diagnosed as a child, or still hasn't been officially diagnosed, then probably all of your and your child's efforts have been spent trying to fit him into a mold that just doesn't fit—the square peg in the round hole syndrome.

It's likely there will be more problems with your teenager rebelling about accepting his ADD, taking medication, or just having something different from his peers if he isn't diagnosed until the teen years.

Think about it. What happened to your ADD child if his ADD went undiagnosed? In response to your child's problems and lack of success, you probably worked harder to get him to do what he was *supposed* to do. Chances are that didn't work very well. Now, neither of you has much practice at positive negotiating when it comes to school or each other. Neither of you knows how to handle the feelings of resentment and helplessness that engulf you.

The bad news is that power struggles inevitably result from this frustration. The good news is that you can learn to negotiate and work *with* your child, not *against* him.

If your teenager was diagnosed as a child, that might not have been an entirely positive experience for him either. For example, if medication was administered for a short period of time and then withdrawn, your teen might be confused.

I've talked with many teens and adults who recall having had a wonderful year or two on medication, when learning came easier, only to have a sharp decline in productivity when the medication was withdrawn the next year. Often, no explanation was given by the professional prescribing the medication and your son or daughter might not know why this happened. This kind of experience wouldn't lead your child to become self-responsible in relation to medication. And he might be leery of trying medication again.

If this happened in your case, discuss the whole story with your teen and admit to lack of understanding by the adults involved. (We'll discuss the whole issue of medication in chapter 11.)

If he was diagnosed at a young age, your child may have begun to view himself as a "case"—a person with "something wrong." Sometimes when that happens, a child develops the personality and characteristics of a sick person or may use ADD as an excuse to avoid doing things he doesn't want to do. As parents, you have to be careful that you don't reinforce this behavior.

If you're already caught in this trap, family counseling might help all of you dig your way out. If you can change your expectations, your teenager can change the way in which he responds to those expectations, and in the process change his self-image.

If your daughter does have ADD but was not diagnosed before the teen years, chances are her initial response to the diagnosis might be something like this: "I don't want anything to be wrong with me." Although your teen might have been aware she was different from her peers in some ways, it could still be a shock to receive an official diagnosis.

Just like younger children, teenagers often want little more out of life than to be like their peers, to blend into the group. The diagnosis of ADD tells your daughter that she is different. And, chances are, her initial response isn't going to be positive.

When I'm working with teenagers, I tell them, "Of course you don't want to have something wrong with you. No one would." Then I explain to them the physical causes of ADD and discuss the fact that ADD isn't better or worse than being wired like other people. I explain the ways in which ADD expresses itself positively as well as the ways in which it can cause problems.

I make note of the specific assets the teen has as well as the difficulties he or she confronts. I might say, "You are able to draw wonderful pictures and create stories that other people can't even dream up," or "You're very talented and smart besides to figure all that out. On the other hand, you know you've been having trouble with doing your homework. Remember how hard it's always been to keep your mind on your work? Well, that's also because of your ADD. You and your dad are alike in that way. You inherited his brown eyes and his ADD."

You can help your teen overcome some of the difficulty of dealing with this diagnosis by letting her know that your whole family will need to learn a lot about this, together. Let your teenager know it's all new to you, too, and that you're going to invest time reading and learning about ADD.

Some teens do best dealing with the diagnosis if they join a teen group for counseling. For others, it's helpful for the whole family to go for a few counseling sessions.

If, after talking with your daughter, she is still unwilling to accept the fact that ADD is a part of her life, let it go for the time being. Just say, "You are responsible for your grades and your behavior. I can't and won't try to force you to take care of yourself. I want you to know that I'm behind you 100 percent, even if I don't agree with what you're doing. I know you'll do what is in your best interest." Then let it go.

After time goes by—after getting over the initial shock of the diagnosis—your teen may be overjoyed to realize what has been getting in the way of reaching her potential. She may gain new hope about her future. And you will probably find some major positive changes in the lives of all family members.

Be sure to take care of your own ADD if you are the parent who passed it down genetically. If you're not, learn all you can about it so you can truly understand what it's like to be wired in that way.

You might be feeling a sense of relief at the diagnosis of ADD because the puzzle pieces of your child's behavior are finally coming together to make a complete picture. You might feel comforted by the knowledge that there was a reason, an explanation, for the difficulties you've been through. And you'll be glad to know that help is available.

DIFFERENCES BETWEEN YOUR TEEN AND NON-ADD TEENS

It's important to understand that your ADD teen *experiences* things in a different way from other people. And if you are the parent with ADD, then the same is true for you. Although each person is different and no general description could apply to everyone, here are some basic characteristics of teens with ADD:

▶ *Focus of attention.* The ADD teen tends to be very aware of, and easily distracted by, sights and sounds. Consequently, he has difficulty staying on an unpleasant task. Although he starts tasks with the intention of finishing them, he often skips from one task to another without completing any of them. Forgetfulness is a major problem.

▶ *Organization.* Because he is so easily distracted and sidetracked, the ADD teen often loses track of time and tends to be late. He has difficulty staying on track when the task involves multiple steps. He tends to be either messy or compulsively orderly. And he has difficulty planning ahead and setting priorities. Keeping track of details are beyond him.

▶ *Learning style.* The ADD teen learns better by doing than by listening. He is a hands-on learner, a kinesthetic learner, who usually wants to get started on a task right away without instruction. He is stimulated by trying new things but dislikes repetition.

▶ *Sensitivity.* The ADD teen is often hypersensitive. He is easily irritated and tends to frequently lose his temper, either verbally or physically. He often counters authority and may have trouble working well in groups. He feels everything deeply and may be so compassionate that he hurts painfully for others. He may cover his sensitivity by pretending not to care or by acting in an oppositional way.

▶ *Impulsivity.* Because he is easily excitable and impatient, the ADD teen often acts or speaks without thinking through the results of his behavior. For the same reason, he often has trouble with peer relationships.

▶ *Activity level.* ADD teens tend to be either overactive or underactive, without much middle ground. Some ADD teens talk, move, and fidget more than their peers. Others have difficulty waking up in the morning and are underactive compared to their peers.

▶ **Creativity.** ADD teens tend to be excited about the
creative planning aspects of new projects, but are not as
successful as their peers in following through and
completing a task. They usually are very imaginative
people who can see a global picture in contrast to those
who think in a linear fashion.

If you can understand these differences between your ADD
teen and his peers—or the teen you might have imagined he
would be—then his behavior will make more sense to you. And
chances are, it will be easier for you to resolve certain conflicts.

For example, suppose you walk into the TV room in your
home and your son is lying on the floor studying with the TV on.
Your initial reaction might be to say, "Turn the TV off. You have
a test tomorrow and you need to study so that you can get a good
grade."

Your son might reply, "No. I'm going to leave it on."

On the surface this looks like defiance. But ask yourself this
question: Is he watching TV, lost in the plot, with his books forgotten? Or is he studying intently with the TV volume turned
down low? If the latter is true, this is probably an effective study
method for your child. He also wants to do well on that test and
he probably knows that he studies better with the TV on in the
background. It eliminates a lot of random noise and other distractions for him. When he said he would not turn off the TV, he
was not objecting to studying. He was objecting to the *way* in
which you wanted him to study.

The same might be true for teens who study lying on the floor
instead of sitting at a desk. Or maybe your son studies best lying
in bed with his feet up on the wall. Give your child credit for
knowing what works best for him. If his strategy doesn't seem to
be working, you might help him try another way of doing things.
But if he's passing his exams, congratulate him on discovering
study methods that work for him.

ADD teenagers have another wiring characteristic that can be
problematic for their family, teachers, and friends: Sometimes they

simply do not hear things. I'm not talking about ignoring you— that's a rut all teenagers get stuck in from time to time. And it's not faulty hearing. It's just that ADD teens, distracted by inner thoughts or outer distractions, might not process incoming information that's unimportant to them at the time.

For example, I knew of one thirteen-year-old girl with ADD who had this type of communication problem with her mother. Her mother asked her to pick up her clothes and put the dirty ones in the laundry. When the girl didn't do it, the mother said, "If you don't get those clothes picked up and in the laundry, you can't go out with your friends tonight." The girl looked at her mother with a blank stare. She didn't seem angry or sullen, just blank.

Later, her mother overheard the girl talking to a friend on the phone. The girl said, "I don't know what's wrong with my mother. She just wouldn't let me go out tonight—for no reason. I don't have any idea what her problem is."

When the mother asked her why she had said that, the girl answered, "Mom, you never asked me to pick the stuff up." The girl might have said, "Uh-huh," when her mother asked her to pick up the clothes, but, in fact, she wasn't listening.

This "Uh-huh" phenomenon creates an expectation that the ADD teen is going to respond to your request. Although sometimes a teen uses that behavior just to get someone off her back, she can also use it at an unconscious level. The teen does not *intend* to con- found the person asking for something, but that's what happens.

The "Uh-huh" phenomenon is related to a desire to please— another common ADD characteristic. Outside of conscious aware- ness, the "Uh-huh" is tossed off to accommodate another person. On the conscious level, the request just doesn't get through in a way that gets translated into action.

The ADD teen's "Uh-huh" response can often mean, "I like you and appreciate whatever you are doing." It often does not mean, "I know what you are asking of me" or "I understand what you are telling me."

If you understand this about your teen, you can communicate in a more meaningful way. Make eye contact and find out if your daughter's response indicates she really did hear and understand you. Then there's a better chance she will follow through with action. Better communication will make both of you happier.

Teens who are ADD react differently to touch than their non-ADD peers. All teens are very sensitive to touch and very conscious of being touched, whether by parents, relatives, same-sex friends, or opposite-sex friends. But ADD teens are often hypersensitive and they experience touch differently than their peers. The exact manner of the touch or the duration of the touch can become a significant factor in the teen's response to the situation.

If your daughter can learn to verbalize her feelings about being touched and communicate those feelings, her relationships will all work out better.

I knew one seventeen-year-old girl with ADD whose boyfriend was trying to soothe her when she got upset about a minor car accident. "Don't touch me that way," the girl said. "I hate it when you come up and hug me. I feel smothered. And don't pat me on the shoulder. It makes me crazy."

The boyfriend was shocked because all he wanted to do was help her and soothe her. Finally, when he explained his intent, she said, "Well, come up from behind me after you let me know what you're going to do and put your arms around my shoulders. Don't lean on me or get your arms up too high so I feel smothered. It makes me feel pressed down because your arm is too heavy. Put your arms here (a few inches below her shoulder). Hold me for a minute. No patting or stroking. Then let me go."

He tried soothing her the way she described and they were both fine. To an outsider, it might sound like this girl was just being bossy. But she was actually communicating effectively with her boyfriend, describing her specific needs — which might have been different from other people's needs — so that he could understand them. Not everyone understands her own needs quite as well as this girl did. But if you see that your teen feels frustrated or "smothered" at being touched, you might try to help her talk about it. That's a big step in the right direction.

One of the biggest differences you'll notice between your

child and his peers is that teens with ADD mature at a slower pace. I don't necessarily mean physical maturation. Your son may have just as much stubble on his face as his friends, and your daughter might have been among the first girls in her class to start menstruating. But the emotional and intellectual maturity to cope with all these changes—and others—comes more slowly to an ADD teen who is hypersensitive. Your teen will probably lag behind her peers in tasks requiring organization or impulse control. However, she may be ahead of her fellow students when it comes to utilizing "street smarts" or expressing a special talent. ADD teens are more concrete learners than their non-ADD peers and may do better on the job than in school.

The areas of slower maturation can cause your teen some problems. Maybe he's still dealing with temper problems while his peers have matured beyond that. Maybe he's as disorganized as he was in elementary school, while his peers seem to be much more efficient at accomplishing their work.

While these are issues your teen will eventually iron out, his lag in maturation can be a source of frustration for him. The danger is that the frustration he feels can lower his self-esteem and lead him to make poor choices. Drug or alcohol abuse or impulsive risk-taking behavior may result. Those are very real concerns of all parents these days. But as a parent of an ADD teen, you might feel an extra burden of concern as your child learns to circumvent those dangers a little more slowly than other teens. We'll deal directly with those issues in chapter 10.

THE BOTTOM LINE

I hope this chapter has helped you to think about your ADD teen in a different way and to become a little less judgmental. The most important message I can give you about your child is this: Your teenager is a wonderful person who needs and deserves your complete, unconditional love and support at all times.

I am *not* saying that everything your child says or does is wonderful—not at all. What I am saying is that for you to do your best for your teenager, you have to separate your teen's *behavior* from his *self*. Your child needs to know that you love him unconditionally and that you will always believe in him and support him emotionally.

You may be saying, "I know. It sounds great, but. . . ."

Yes, it's hard to be a wonderful parent when your child is failing history again because he's not completing that term paper. Or when you've been called up to school again because he's being disruptive in class. Or when he promised he'd mow the lawn yesterday but spent the whole day in his room looking for a particular book.

As a parent of an ADD teen, you have to take a giant step back and take a fresh look at the big picture, because the big picture for an ADD teen might just be different than the big picture for his peers.

Ask yourself this: In the greater scheme of things, exactly how important is that history class? I think we'd all agree it's important for us to study history as a society. But how important is that one class for your child?

Did he try to do the assignment? Did he start the research for the paper? Did he seem to have every good intention of writing the paper? Was he struggling? Is *he* frustrated, too? Would he have preferred to receive an A, B, or C for a grade—rather than the F? Is he at a loss to understand what went wrong? And, most importantly, do you think he really tried his best to accomplish the assignment? If so, then you need to support him and let him know you believe in him, no matter what grade he gets—ever.

If you tend to be somewhat controlling, it will be hard for you to give up your hopes of perfect behavior from your child. But if your teenager is ADD, then he's different in some ways from the cultural standard for teens and different from the perfect child you have in your mind. His internal wiring—the basic way his system is put together—is different. Wanting your child to change to be just like you or expecting him to fit completely into the mold our culture has said is *right* just isn't going to work for an ADD teenager.

If you want what's best for him—if you want him to be able to lead a satisfying, independent, and productive life with stable, loving relationships, then he must have your support and love and know that you believe in him always. With your understanding, appropriate support, and unconditional love—and with admirable effort on his part—your child will grow into a responsible, satisfied adult.

1. In February 1991, Dr. Daniel Amen began doing brain SPECT imaging studies on people who met the DSM-IIIR criteria for Attention Deficit Hyperactivity Disorder and Attention Deficit Disorder without hyperactivity. His work confirms the physiological base of ADD. His findings were presented as early as 1993 at the American Psychiatric Association and the annual meeting of the Society for Biological Psychiatry.

Brain SPECT is a nuclear medicine technique that supports the work of Dr. Alan Zametkin. Affiliated with the National Institute of Mental Health, Dr. Zametkin published an article in *The New England Journal of Medicine* on the use of PET (positive emission topography) to study people with ADD. Still earlier computerized EEG brain wave studies differentiated people with ADD from other patient populations.

Though not generally used to diagnose ADD, these and many other studies have demonstrated the tangible, physiological nature of ADD which affects the way people behave, process and express information.

cᘐᘐᓑ

IDENTIFYING AND BUILDING ON YOUR TEEN'S STRENGTHS
The Positive Side of ADD

As a parent of an ADD teen, you're probably well aware of your child's weaknesses — or at least those characteristics that have always been labeled weaknesses: "Sean can't sit still in class"; "Mary never finishes algebra homework"; "Kenneth can't seem to get anywhere on time"; "If you even look at Cynthia angrily, she gets her feelings hurt."

If you've been called up to school to discuss these behaviors, your child's teacher might not have mentioned two very important points: First, there's a positive "flip side" to most of these behaviors, and that's what you and your teen need to focus on long-term.

Take Cynthia, for example. The same internal wiring that makes her hypersensitive and causes her feelings to get easily hurt also gives her a wonderful sensitivity to people. She's probably the friend others turn to when they need someone to understand their problems. She's probably the one who's willing to devote time to community service projects when her other friends are out shopping. She's probably the one who could become a successful social worker or marriage-and-family counselor, if she can weather the required academic training.

And second, there are ways in which you can help your teen develop behavior patterns that will serve him better and put him on the road to success.

Just telling your ADD daughter that she needs to complete her homework assignments from now on does not help her learn how to organize her time or to work better. Just telling your ADD son that he'll be grounded if he doesn't do well on his math test doesn't help him learn the math concepts he's being tested on. But there are things you can do to help, and we'll discuss some of them in this chapter.

No matter what your ADD teen's specific behaviors, the *most* important way you can help him is to believe in him, try to focus on his strengths instead of his weaknesses, and help him learn how to do the same.

REDEFINING "WEAKNESSES"

ADD is a "differently wired" way of doing things. It's not the *wrong* way, it's just a *different* way. For your ADD teen, it's the *only* way. Although we tend to focus our attention on the problems a particular personality trait causes, many ADD traits do have a positive side.

One common characteristic of ADD teens is difficulty in keeping focused. Your teen might sit down with every intention of reading that history chapter. But each time a car drives by, a bird chirps, or the refrigerator fan cycles on or off, her attention is pulled to that noise and away from the task at hand.

Other teens might be able to block out those noises or just pay no attention to them, but it doesn't work that way for your daughter. She hears a bird chirping and her thoughts turn from the sixteenth-century French history she's supposed to be reading to the morning her uncle showed her the nest of baby birds outside his kitchen window. Suddenly she's off reminiscing about that day, her uncle, and the baseball games they used to watch together.

The biggest problem is that mental drifting occurs without her knowing it. Her brain does not announce in advance: "I'm going to have a lapse of attention now. So if what you're supposed to be doing is important, be aware that you're going to miss something." When she returns from her daydream, she can continue reading if she can remember where she left off! It's much more serious when she loses concentration during a classroom lecture or when oral directions are given for an exam. This kind of lapse is why many people with ADD have reading comprehension difficulties.

One reason your ADD teen is so easily distracted from a given task—particularly one she identifies as boring or one that lacks the stimulation of motion—is that people with ADD have a high level of sensitivity to all stimuli. All senses are heightened: taste, smell, sight, hearing, touch, and intuition. That sensitivity becomes a significant distraction, steering attention away from a "boring" task.

The ADD teen doesn't make a distinction between what is important to the task at hand and what is interfering with the completion of the task. He just doesn't think to do it.

In addition, many people with ADD think on multiple tracks at the same time, which makes it hard to focus on any one thing at a time. They rarely take just one thought and follow it through from beginning to end to a logical conclusion. Rather, they may process several loosely connected thoughts simultaneously. That jumble of thoughts may or may not lead to a logical conclusion. More than likely, it will lead to a *creative* conclusion.

Now, think about it this way: Your ADD teen has the special ability of multiple-track cognition. She has a much higher level of awareness of her surroundings than her non-ADD peers and can often recall details of events or surroundings that her non-ADD peers did not even notice. So if she chooses to write a memoir about those ballgames she attended with her uncle, she could probably fill it with details that would make it stand out from the crowd.

If she likes to draw or paint, her artwork might be filled with intricate details her non-ADD peers wouldn't think to include. If she should become a stand-up comedian or a radio deejay, she could more easily keep several conversations going at once than if her thoughts were tightly focused and single-tracked.

In other words, whether this multiple-focus trait is seen as a weakness or a strength depends upon what kind of work she does. It might not help much when it comes to studying sixteenth-century French history. But if she goes into radio communications, it could become a great asset.

Another teen issue—one that affects both ADD teens and their non-ADD peers—is run-ins with authority and belligerency. Often, the teen is using these behaviors to protect himself the only way he knows how. With ADD teens there will always be a reason for the oppositional behavior. You just have to know how to look for it. Frequently, an adult is trying to get the youth to do something he doesn't want to do, cannot do, or cannot do in the *way* the adult wants the task handled. Or the adult is hurting the teen with sarcasm, shaming tactics, or threats. Resisting verbal or emotional abuse from others, including adults, is actually a healthy behavior. It's a strength, not a weakness. And that's what ADD teens are often doing when their behavior looks confrontational.

People with ADD tend to be experiential learners—another characteristic that can be viewed as a weakness. For example, reading about sixteenth-century French history is not the best way for an ADD student to learn the material. Visual images and movement—seeing a movie about that time period, writing a play, or constructing a set for a play—are ways the student can better experience sixteenth-century France. Physical experience, supported by reading, is a much more effective way for an ADD student to learn.

Or consider math. Children with ADD have less success learning math when a teacher lectures from the front of the room and then gives out worksheet assignments. If that's the only teaching style in the classroom, experiential learners will usually not do well. But if you take those same mathematical principles and give teens a project utilizing the math concepts being taught—the ADD children will be able to learn the concepts just fine. This type of teaching actually tends to work best for all students. But for ADD students, it's usually the *only* way they can learn a concept and retain it.

In most classrooms experiential learners don't have the same chance to learn as other students. Curriculum is presented, and many teachers learn, in a linear way. Also, it's easier to stand up in front of students and lecture rather than give them creative, hands-on work that takes longer to prepare and might be more difficult to grade.

The truth is that experiential learners—whether ADD or non-ADD—usually retain what they learn better and longer than students who just memorize material, even if those other students do quite well on school exams. So when it comes to really *learning* the material, being an experiential learner can actually be a strength, not a weakness.

Teens who learn experientially are usually creative. I often think of the young girl whose mother was teaching her to make mashed potatoes. The girl wanted to experiment and see what would happen if the skins were left on the potatoes. Because she's an experiential learner, she didn't think of asking her mother, "What will happen if I leave the skins on?" Instead, she just left them on while boiling the potatoes.

After they were boiled, she added cinnamon and onion. When her mother first saw the dish, she was a upset because she specifically told her daughter to make mashed potatoes. (It never occurred to the mother that *mashed* potatoes could be made without peeling them first.)

The mother decided to try the dish before she said anything, and the potatoes turned out to be a delicious surprise! Some years later the mother found this same type of dish on the menu in an upscale Spanish restaurant.

DIFFERENT FORMS OF ADD— DIFFERENT STRENGTHS

As we discussed in chapter 4, ADD presents itself in three forms, each with its own characteristics. Let's look at the strengths and talents of these different individuals.

Outwardly Expressive ADD Teens

These teens tend to be honest, forthright, expressive and usually have a positive attitude about attacking new projects. They are spontaneous, have a heightened awareness of what's going on around them, are good at troubleshooting, and often excel in sports, not to mention having a tremendous sense of humor.

These teens often enjoy martial arts, dramatic improvisation or standup comedy, and expansive artistic endeavors. And they usually enjoy challenges of all kinds—from physical fitness to starting their own business.

Teens with Outwardly Expressive ADD can be quick to respond emotionally to situations. This range of emotions can be very expressive and exciting, especially if the person is drawn to the theater, oratory, or dramatic writing. When this type of student finds his talent and expresses it, he often reaches a high level of achievement. Sometimes these teens even become overachievers in one area to "make up for" what they cannot achieve or have trouble achieving in another area.

Your Outwardly Expressive ADD teen is likely to have a number of close friends instead of just one. This type of teen usually is a good friend, providing freedom and independence to others in a relationship. He thrives on change and the challenge of new situations; rarely does he get stuck in a rut with friends, activities, or interests.

One young man I know with Outwardly Expressive ADD wants to become a sports announcer for a major radio network. Shane is funny, witty, creative, opinionated, and has no inhibitions about saying what's on his mind. He's able to pick up on many cues simultaneously and then put the information together in a unique manner that's fresh and vital. He's never bored because there's always something new to learn about and report on. As a result his interest level is consistently high.

Although there are many sports-announcer "wannabes" out there, I believe Shane has an excellent chance of achieving his dream. And in Shane's case, that's *because of*, not *in spite of*, his ADD. Shane is "different"; he stands out in the crowd. And that's a big advantage in the field he plans to enter.

Many people with Outwardly Expressive ADD become successful entrepreneurs, often joining with a partner who can handle the day-to-day administration of the business. (The day-to-day work would hold little interest for someone with Outwardly Expressive ADD.) The ADD entrepreneur is the pathfinder, the creative visionary of the business who gets excited about the possibilities of unexplored territory, while the partner is the detail person. Many wonderful partnerships have been formed this way.

One fourteen-year-old boy I know with Outwardly Expressive ADD already has his own business and is busy figuring out how to get other people to work for him. Peter loves selling and he loves creating empires in his mind. He has the ability to find people who can help him follow through with his deliveries and keep his account books.

Peter is a high-risk taker by some people's standards—successful entrepreneurs often are. He is not afraid to reinvest his capital in order to expand his business. His high energy level and quick thinking allow him to react swiftly to opportunities and to keep working until he gets what he wants.

Inwardly Directed ADD Teens

These teens are quieter and more subtle than those with Outwardly Expressive ADD. They are usually easy people to be around. They tend to keep their feelings to themselves and to be good friends, sensitive to other people's needs. They like to spend a lot of time with their friends or talking with them on the phone. These teens often excel at community service work, or any work that requires being a supporter or helper rather than a leader. Teens with Inwardly Directed ADD are cooperative and make wonderful team members.

Similar to Outwardly Expressive ADD teens, teens with Inwardly Directed ADD naturally have big dreams and a commitment to accomplish what they want—they just use different methods to get there. They often use their cooperative natures to great advantage by trading services and talents with their friends. For example, one teen I know offered to drive her younger brother (who didn't yet have his driver's license) to all his football games and practices if he would do the laundry for her. They both agreed to the trade, and it worked out well.

Nick, another teen I know who has Inwardly Directed ADD, likes computers and has learned elementary programming. When his teacher assigned a project he was particularly interested in, Nick worked on it for many more hours than was really necessary because he wanted to see what would happen when he experimented and tinkered around. He loves inventing things.

On the other hand, I know one teenage girl with Inwardly Directed ADD who doesn't do so well in school. But when it comes to making and keeping friends, Hannah always gets top marks. She treats her friends well and is nonjudgmental, fair, sensitive to their needs, and a great listener. It's probably her listening skills that make her so popular.

Hannah never criticizes; instead, she has great empathy and listens to her friends for hours. When they do ask her opinion, she always seems to give solid, sound advice. Her own boyfriend doesn't really understand why she spends so much time talking to her friends, but he knows she's a good friend to him, too, and he values that about her.

Some teens with Inwardly Directed ADD are dreamers — or at least they look like they're daydreaming. But what's really going on in that mind is intense creativity. These teens might be musicians, visual artists, or dancers. Once drawn to a particular type of artistic expression, these teens do not give up. They persevere and continue to practice and refine their art. That level of commitment and practice often leads to success.

Finally, the sensitivity of Inwardly Directed teens often leads them to an interest in animals and plants. From landscape designers to game wardens and forest rangers to veterinarians, these teens quietly turn their interests into careers.

Highly Structured ADD Teens

These teens tend to do very well in school. Consequently, parents of these teens, unlike parents of other ADD teens, are often well aware of their children's strengths.

Teens with Highly Structured ADD usually work hard —

almost rigidly, attend to their school assignments, and are detail-oriented perfectionists. They are often excellent debaters. They're fierce about what they believe, can be dogmatic, and usually do a good job of communicating their case. These teens make highly effective, self-motivated, and self directed leaders and project managers because of their attention to detail. Because these teens are so conscientious, they will stay with a project until it is completed, regardless of what else presses upon them.

Travis is a perfect example of how effective teens with Highly Structured ADD can be. Travis is in charge of the band instruments for his high school. It's his responsibility to keep the instruments properly stored, to arrange transportation for out-of-town games, to set up for concerts, and to make sure the instruments get to the right person at the right time. And let me tell you, he does a superb job!

Travis is focused on this task even to the point of being a little gruff with people at times. But the students have never arrived at a game or concert without their instruments where they needed them, when they needed them, and in top-notch condition.

John's interest is physical — he's a teen with Highly Structured ADD who is a marathon runner. At age seventeen, he has already spent much of his adolescence running. He loves the way running makes him feel. No matter what, even if his time is over-committed, John never fails to get in his daily practice.

He also likes to encourage the younger high school and middle school kids to get in the habit of running. In fact, he often runs with them just so they have company and stay motivated. John is quiet about his accomplishments in this area, and he's not involved in a lot of other school activities, but he's committed to his running. And he finds that it helps him focus.

Katie is also a teen with Highly Structured ADD and her schoolwork has always reflected her perfectionism. If Katie is writing a paper, she will rewrite and proofread until even the teacher has to tell her to stop working and turn the paper in. But the quality of Katie's work has always been impeccable, and she has won numerous awards for her writing. Even if she has other work to do or outside pressures, Katie will concentrate on the task at hand, simply refusing to stop. Other people and other assignments just have to wait.

Grant, a young man I know with Highly Structured ADD, is a good example of how successful people with this type of ADD can become in the military. Their attention to detail, ability to lead and/or follow orders to the letter, and commitment to accomplishing an assigned task are all strengths that propel their military careers.

When Grant was a teen, he began planning for a career in the military; he joined the ROTC and loved it. It was easy for him to accept and follow orders because he believed in what he was doing. The ROTC adult leaders praised him, his friends in ROTC respected him, and the girls admired him. Grant went on to win a four-year ROTC college scholarship and now has a successful military career.

RECOGNIZING YOUR CHILD'S STRENGTHS

Some teens' strengths jump out at us, and everyone is aware of them: academic achievement, musical talent, artistic talent, writing ability, excellence in sports. These kinds of strengths are obvious because opportunities exist for teens to showcase these talents. There's the school band, sports teams, newspaper, computer club, photography club, and theater groups. If your child has excelled in any of these areas, you and your teen have every reason to be pleased.

But chances are your ADD teen has many strengths and talents that don't fall within one of these easily recognizable categories. Those strengths might take a bit more work to expose and develop, but they are there.

For example, does your ADD teen love to watch movies on television? Sitting in front of the tube isn't usually seen as a legitimate interest, much less a talent. We usually think of teens who watch a lot of television as just plain lazy. But I've found that many ADD teens who love TV know the name of each performer, can recall the sets and props in many scenes, understand the stage directions, and can discuss the show's special effects. They are familiar with the production process from idea to finished product and are often good at comparing various production techniques. They follow the story line and note discrepancies.

Teens who are that knowledgeable are not just "vegging out" in front of the TV; they are studying, analyzing, sorting data, and making comparisons—all of which are skills that will serve them well in any academic endeavor or career they choose.

Similarly, many ADD teens who are focused on sports remember the name and "stats" of almost every player and the game scores and team histories, including specific staffing changes. Girls who seem to shop endlessly can often describe the merits of various designers, their clothing prices, and construction and artistic attributes of style, color, texture, and fit.

Yes, watching TV, following sports, and shopping are activities that are enjoyed by most teens, whether ADD or non-ADD. But what often separates ADD teens from the crowd is the level to which they take their interest. It's all a matter of degree.

For example, your teen's non-ADD friend might love to shop simply because she loves to wear new clothes. She might not remember which style blouses she saw last weekend, the decorative details, or the fabric composition of the brown plaid size-seven skirt she saw three weeks ago. But there's a good chance your ADD daughter will remember all that (particularly if she has some Highly Structured ADD), plus the regular and sale prices of the skirt, cleaning instructions, and how many size nines were also on the rack.

As you know, shopping is not a talent that can easily be developed into a successful full-time career—although it has been done. But the important thing to recognize is this: The skill your daughter uses when she reports the minute details of every pair of jeans she tried on in a one-month period is a marketable strength that can help her in whatever career she chooses to pursue.

You might be feeling tired, bored, and frustrated from hearing about yet another shopping expedition. In fact, what you might really want to say to her is this, "Shopping? Again? It's not like you don't have jeans spread from one corner of your room to the other. How about paying some attention to cleaning up that mess?" Instead, listen carefully to what your daughter is telling you. And if you can focus on the positive aspect of her ability to record and remember so many details, you might be able to respond like this, "How in the world do you remember all those details? There's no way I can do that. When I look at ten pairs of jeans, they all start to look the same to me. But you pay much more attention to details than I do, and that's really an impressive ability."

Don't worry about over-praising your daughter's shopping abilities; your comments aren't going to lead her to spend even more time at the mall than she already does. But those comments will help her feel good about herself. She will appreciate the respect you show her. And you'll have other opportunities to explore with her the many other ways — non-shopping-related — in which that skill can be used!

WHEN TO HELP, WHEN TO STEP BACK

Parents of ADD children — whether younger children or teenagers — often have difficulty focusing on their children's strengths. If you find yourself in this category, it's worth asking yourself why. Could it be you're afraid? In fact, many parents' reactions to their ADD children are rooted in fear that the child will fail a class, not be able to graduate, not be able to make a good living, not be successful in life, *or not live up to the expectations you have as parents.*

The reality is that many ADD teens perform adequately in school, and some do work that is clearly above average. If your child is not successful in school, you must remember there are many ways to have a healthy, happy life without succeeding in traditional academics.

As a parent of an ADD teenager, you need to answer these questions: What am I afraid of for my child if he doesn't learn to concentrate better? What do I think will happen?

When you've determined exactly what your personal fears are, you'll be in a better position to help your child learn to use the talents he has and do the best he can in those areas that are not his strengths. For example, maybe your child would be better able to focus on his homework with a bit of background noise. Or maybe, because he needs complete silence, he works best in the middle of the night.

When you were a child, your own parents might have insisted you do your homework immediately after school, sitting at a desk or table, the TV and radio turned off, no snacking while working, and no phone calls. Maybe you're afraid that if your teen doesn't follow those same strict work habits, he's doomed to failure.

Your ADD teen needs more leeway to find a study environment that fits. Your ADD teen can only produce up to his abilities when he is given the freedom to experiment until he finds what works best. Encourage him to do that.

Your teenager wants to do well—to be successful. As a parent of an ADD teen, you can best help your child by realizing there is more than one way to accomplish your shared goals.

ADD teens are much more effective learners when they are learning something that appeals to them and holds their interest. This might also be true for their non-ADD friends but it's all a matter of degree.

Your teen's non-ADD friends might be able to force themselves to study economics, whether or not they are interested in it. But your ADD teen is going to have a much harder time constantly forcing himself to refocus on something that just doesn't hold his attention. On the other hand, if he finds the subject interesting—whether it's geology, computer science, or the history of jazz—he's usually willing to throw himself into it (particularly those teens with Highly Structured ADD) and earn satisfactory grades.

Your teen will not always be able to choose which classes he takes or what work he's assigned. Whatever state or school district you live in, there are certain subjects your child will be required to pass in order to graduate. Chances are, your child, like all students, will find some of them less than exhilarating.

When your child is faced with any task she finds difficult or frustrating, you can choose to react in one of three ways: First, *you can nag, cajole, or threaten* in the hopes you will force her to improve her concentration and study habits.

Unfortunately, these techniques are not effective when dealing with an ADD child—even though they might be your first reaction to the situation. If your son could focus and concentrate on his work the way his non-ADD peers do, he would probably do it without nagging on your part.

Remember! ADD is a condition with an underlying biological cause. If your child had asthma and wasn't able to practice sports as effectively as his non-asthmatic peers, you probably wouldn't threaten to ground him in the hopes his condition would improve. Similarly, ADD is a physiological condition. Your child can learn to become successful by building on his strengths. But nagging and threatening are not going to get results.

Second, *you can do the work for your child* to make sure he gets good grades. You would not be the first parent to try to "help" your child this way. But neither would you be helping him.

I know one parent who wrote all of her ADD daughter's school papers from the sixth grade on. Every time the daughter brought home a writing assignment, she would turn it over to her mother who would say something like, "I don't want you to worry about this now. We'll get this done. No daughter of mine is going to have to think she's less than the other kids who are making all those A's."

This mother tried to help her daughter the best way she knew how. But the message she was sending to her daughter was that the girl couldn't possibly accomplish this on her own; in fact, it wasn't even open for discussion. This girl made it through high school and into college with her mother doing most of her work. Consequently, she entered college without the study skills she needed. The last I heard, her mother was still doing most of her work for her via fax.

You may need to *help* your teen write her paper—teaching her the research and writing skills at a slower pace than they are presented at school. But if you choose to do the work she can do for herself, you are choosing to keep her from learning how to do it herself—no matter how noble your intentions.

Third, *you can plead his case to the principal or dean,* respectfully describing your child's ADD and explaining why it would be best for him to substitute Course B for Course A. This is a tempting option and may be necessary if your teen is severely learning-disabled in a specific area.

Often your teen can be tutored or assisted in alternative ways to learn difficult material. Encourage your teen and help him use his strengths to do the best he can with these subjects. As long as you let your child know you will be satisfied if he does his best— no matter what the outcome—you have made it safe for him to take a risk and try. You both might be pleasantly surprised at his accomplishments.

HELPING YOUR CHILD DEVELOP
HIS OR HER STRENGTHS

It's not easy for an ADD teen to learn to manage or compensate for her weaknesses so that her strengths can shine. It takes a lot of hard work and, usually, a lot of trial and error. There are things you can do to help that process along. Simultaneously you'll notice that learning to value your teenager's talents and skills brings joy and comfort to both of you.

First, your teen needs an opportunity to realize his strengths.

One of the best exercises I know for increasing your own awareness of your child's strengths is to get out some paper and a pen and make two columns. List his weaknesses on one side and his strengths on the other.

Parents often become so focused on the negatives that they fail to see the positives. If you're in that category, it might take some practice to change your perception.

For example, if you can only see two positives today, but you can see twelve negatives, look closely at the negatives column again. Focus on one weakness and turn it around to look for the positive, as we discussed at the beginning of this chapter. Keep working with the columns until they are balanced or until you have more positives than negatives. When you are comfortable that you've presented a positive picture of your teen, show it to him and ask him for feedback.

The most important thing a parent can give an ADD teen is a sense that he is important and valuable and will be able to function well in life. To develop that self-confidence, he needs as much positive feedback as you can give. Step right up and tell him what you value in him. Tell him what you see as his positive attributes—whether it's his ability to listen carefully to his friends and offer sound advice, or the care and detail he puts into the model airplanes he builds. Don't take those traits for granted, and don't let him take them for granted either. Train yourself to notice the positives in your child. That in itself is a wonderful ability.

Make sure you provide your teen with opportunities to develop his strengths. If he's interested in the theater, take him to local productions. If he's interested in sports, encourage him to participate. If his interest is classical music, check to see what local concerts are available.

You might want to consider pairing up your ADD teen with a mentor, an older person who shares his interests. Maybe you have a neighbor who's as interested in gardening as your son. Or if he's particularly good at math and loves that challenge, he might ask his math teacher for information about local math clubs or chess clubs.

I know one fourteen-year-old with ADD who was particularly interested in working with lighting for the theater. His father found a local community theater group that was willing to let him hang around. Because the teen caught on so quickly and proved to be helpful, he became an assistant. His father drove him to the rehearsals every night, and his family attended all the performances to show their support for this boy's interest and success.

BUILDING YOUR CHILD'S CONFIDENCE

Helping an ADD teen grow to independence means showing him that you have confidence in his ability to do things for himself. If you consistently try to cover your teen's mistakes, do his work for him, or make excuses for him when he doesn't succeed, you will be teaching him that he's not capable of doing these things for himself. If he's already concerned about his abilities to make it on his own after school, you will just be feeding those fears.

Help him build confidence and recognize his capabilities by giving him responsibilities—a little at a time—and praise him for his accomplishments.

All teens develop a sense of strength and independence by learning how much they can do for themselves. But it's especially important for your teen.

ADD teens usually experience some sense of failure when they try to work within a system that doesn't "fit" them. They are more likely than other teens to really worry about their ability to make it on their own. You can show your teen that he will develop all the skills and abilities he needs and that you look at him with pride and confidence. That will help him develop the emotional power he'll need to succeed.

One of the easiest ways to give your ADD teen a feeling of control and responsibility is to give him opportunities to make choices. If you are buying clothes, for example, give him a budget and let him choose his own clothes. If you are in the grocery market, let him choose the fruits or vegetables. If you are buying a desk for his room, give him two or three to choose from that are within your price range and let him make the choice.

Letting your child make choices tells him you have confidence in his abilities to weigh the factors and make a sound judgment.

To build your child's confidence, you have to be willing to stick with *his* choice. It does no good for you to let him choose a desk and then point out why you prefer a different one and buy the one you like instead. That undermines his judgment, and everyone would probably have been better off if you would have made the decision in the first place.

If you are going to give your teenager choices, you have to be willing to stick with the choice he makes. (That includes the styles and colors he chooses.)

Letting your teen make choices includes being willing to let him live with the consequences of his choices. If he's buying clothes, and he realizes later that he made a poor choice for some reason, that's okay. He will have learned a valuable lesson and will be more discriminating next time he goes shopping.

In addition to building confidence by letting your ADD teen make choices, it's important to give her as much responsibility as she can handle. Doing things for your teen that she knows she could do for herself says you don't have much confidence in her.

Think about it this way. If your teenager is physically healthy and normal, you would never consider cutting her food for her! That's an obvious example. But right now—without realizing it—you might be doing other things for her that send an equally strong message that you think she's helpless.

Consider this principle in your own life. Suppose you had a supervisor at work who was constantly stepping into your territory, pulling papers from your "in" box and doing the work herself. That would drive you nuts and send a clear message she didn't think you were capable of completing the task accurately or quickly enough. If she did that consistently, you might eventually feel that no matter what you did it would never be enough to please her. After a while you might stop giving it your best effort. *After all,* you think, *what difference would it make? She'd still be in there trying to do everything herself, anyway.*

Our teenagers feel the same way if we don't give them the opportunity to do "the work" themselves.

There are many daily opportunities to help build your teen's confidence and inner strength. For example, if you have a dog, you could give your child some responsibilities over time. Here's one example of how to do that (Don't worry if you didn't start years ago; you can jump in any time.):

Age 8:   Help feed the dog.

Age 9:   Help buy the dog food at the market.

Age 10: Feed the dog (might need some reminders).

Age 11: Go with parent to the grocery store, pick up some items on the grocery list — including dog food — and meet back at the check-out counter. Feed the dog when parents aren't home.

Age 12: Walk to store and buy dog food alone if the store is in the neighborhood.

Age 13: Take care of pet on a regular basis.

Driving: Drive car to do dog-related errands.

You can also help your ADD teen by holding him accountable for his actions. Learning to be responsible and accountable is an important part of anyone's maturation process. But for an ADD teen, the *way* in which this is learned is especially important.

For example, you can tell an ADD teen that if he doesn't return his library books on time, there will be a fine. Just hearing that information is not usually an effective way for an ADD teen to learn. It is much more effective to give him that information and then, if the books are overdue, make sure he pays the fine himself. As an experiential learner, the physical experience of going to the library and paying the fine will be a much better way for your ADD teen to learn — and remember — that his actions have consequences; and it will require him to follow through.

The extent to which you hold your child accountable for his actions, or at least the extent to which he pays for the consequences of those actions, should vary with age. For example, if your child accidentally breaks a neighbor's window playing baseball after you've told him not to play in that yard, you might ask him to provide the replacement window in this way:

Age 9: Pay about one-third of the cost of the new window.

Ages 10-11: Pay about half the cost of the new window and help to install it.

Age 12: Pay the entire cost of the new window and help install it.

Age 13: Pay the entire cost of the new window and install it himself, if he has the skill.

I know one thirteen-year-old with ADD who wanted to impress his friend by shooting his BB gun in the front yard. He was trying to hit a specific street sign. Instead, the BB hit a concrete post from which it ricocheted onto the back of a passing car. This teen was a well-meaning kid who had never been in any serious trouble. He was scared.

His father helped him talk to the driver of the car and they worked out a plan together. First, the teen had to pay for the car repair—appropriate responsibility for his actions. Then he agreed with his father that if he wanted to "show off" with his BB gun, he would go to a BB range—a much safer environment than his own front yard. His father also told him that if he had been shooting the BB gun because he was feeling the need to do something adventurous, they could go camping, take a hike together, or go bicycle racing. Again, the father was giving his ADD teen choices within a safe framework. Of course, giving him appropriate choices for the future was not the same as condoning his present action. The child was required to pay for the consequences of those actions.

You can help build your teen's confidence by asking him for help in areas in which he is strong and you are weak. Don't be afraid to say, "Could you help me out here? You're so much better at remembering things than I am. I could really use your skill."

For example, my ADD son is the best salesman I have ever seen, and I let him know that I value that ability. Once when our family was having a garage sale, we had a piece of fairly old stereo equipment marked at $12, but we were willing to lower it to $9. I told my son to do the best he could with it. He managed to sell it for $25! I told him, truthfully, that I was awed at his ability and I asked him to teach me how he did it.

Letting your ADD teen make as many decisions about his

schooling and studying as possible will help boost his confidence in his ability to make good decisions. For example, if he is having trouble academically in school, it will do you no good to say, "You have to do better next time." You're usually safe to assume that your teen would have done better if he knew how. What you need is a game plan in which both of you are on the same team working toward the same goal.

Instead of immediately telling your ADD teen what to do about his grades in school, if they are a problem, try asking him what *he* thinks the problem is. And then listen—really listen—to what he has to say. Ask him what he thinks could improve the situation, and then help him try to implement his suggestions.

Of course, there's always a chance your teenager won't know why things aren't going well for him. In that case, you might want to offer some suggestions. In chapter 9 I will offer many specific suggestions that can help with schoolwork in particular.

HELPING YOUR TEEN ACCOMPLISH GOALS

Sometimes your teenager's difficulties stem from an inability to break a task into manageable segments. That's not just a problem teens have.

Many an adult is in trouble with the IRS or has other accounting or business difficulties because of a neurologically-based problem with organization. Some adults who look like they have everything under control might actually have someone else keeping them organized, such as a secretary or administrative assistant.

Your teen might want to get help by delegating some tasks. Maybe he could work out some kind of trade for services with a brother, sister, or friend. Trades can also be made with parents. In that way, your teen will be instrumental in the accomplishment of that particular task, even if he didn't *do* it himself. And just knowing that the task was accomplished will bring a sense of achievement and confidence.

Problems with task management can spill into other areas of life besides schoolwork.

One nineteen-year-old girl I know with ADD had her own apartment. She wanted to keep it clean and neat, but she just couldn't. Every time she had a day off (she was in school and also worked part-time as a waitress), she would plan to clean her apartment. And every time she would fail to do it.

She would either start and get distracted, never finishing the job, or she wouldn't even get started. After all, there were a lot of little things to be done before she could begin the real job. Before long she would be in tears because the apartment was still a big mess and she felt ashamed. She realized she didn't know how to begin the job.

Her problem was that she saw the whole job at once. Because her goal was too big, she had never experienced a sense of success. Her mother tried to help her by suggesting she complete one task at a time. She started with picking up the newspapers in the living room, after which she rewarded herself. Her mood changed, and she wanted another task at which she could also succeed. Eventually, using this method, she succeeded in getting the whole apartment under control.

The next step was to make up a schedule in which she did a little bit every day, making a cleaning cycle of the whole apartment in one month. It worked for her. And she continued to schedule in rewards for herself until she became habituated to keeping her apartment clean and organized.

You might suggest a variation of this for your child if you think task management is difficult for him. But if you do offer suggestions, whether it's a file cabinet to help him organize his schoolwork or a plan to break his work into smaller tasks, be sure to let him choose which of the suggestions he wants to try. And have him evaluate how well the plan is working for him instead of telling him.

The goal here is not only to help him improve his schoolwork or management skills but to help him develop the self-confidence and strength that comes from knowing he can face his problems and find solutions for them. The key word is *choices*.

After trying the plan he chooses, he can determine whether

or not the choice he made was a good one. From that experience he will learn what, if anything, to do differently next time.

Whatever you do, don't give up on your ADD teen. The slow process of helping him develop confidence and the ability to focus on his strengths is well worth it. Make sure you set an example by focusing on the positives. This means letting him take every ounce of responsibility he is capable of taking but not expecting more than he is ready for.

Take it one step at a time.

And, above all, don't forget to laugh together and enjoy one another's company.

❧ ❧

CHAPTER SIX

REDUCING THE STRESS
OF ADD IN YOUR FAMILY
Understanding and Coping with Its Effects

Let's say you gave your sixteen-year-old daughter permission to take the car and go to a friend's house for a party. And you agreed on the time for her to return home. As that time comes and goes and she's still not home, you figure she's having such a good time that she's lost track of the time. But when thirty minutes have gone by, you begin to worry that she might be having car trouble, stuck on a dark street and needing help.

Finally, when you can't stand the suspense any longer, you call the friend's house. The line is busy. Now you're really worried. Is she lying in a ditch somewhere, hurt and bleeding? Did she drink at the party? To the best of your knowledge there wasn't going to be any alcohol served, and your daughter does not have a history of drinking, but you've heard all the stories about parents not knowing what their teens are up to. Is she all right? Is she just thoughtless? Now you're mad. How dare she cause you so much worry!

Sound familiar? If this hasn't happened to you yet, chances are it will before your child makes it through the teen years. These are years filled with stress, for all parents and teens.

Generally, stress results from feeling out-of-control in some situation. And the teen years certainly create a lot of opportunities for this feeling. Yet there are no "bad guys" purposely plotting and planning to create stress. Neither parents nor teens wake up in the morning and vow to make life miserable for the other. Nevertheless, it can be a very stressful time.

In this chapter I'll discuss stressful situations for any parents of teens, and stressful situations that are specific to parents of ADD teens and what you can and cannot do about them. Certainly not all stress results because your teen is ADD. In fact, some of the attributes of ADD can actually reduce stress when properly handled. So the first job in understanding and coping with stress is to identify what's normal adolescent/parent stress and what is specific to ADD.

Notice I use the term *adolescent/parent stress*. That's because the majority of stress-related incidents are jointly created and they need to be jointly resolved.

During the teen years parents must transfer power and independence to their teens, and teens must become self-sufficient and responsible. It's a big job for both parent and teen. As the parent of an ADD teen, your history of preadolescent stress has probably made you even more wary of this stage of development that has such a bad reputation.

You *can* learn to cope with the stress of the teen years. It doesn't need to be overwhelming.

RECOGNIZING THE PHYSICAL AND EMOTIONAL SYMPTOMS OF STRESS

When Ben stops eating, can't sleep, and paces more than usual, his parents realize he's probably feeling stressed out. Holly, on the other hand, bites her fingernails, withdraws to her room, and becomes very irritable when she's feeling stressed.

Everyone reacts to stress in a slightly different way, including you. Let's look at some of the common physical and emotional symptoms of stress so that you'll be able to recognize them more easily in your child and in yourself. They include headaches, body aches and pains, teeth grinding, nail biting, hair twirling, picking at the body, rashes, itching, stomachaches, frequent infections, accidents, fatigue, listlessness, sleep difficulties, appetite changes, confusion, forgetfulness, disorganization, loss of mental acuity, worry, depression, anxiety, feelings of panic, and compulsiveness.

In moderation these symptoms are nothing to worry about. However, if they are severe enough to have a disruptive effect on all aspects of your teen's life—school, family, friendships—or if they last for more than three or four months, then it's time to consider outside help. (Three or four months is an arbitrary time, but most semesters last about that long. If the stress comes from a temporary school-related situation, it should be alleviated in that time frame.)

Many of these symptoms or conditions may be present over extended periods of time for reasons other than stress. If you are concerned, it's always best to check with your medical doctor.

In addition to the symptoms listed above, teens may also exhibit stress by appearing extremely silly, demonstrating a "couch potato" lifestyle, showing aggressive or outrageous actions, using confrontive behavior, having nonstop activity, or manifesting an I-don't-care attitude.

Some of these teenage symptoms might surprise you since you certainly don't feel like laughing or running around when *you're* under stress. But these symptoms are an expression of stress, nonetheless.

Go back over the list slowly and note how many stress symptoms apply to you. You must be the judge of whether you are handling your stress effectively or whether you need professional help. Knowing when to reach out is an important aspect of dealing with stress. A trained counselor can help you relieve the stress until you can take over and cope with it more effectively yourself.

THE CAUSES OF STRESS
IN PARENTING ANY TEEN

Some of the issues that cause stress for you and your teen come from outside the family—school, peer relationships, extracurricular activities, and worries about the future. Other issues that create stress for parents and other family members are finances, marriage or health problems, family and job changes, and losses of all kinds.

Of course, stress can also result directly from the parent/teen relationship. In this chapter I want to concentrate on that facet of stress, because it's the area over which you have the most control.

Not Understanding the Other Person
It's a tough job trying to understand another person when often we don't even understand ourselves. But understanding our "baby" who's grown into an adolescent requires us to learn about a whole new person. Little of what we once knew about this child still applies or, at least, it is secondary to the budding personality striving to become independent and separate from his or her childhood and family.

When your child was little, you often knew what was best for him. And he was glad you provided protection and guidance in a world that was so big. But over the years that same child began to accumulate experiences that taught him a lot about himself and the outside world. Even by age four, and certainly by age nine, your youngster sometimes knew what he needed and wanted better than you did. He even knew some of what worked to help him get along in the environments in which he lived and worked.

There were times when you had to pull rank and provide limits and guidelines. But slowly, over the years, you realized that he was becoming capable of judging effectively for himself. Of course, if you held a tight rein on your child or were very controlling, he might not have acquired as much decision-making experience as a child who was given opportunities to exercise his judgment and learn from his experience.

By the teen years your child is restless to become captain of his own ship. And chances are your child will arrive at this point before you do.

I know that I continued to worry about my precious children even when I trusted their judgment. Perhaps this comes from knowing the world can be unfair and many hurtful things can happen, even though our children are using good judgment. There is also the problem of their limited experience. We know more as parents than they do as teens. And some of what we know frightens us.

The trick to weathering this period is to realize our teens *must* gain experiences that will provide them with the kind of good judgment that will lead to self-reliance and successful living. The truth is, we will probably have a harder time getting control of ourselves than getting our teens to control themselves. And when we have difficulty controlling ourselves, stress results for both parent and teen.

Every time you think you know what is best for your teen, ask yourself the following questions:

- ► Do I have all the facts, or at least as many facts as my son or daughter?
- ► Does my teen have all or most of the necessary facts?
- ► Has my teen had experience with this kind of situation?
- ► Have I had experience with this kind of situation? If so, how is my teen's situation similar and different from mine?
- ► How serious are the repercussions of poor judgment in this particular situation?

Notice that none of these questions assumes that you know better than your teen about a particular situation.

For example, when Kathy wanted to drive to the party, her parents might have worried that she wouldn't drive safely, would drink at the party and put herself and others at risk by trying to drive home, or would stay out all night and get into trouble. Suppose Kathy's parents decided she shouldn't drive to that party because "they know how dangerous it is." Chances are they would be basing that conclusion on several assumptions: Kathy would make the same mistakes they made as teens; because a friend's teen got into big trouble while driving the family car to a party, all teens get into trouble when they drive the family car to a party; all teens are reckless and irresponsible like the troublemakers they read about recently in the newspaper or heard about at the office.

Judging your teen based on what others, *including yourself* did or still do automatically leads him to resist and even reject your input into his situation. If you do not consider his own personal abilities — and I don't mean the abilities your child had five or even two years ago — while helping him make sound decisions, you will create a stressful situation.

Although it might be hard for you to admit, the stress is not coming from the issue at hand but from the way in which you are handling it. You must look at your teen as an individual and give him the benefit of all that he knows while being careful not to assume you know more about the situation than you actually do.

On the other hand maybe Kathy's parents didn't think she should drive to that party because she wrecked the car earlier in the year while speeding to a party, she has lied on several occasions about what she was doing when she went out, or she has a previous history of driving when drinking. If this is the case, Kathy's parents have valid reasons to be concerned and need to communicate their concerns effectively to Kathy.

I'll give you some guidelines for communication later in this chapter.

When Randy's father says, "Son, I know what's best for you; do what I tell you to do or you can't go to the prom," Randy has no chance to explain or act on what *he* feels is best for him.

Randy's father has made him powerless. Now Randy has only two options: to feel inadequate, helpless, and dependent (which will probably lead to feelings of depression), or to fight back, "rebelling" against his dad's authority, in which case he will be labeled as having "authority problems."

As you can imagine, either response will result in stress, for both Randy and his father.

No one wins in a power struggle. This is one of the most important points to remember if you want to reduce stress during your child's teenage years.

If Randy ignores his father after his father tells him no, Randy will still lose out, not just because he'll be grounded, but because he will see his father as having lost the power struggle, and he'll lose respect for his dad. No person, even an adult, feels good when he wins "over" another person.

If Randy succumbs to his father's threats and gives up what he wants, he'll also feel that he lost. And his father will have lost the hope, at least for the time being, of having his son mature into an independent person. No one wins. *Power plays always create stress, no matter how they work out.*

Family Putdowns

Putdowns are another source of family stress. When one person builds his power or sense of value by saying he is better than another person, stress is a sure result. Calling teens names, telling them they are "stupid," "weird," "fat" or "lazy," is disrespectful and stress-inducing. So is challenging what they do or don't do, "You don't know enough to come in out of the rain." "Look at the grades you brought home! Anyone could have made those grades just by sleeping through the semester!"

When someone builds himself up by making a big deal of a teen's inexperience, a stressful situation is created. In addition, the person dishing out the putdown doesn't really gain any long-lasting good feeling by doing it. And the teen is damaged.

In some families the tables are turned, and a teen is allowed to speak down to a parent. Often this happens in families in which one parent openly puts down the other. Unfortunately, scape-goating becomes a way of life in these families. Everyone loses when respect is lost.

Chaos

Another source of stress comes from living in a chaotic family — one in which there is little consistency or order. When the parents don't follow through, the teen doesn't know what to count on. A teen growing up in this kind of family will feel insecure and will keep trying to find stable limits within which to live.

Mark's mom, for example, usually went out to have a drink after work. Sometimes she'd come home after one or two drinks and fix dinner for the family. But sometimes she'd stay at the bar all night drinking. Mark never knew what to expect.

Once she embarrassed him in front of his friends by showing up drunk at a school function. At other times she would come to school sober for open house and everything would be okay.

Sometimes she was easy to get along with, and sometimes she was awful—irritable, critical, and even abusive. It all depended on how much she had to drink and how stressful her day had been at work. Mark felt helpless because he could never predict her behavior. He didn't know what to do about changing the situation.

Mark expressed his stress at living in a household with such a lack of order or consistent expectations by yelling. He yelled at his mother, whom he did not respect. He yelled at his sister because he didn't know another way to communicate how awful he felt. He knew she really couldn't do anything to help the situation, but he had to yell at someone, and it was safe to yell at her. He yelled at his dad when he could find him, but his dad stayed away from home a lot. And when Mark yelled at him, his dad just walked away.

Yelling made Mark feel like he had some power in an impossible situation. Actually, it only helped to temporarily discharge the tension he felt inside. Yelling didn't get him what he wanted in the long run—feelings of safety and security and a role model that showed him how to grow up with some hope of having his needs met. And he surely had no idea how to feel good about himself.

THE CAUSES OF STRESS FOR PARENTS OF ADD TEENS

As you well know, your offspring has marched to a different drummer from the time he was born. Society's norms are probably quite different from what works for him, and you've had a lot of experiences in which you are trying to fit a square peg into a round hole. By the time you've reached the present stage in your development as a parent of a teenager, you know what society expects and have found ways to fit in, at least somewhat.

When your teen does not accommodate well to his "misfitting" environment, you are likely to feel uncomfortable. Often the more successful you have become, according to societal norms, the more your teen will want to "be herself." You, as a result, are likely to feel stress, maybe a lot of it.

Mismatched Comfort Levels
Each one of us has a comfort level—a zone in which we feel comfort in relation to what is going on around us. Parents' comfort levels include their comfort or discomfort with their children's behavior and choices. And it's a very individual thing.

For example, you might feel comfortable with your daughter's purple hair or your son's long hair, while your brother might feel uncomfortable if his children made these choices. As a result, you might appear more or less flexible and accepting than another parent. And it wouldn't be unusual for your spouse to have a different comfort zone from you.

ADD teens are often quite creative and express themselves differently from those in the mainstream. ADD kids like excitement and variety; they tend to take risks and often don't mind challenging the status quo. But if this type of behavior falls outside your comfort zone, then stress is the result. Of course, if you're ADD, you may already have a broad comfort zone, in which case the stress will come in relation to others who think you're doing something "wrong."

When Gwen's coworkers questioned her practice of allowing her thirteen-year-old ADD son to watch television instead of "hitting the books," she felt stress. She wondered whether she was doing the right thing. Then she remembered how much he seemed to be learning from scanning the various channels. So she decided to quit fighting him all the time about doing schoolwork and accept his making C's on tests. Previously they had battled constantly, and he still made C's.

Gwen reassessed her position about TV because she noticed that her son was beginning to talk about a career in television as a sports broadcaster. That was something new, and Gwen was overjoyed. She knew he was more likely to attend to his studies over the next few years if he were headed for a career that excited him.

When her son did watch TV, Gwen made sure he wasn't just being a couch potato and that he was thinking about what he was watching. They talked about how much time he could comfortably spend on schoolwork, and they agreed upon an amount they could both live with.

Although Gwen felt satisfied, other parents didn't realize how much thought and discussion had gone into her decision. They reacted superficially, clucking their tongues about how bad television is for kids and looked at her as if she were guilty of some great offense. But Gwen didn't feel stressed from their behavior because she was confident about her decision.

Disapproval from school personnel who think your teen "could just do it if she tried," puts you on the defensive and is another source of stress.

Unless you are a trained educator, you may feel that school personnel, as the authority figures, always know best. But something inside of you knows your child, too. Consequently, you're likely to find yourself in a stressful conflict when the school representative pressures you to get your child to do something you know is not realistic.

Benjamin received a call at work about his son Luke who was flunking algebra. Luke was also on the varsity cross-country team that had a big meet scheduled immediately after six-week grades were due to come out. In addition, when the teacher had told Luke he was just a lazy kid who thought he was too good to have to do his homework, Luke got up and walked out of class.

Benjamin knew Luke was having trouble with algebra. He also knew that Luke had been trying hard to understand it but just couldn't. He knew that his son didn't do his homework because he didn't have any idea *how* to do it. Luke felt ashamed and didn't want anyone to know how "dumb" he felt. That's why he didn't go to peer tutoring at school. And Luke had told his father about the time he impulsively walked out of class. He said he had done that rather than hit the teacher or break up the desks. Stressed to the max, Benjamin inhibited the impulse to yell at his son, but he felt like yelling so that the problem would get fixed, so that he wouldn't get calls from school, and so that his son could run in the cross-country meet he was really looking forward to. Benjamin's stress came in large part because he was so worried about his ADD son. Luke had finally found something he loved—running—and it was about to be taken away.

Benjamin realized that if his son knew what to do to solve his problems with algebra and his teacher, he'd already have been doing it. He realized that no teenager gets up in the morning and asks himself, "How can I make trouble for people today?" Unfortunately, this seems to be something many adults don't understand. Chances are the school personnel would criticize Benjamin's enlightened view of his son and judge it to be overly protective.

If you've ever received the disapproval of other adults because of the way you're trying to help your child, you know exactly what I mean. But you *must* stand up for your belief in your son or daughter as you work to find a solution. That doesn't mean denying the problem exists. It means that you ask others to help solve the problem rather than play a blaming game to prove who's wrong or should be disciplined.

Parental Differences
Stress emerges when a teen's parents have differing ways to solve problems. Usually, one parent emerges as the "tough" parent and the other as the "understanding" one.

The tough one has high expectations, often a fairly rigid way of solving problems, and believes that everyone would be better off if they just did everything his or her way.

The understanding parent is more empathetic and tends to feel what the youth is feeling. This type of parent tends to make excuses for his or her child and may even do things for her that she can certainly do for herself.

103

The tough parent often has expectations that are too high, and the understanding parent may have expectations that are too low. Often the understanding parent will be more lenient to make up for the strictness of the tough parent. Then the strict parent compensates, becoming even more strict or critical of the teen, and the seesaw goes back and forth.

The result is marital stress between the parents. Divorced couples, though already familiar with their differences, may also continue to seesaw back and forth on these issues. Even single parents with a man-friend or woman-friend run into this.

No one wins in this scenario, and everyone becomes stressed. But the biggest loss by far is suffered by the teen. She is likely to receive emotional or verbal abuse from the warring adults. And she certainly receives no constructive guidance.

Fatigue

There's a good chance that stress has become a common part of your everyday life if you've dealt with ADD for years. Fatigue—just getting worn down—often emerges as a major secondary source of stress for the parents of ADD teens.

As a single parent of an ADD son, Georgia had been making visits to school for years, attending parents' meetings at church, and trying to explain her son's ADD to her friends. She watched one of her personal relationships end because "dealing with that kid was just too much," and she suffered the pain of seeing her son's low self-esteem and poor social life. She was afraid he'd never grow up.

She wasn't sure how much longer she could hang on. She didn't know what else to do to help him. She was even considering asking her doctor for a tranquilizer to help her deal with the stress.

Since ADD appears to travel genetically from generation to generation, an ADD teen is likely to have at least one ADD parent. It's stressful enough when a parent is not ADD and must struggle to understand what ADD is and how to live with it; but it can be even more stressful when an ADD parent is trying to raise an ADD youth.

Let's look at the different parent/child combinations of ADD types to see the effect on stress levels within the family.

WHEN BOTH PARENT AND TEEN HAVE ADD

The Outwardly Expressive Parent and Teen

When both parent and child are Outwardly Expressive ADD, they probably have great fun together, often making a lot of noise and calling attention to themselves in public. They are likely to be involved in many exciting activities. Stress comes from taking on too much and from other people who don't approve of not staying within limits the way you're "supposed to."

This parent and teen are likely to experience stress because they tend to overlook details, which can lead to missed opportunities, lowered grades, and frustration. When this combination disagrees, everyone hears it.

The Outwardly Expressive Parent and the Inwardly Directed Teen

The Outwardly Expressive parent is likely to overwhelm an Inwardly Directed teen, inundating him or her with lots of talk and action, not noticing that the teen is unresponsive.

Stress results when this type of parent tries to get the teen to respond in a way that is familiar to the parent—not realizing that the teen's way is different. And the teen just might not be able to keep up with the parent. This type of parent is in danger of "winning" conflicts.

The Outwardly Expressive Parent and the Highly Structured Teen

The parent in this combination is likely to get frustrated with his teen's perfectionism and attention to detail, seeing no reason for it. The parent then pushes harder to get the teen going in the direction the parent thinks he or she should go. And the teen, being rigid by nature, stubbornly resists all the more.

The Outwardly Expressive parent is likely to lose his or her

105

temper, expressing anger and frustration overtly. The teen may fail to respect the parent and not recognize the strengths the parent has to offer, instead dwelling on the fact that the parent does not seem to behave in a logical, detail-oriented manner.

The Inwardly Directed Parent and the Outwardly Expressive Teen

The parent with Inwardly Directed ADD is likely to feel controlled by the teen with Outwardly Expressive ADD, even when that is not the intent of the teen. This type of teen is simply a lot more expressive than a parent with Inwardly Directed ADD. This teen is likely to voice his opinion loudly about what he does and does not like. In response, the parent may become passive, frustrating the teen. The teen is likely to win arguments and lose respect for the parent. And the parent might feel like washing his hands of responsibility for the teen. If that happens, the teen has no solid limits or guidance from the parent.

The Inwardly Directed Parent and Teen

The relationship between a parent and teen with Inwardly Directed ADD can be quite peaceful, especially if they share a particular interest. But stress can result from the fact that neither of them tends to finish things in a timely manner. And if neither develops an interest or talent, boredom and frustration may develop.

The Inwardly Directed Parent and the Highly Structured Teen

Though this teen may live more peacefully with an Inwardly Directed parent than an Outwardly Expressive parent, lack of respect can again become an issue. When the teen doesn't understand the ways of the parent, he or she can often become either patronizing or critical. If the parent has low self-esteem, he or she may turn the parenting over to the teen.

The teen with Highly Structured ADD might seem to be in control but, in reality, is very inexperienced. Frustration comes when the teen does not see the parent's guidance as valuable and he ends up with no guiding limits.

The Highly Structured Parent
and the Outwardly Expressive Teen

The parent in this combination is likely to demand more and more of the teen as the teen rebels against the parent's control. This can be an extremely volatile situation, and major power struggles often develop with big blowups.

This type of teen tends to fight back, which only exacerbates the rigid, critical, and threatening nature of the parent. In this situation the Outwardly Expressive teen is likely to take his or her anger out on others or run away to "do his own thing," totally discounting the parents.

The Highly Structured Parent
and the Inwardly Directed Teen

Because the Inwardly Directed teen does not openly fight back, he is more likely to become depressed in relation to this parent's controlling nature. If the teen is having difficulties or failing at a task, this type of parent, rather than trying to understand the problem, may start giving orders that simply overwhelm the teen and cause serious feelings of frustration and helplessness.

This teen is likely to run away into chemical abuse or become a couch potato. Or he can become dependent on the parent. And the parent will become stressed when the youth does not become responsible.

When family members have more than one kind of ADD, aspects of each of these differences will appear. No one intends these outcomes, but they occur just the same. The most important aspect of handling them is to realize that no *one* approach to parenting works for all youth. And parents are not all alike. Both the parent and the teen can come to understand their natural inclinations, acknowledging the way in which the other is wired and making allowances to do what feels comfortable *and* suits the other person.

Siblings

Another source of stress within the family comes from sibling issues. Whether one child or several children in a family are ADD, there are many opportunities for stressful situations to develop. Considering the genetic nature of ADD, your children are likely to reflect various types of ADD, which can cause additional stress.

Consider Jacob, a fourteen-year-old with Highly Structured ADD, and his sister Rachel, a twelve-year-old with Outwardly Expressive ADD. Rachel was always interrupting Jacob, bouncing into his space and bumping into him or the table he used to build his model airplane. You could see the pain on Jacob's face as the pieces of his airplane would shift and begin to fall. You could also see the guilt on Rachel's about this problem she didn't intend to cause. At this point, Jacob and Rachel would usually start yelling at each other. Their arguing would irritate their parents. Why couldn't she just be more careful? Why couldn't he just be more tolerant? And, the parents wondered, why couldn't *they* just ignore the yelling and squabbling? It was a familiar situation—one that almost always became very stressful.

Occasionally, several siblings will like the same activities, but all too often they won't. Your desire for a picture-perfect family in which everyone is sweet and kind and dearly loves one another seems destined for unfulfillment. When ADD enters the picture, the differences between the siblings can become even sharper. They must be acknowledged and accommodated.

Although it is certainly difficult when more than one of your children is ADD, it's just as difficult when one is ADD and another is not.

For example, how can LaTisha possibly understand what Derrick, her ADD brother, is going through when she has almost none of the characteristics shared by people who are ADD? Generally, if she wants to do something new, all she has to do is try it, spend some time practicing, and she usually learns the skill. Derrick, who seems smarter than her in many ways, is so impatient that he doesn't spend any time at all doing his schoolwork. In fact he rarely sits down at all. LaTisha is two years younger, but her attention span is greater, and she almost always finishes whatever she starts.

People ask LaTisha if something is wrong with her brother because he's doing so poorly in school. She's embarrassed to tell them he never does his homework or even tries. She assumes he's just lazy. And when she gets mad at him, she calls him names.

As a parent, you hate to see this happen. But you also get tired of trying to stop it—particularly when your spouse tends to think poorly of anyone who has to struggle with learning. Consequently, trying to help your ADD and non-ADD children to cooperate and appreciate each other's talents and skills is emotionally exhausting for you.

Every child in a family struggles to feel special and good about himself or herself. When ADD becomes apparent as the cause of some of the difficulties experienced by a person, it's not uncommon to start blaming ADD for *everything* that is wrong.

ADD can never be solely responsible for the difficulties and stress that are part of a family's life. But the differences it creates—between parents and children and between siblings—must be understood and handled respectfully by everyone in order to minimize that predictable stress.

ALLEVIATING STRESS

Two strategies can be used to alleviate stress. You can change the circumstances creating the stress or you can use coping skills to reduce its effects. Unfortunately, changing the stress-causing circumstances in your life isn't always an option. But you can learn to prevent a build-up of stress by incorporating stress-prevention techniques into your daily life, as individuals and as a family unit.

I consider these techniques just as important as brushing your teeth every day to prevent dental cavities or working up a budget to make sure you can pay your rent. That's how important they can be in helping you maintain your mental and emotional health and a positive outlook on life.

Relaxation

Each individual, even a young child needs to practice some form of relaxation. One of the easiest, least expensive, and most effective techniques for relaxing is to breathe in a relaxed manner. Coupled with quiet time, a teen or parent needs to be aware of when it's time to take a deep breath or go off alone. You can model this for your teen by simply announcing that you're going outside to the patio to be quiet for ten minutes. When you're finished and return to the house, mention that you feel refreshed. Your offspring will get the message.

You might suggest that your teen go to her room for quiet time at the same time each day. Just as when she was a child and didn't want to go to sleep, you might need to say, "I want you to stay there for thirty minutes to rest. If you can't go to sleep, that's okay. Just take some time off." This routine "down time" will only be worthwhile if it is never used as punishment or as a repercussion of certain moods or behavior. And don't *you* forget to go to your room and relax too.

The whole point is to be proactive with your relaxation rather than waiting until you're exhausted. This is something you can control. Though you may feel you can't possibly take the time, you will find the time if you want to make relaxation a priority. Unfortunately, people with ADD often avoid relaxing because they are fearful of getting bored. But if they don't take some time to relax, they might begin to feel anxious or irritable or even more hyperactive.

Do something you find relaxing every day. A quiet walk or lying by a swimming pool might do the trick. Start with five minutes if you can't do thirty. Then slowly increase the time you spend. There's nothing wrong with reading in bed before falling asleep or even watching TV while you're lying down. Just do *something* relaxing every single day.

You might even want your family members to sign a "relaxation pledge." Corny as it seems, a pledge works well to reinforce relaxation as a priority.

Recreation and Physical Activity

Many people with ADD do not get enough physical exercise, even though they might be hyperactive or restless. I'm talking about the kind of physical activity that includes recreation or pleasure, like walking or playing recreational sports. Highly competitive sports do not count for this purpose. Even though they are enjoyable under some circumstances, they tend to increase stress.

You may want to exercise formally by going to a gym or playing a sport, or perhaps you'd rather walk in the woods or along a beach for thirty minutes every morning.

I would suggest that whatever you do, turn your mind off by paying attention to your body. As you swing a racket or lengthen your stride, pay attention to how your legs feel. What does the ground feel like under your feet? Is the air moist or cool against your skin? As you become aware of your body, you will be less anxious and more in tune with your surroundings. And that, believe it or not, will have the effect of soothing your entire system and reducing stress.

If you live in the city, try to find a park where you can get the benefit of the earth. Always being on concrete does not allow your body to fully relax. Water is a good alternative, either in a swimming pool or spa or in your own bathtub.

The trick is to choose a regular relaxation activity so that your mind and body gets used to relief of stress before it accumulates.

Good Eating Habits

Do you shovel your food into your mouth, rarely taking time to savor its flavor? Do you eat only one meal a day, taxing your digestive system all at once? Do you get a balanced diet, or are you drawn to lots of sweets, fast foods that may be low in nutrition, or concoctions full of synthetics and preservatives?

Eating healthful foods regularly, and being sure that you enjoy the food you eat is a must for people with ADD. And remember, you don't necessarily have to sit down at the table together as a family. That can become stress-producing itself, depending on everyone's schedules!

Often teens who participate in sports or strenuous activities such as dance are coached about nutrition so they can get the most out of their bodies. Seeking role models with healthy eating habits who also have interests similar to your teen's can help your case. Again, never discount the effect *you* have as a role model. If you eat poorly, constantly dieting one minute then drinking alcohol or laughingly "fudging" on your diet the next, your teen will tend to model your behavior.

Teens should eat healthily not to *look* good but to *feel* good. The emphasis needs to be on doing this for themselves, not because others will judge them for it.

Eating disorders are a real concern for parents of all teenage girls, but even more so for parents of ADD daughters. Some evidence is developing that eating disorders and ADD may be linked. Certainly compulsive eating, bulimia (binging and purging), and anorexia are all stress-producing conditions.

Though little is truly known about the development of these disorders, and many past theories are being rejected, some evidence about brain chemistry (which also dictates ADD) indicates that a healthful diet and stress-avoidance practices might help to prevent eating disorders in some people.

Learning to balance self-control with relaxation, avoiding over-control, and being sure that fun and playfulness are a part of family life can help keep these serious physical conditions from developing.

COPING WITH STRESS

For families that include an ADD teen or parent, stress is a permanent issue and one that must be addressed on a daily basis. To help you cope effectively with that stress, I'd like to present several options for you to consider making a part of your family life.

Family Meetings
I'm a great believer in family meetings. They are based on the premise that each member of a family is important and that par-

ents and youth alike should be given the opportunity to be heard. In successful family meetings each person negotiates to get his or her needs met, and no one loses in the process. A family meeting can be a positive way of honoring individual differences. But successful family meetings don't just *happen*. Family members have to be willing to learn, and stick with, the appropriate procedures.

On a regular basis, once a week initially, the family needs to find thirty to sixty minutes when all the members can sit down together. (The length of time depends on how many people are in the family and how restless the participants are.) Turn off the television and radio, and don't answer the phone. Simple snacks are okay and often help people concentrate, but having the meeting at meal time is not a good idea.

Here are specific steps to follow:

▶ One person is designated as notetaker and timekeeper.
▶ Each person has a short period of time to bring up something he or she would like to work on in the meeting. This stressful situation can involve two family members or it can include someone or something outside the family. Three or four minutes is plenty of time for the person to explain the problem.
▶ As soon as the person speaking begins to repeat himself, he needs to turn the speaking over to the next person.
▶ Each person is given the opportunity to raise one issue. If someone has an emergency situation and needs another turn after everyone else has spoken, that's okay. (Family members can call a family meeting any time during the week if something important comes up.)
▶ Parents and youth alike are treated with respect. Blaming, scolding, and shaming have no place in a family meeting.
▶ A speaker must use "I" statements. For example, suppose the issue is a bathroom shared by two sisters. One sister, who is non-ADD, is angry that the bathroom is always

113

left messy by her ADD sister. An example of an "I" statement would be, "I don't like it when you leave the bathroom a mess. I want us to find a way to share the bathroom without my having to always clean it up."

An example of a blaming "you" statement would be, "You never clean up after yourself. You make me sick." The first couple of meetings may require practice on how to speak respectfully to one another.

▶ After everyone has presented what they'd like to work on, start a second round to find solutions. All constructive suggestions are welcome, but no arguing allowed.

▶ Ask everyone involved in a situation to give his or her perspective, emotions included. For example, during the second round of addressing the messy bathroom issue, one person might say that she feels really bad and gets overwhelmed when clothing, towels, toothpaste, make-up, and the hairdryer are left out. She also hates it when the soap is left in the bottom of the tub to get gooey and toilet paper isn't replaced when it's used up.

▶ It's often a good idea to turn to the person whose behavior is offensive and ask, "Do you mean to make me feel bad?" At the first family meetings, teens may be a little uncomfortable and say, "Yeah, I just do it to bug you." Usually, they're kidding around. When that happens, a parent needs to calmly reaffirm that this is an important meeting and the goal is to see that each person gets what he or she needs, so give thoughtful answers, please. Then thank the person who was goofing around for taking the meeting seriously from this point on. "Seriously" does not mean being agitated or morose.

▶ Next, ask the other user of the bathroom, "And what is your perspective on what your sister said?" This sister might say, "She's always rushing me. I don't have time to clean up after I use things. Besides, it's really hard for me to remember to do all that stuff. I can never be as neat as Miss Prissy Two-Shoes."

At this point the second sister has begun to touch a much deeper issue related to ADD messiness. Her sister, in fact, might be a very organized person, and in comparison the ADD teen has long since given up trying to keep up with her sister. What a great opportunity to discuss their differences and find some solutions that can help both girls feel better and coexist more peacefully!

The important thing in this family meeting situation is that neither sister is declared right or wrong, just different. Maybe the neater sister could help her disorganized sister clean the bathroom at the end of each day. Maybe the organized sister could work up a checklist and pin it to the wall. At least special places could be selected for the most used items and marked so the ADD teen would have a quick reminder of where things go. The non-ADD sister could also make an effort not to use the critical tone of voice that makes the ADD teen feel and act helpless and childlike.

When they both understand that it's easy for the organized teen to keep things straight and that the messy teen needs a little help because of being ADD, they can both appreciate each other better. The ADD teen needs to realize that the messiness doesn't mean she's a bad person, but that it truly distresses her sister. Together they can help one another.

The family meeting can encourage a willingness to work together. Perhaps the ADD sister could make a trade with her non-ADD sibling, using one of her talents, such as playing guitar at her sister's party or helping her write a creative story in exchange for help in straightening the bathroom.

Problem-Solving Events

Inevitably, problems arise with ADD teens. Though they can't be avoided, the way in which you respond—the way in which you "problem-solve"—can make the problem either better or worse.

Let me tell you what happened to a fifteen-year-old who impulsively wrote on a dirty car parked outside a video parlor. His parents dropped him and a friend off at 9:00 p.m. on a Friday night. They left to do some shopping and planned to return well before closing at 11:00.

Shortly after the parents left, the game place closed early for a private party. After waiting in the parking lot for a while, the boys got bored. One of the boys found a penny on the ground and used it to write a four-letter word on the side of a sports car with a thick layer of dirt on the door. Then he handed the penny to the other fifteen-year-old and said, "Finish it." So the ADD fifteen-year-old did it just as the owner of the car appeared on the scene.

The police were called, and when the parents drove up at 10:30, they saw their son and his friend, heads hanging, standing next to a policeman. The teens were issued a citation and released to the one boy's parents.

The parents took this opportunity to teach their son by turning the incident into a problem-solving event. One look at their son's face in the parking lot convinced them he had already learned his lesson. Stark terror reflected from his eyes as he watched his dad and mom talk with the police officer and agree to restitution, if necessary.

The parents could have scolded their son when they got home; instead they sat down on the couch, asked him how he was, and whether he wanted something to eat or drink. After learning that he couldn't swallow anything because of the knot in his throat, they asked him to tell his story. More scared than he'd ever been in his life, their son told what had happened—how they'd become bored, how his friend found the penny, and how he finished writing "the word" just as the owner appeared. He said he'd never even thought about what he was doing. He "just did it."

Obviously the teen was not a hardened criminal looking for mischief. Nor was he a troublemaker. The parents quickly decided that no consequences were necessary other than taking responsibility for any costs involved in damage repair. They did feel, however, that their son needed to learn to think before he did something impulsively again that could get him in trouble.

Their positive approach led to talking about the potential consequences of impulsive behavior. They spoke in a matter-of-fact tone of voice without threats. They talked about what would have happened if the car's owner had been a "hothead" and punched the teens out—or worse, pulled a gun. They raised the possibility that the teens could have been taken to jail if the parents hadn't shown up and how this was something they hoped their son would never have to experience.

They talked about the potential cost of having to repaint a new sports car. They also talked about what else the teens could have done to amuse themselves while waiting for their parents to pick them up.

Then they shifted into a nurturing mode. "I'm sorry this happened, Son. I can tell how scared it made you feel. I know you didn't mean to do anything as serious as this seems to be."

Often parents don't consider thoughtless behavior to be hurtful to their child. But the outcome *can be* a very frightening, even traumatic, event for a young person who didn't intend harm.

The parents told their son they'd stick by him. He would, of course, have to earn the money to repair any damage to the car. Then they told him they believed he had learned a tough lesson that night and that he'd be more careful next time.

This story turned out well. Though the young man carried the citation in his billfold for an entire year, he did not hear again from the police. It turned out that the writing on the car door did not penetrate the dirt to harm the paint. The teen never again got into any trouble with the law.

Several years later the young man recalled how frightened he had been and how much he appreciated the approach his parents took. They left him no doubt that he had acted impulsively and inappropriately. But they also conveyed how much they understood that he didn't intend to cause all that trouble. He felt grateful for their support.

These wise parents turned an incident into a problem-solving event and helped their son learn several lessons. First, he learned that when someone acts impulsively, the results can be handled in a calm and rational manner. Second, he learned that his parents

117

would listen to his side of the story and believe him. Third, he discovered that his parents would teach him how to avoid similar situations in the future. And he knew he would be required to take responsibility, financial or otherwise, for the results of his actions, even if those results were not what he had intended.

How different this approach was from threatening or embarrassing him in front of the policeman or his friend, or punishing him with grounding or other retribution. With any of those approaches, he would have learned little and the teachable moment would have been lost.

The stress of any incident or accident your teen causes will always be compounded by the stress resulting from the way the incident is handled. And when no lessons are learned, future stress-producing situations are inevitable.

Obviously, if your son were to repeat the impulsive behavior, that would be a clear sign he is not ready for the freedom or responsibility you've given him and you would need to withdraw some until he gained more maturity.

If you have to take back some freedom, do it in a matter-of-fact way, such as, "I'm concerned that your problems with judgment and impulsivity will cause you to hurt someone else or yourself, so I'm going to restrict you from going to the game parlor at night until you're ready to handle it appropriately." In six months you might see enough signs of maturity that some of the privileges can be returned. Restrict your teen only as far as necessary for him to be safe and stay out of trouble.

Learning to Negotiate

To solve problems, you and your teen need to learn the fine art of negotiation. Sure, you can pull rank and say no to your teen's request, but she doesn't learn anything from that kind of experience. If you really feel something is out of the realm of possibility, you can say no with little or no explanation. But you need to save that type of no for rare occasions.

You'll be surprised how often situations can be negotiated. I'll never forget the stress I felt when my sixteen-year-old, with driver's license in hand, came to me accompanied by his four-teen-year-old ADD brother with a request to go to their first concert alone.

Now you must understand I was a fairly laid-back parent who had only a few absolutely non-negotiable items. I told my sons that their job was to go to school and keep up with their work and that I would not tolerate drinking and driving, abuse of anyone or anything, breaking the law, or lying. Otherwise, I successfully negotiated issues with my sons so that we all felt okay. But this concert request pressed me to the limit.

The first thing we did was assess how important it was to them and to me. On a scale of one to ten, they rated their desire to go as a nine or ten, meaning they *really* wanted to go. On the same scale I rated my desire for them not to attend the concert also as a nine or ten. In other words, this was an issue we both had strong feelings about. We knew we had to do some pretty serious talking. They said they wanted to go to the concert because they'd never been to one, felt they were old enough, loved the entertainers, and they knew how to take care of themselves. They would be careful and I knew they wouldn't drink or use drugs. Didn't I trust them, they asked? And why didn't I want them to go?

"It just scares me," I said.

Because these boys had been well trained to think things through, they insisted that I tell them what I was really afraid of. And I realized it came down to two things. First, they would be going into a situation where many of the people might get out of control, drinking and acting irresponsibly and potentially causing a problem for my teens, especially as they drove away after the concert. Second, I feared what other parents would say if I let them go. I trusted my sons. But I didn't trust the situation or the other people involved.

What I said next was, "Let's figure out a way that you can go and I can feel safe." Instead of arguing, "I want to go" and "No, you can't go," we spent the rest of the week trying to come up with a way they could go with me feeling okay about it.

I would have felt better if I could have driven them, but that wasn't an option from their point of view. There was no public transportation available. Finally, a young friend, age twenty-eight, who had come over to visit volunteered to take them. She would drop them off at the concert, have them call her as the concert was breaking up, and return to get them.

Both my sons and I decided we could live with that solution. They went to the concert. They survived. In fact, they came home wide-eyed at some of what they'd seen. We all felt good that we had not quit negotiating until we found a solution that met all our wishes.

Sometimes negotiations produce unexpected results, as was the case of a young lady who wanted a motorcycle. Though her family wasn't happy about that idea, they did some investigating and discovered there was an active educational program in her community for teaching young people about riding motorcycles. They picked up information about the classes and other require-ments to ride safely and presented them to their daughter. When she heard her parents' requirements — in addition to earning the money for the motorcycle, the insurance, and the upkeep — she decided against it.

Here's a third scenario for learning to negotiate. Suppose your family has trouble deciding where to go out for dinner because you all like different kinds of food. Why not rotate who gets to choose? You could get a variety of food and go to the park to eat, or use the familiar scale of one to ten to determine if someone is craving a particular kind of food and then choose that for the evening. If more than one person is craving a food, try to see whether you can find a place that serves both kinds so no one is left out.

There are many different ways to negotiate within a family so that everyone feels comfortable with the final decision. By watching and learning the negotiating process, your teen can apply those skills to other situations in life.

Having Fun as a Family
Hobbies, common interests, and just plain silliness can bond fam-ily members together and greatly reduce stress. You could meet

at the same restaurant after the weekly volleyball or football game and mourn a loss or celebrate a victory. Try not to overly critique the game or put down players; instead, support each other and enjoy the chance to be together.

One ADD family I know builds a yearly Halloween trail and opens it to the whole neighborhood. Each year they try to outdo what they did the year before. They begin planning months in advance and everyone has a great time coming up with creative ways to do the trail. If one family member has been feeling stressed, this is a sure way to help that person reestablish balance and to relax and have some fun.

Don't forget such family activities as swimming, camping, hiking, boating, skiing, not to mention backyard football games or shooting baskets. Water gun and water balloon fights are wonderful in the summer. Throwing wadded up newspaper or Styrofoam balls at one another, even in the house, can release pent-up stress and get everyone laughing. Don't overlook the pleasure, even with teens, of playing charades or making up costumes to see who can be the silliest.

Laughter probably does more to reduce stress than anything else you can do. Try it!

Forming Your "Family Team"

Although stress is often thought of as something negative, in some circumstances it can unite a family. There are two types of families—those who get their "good" feelings by putting down other family members and those who get their good feelings by belonging to the family.

Sometimes the family joins together against an outside force, sometimes they unite *for* something outside the family, and sometimes they just love being a member of their particular family. Often this unity shows by the support family members give one another.

When Candy was practicing for the cheerleading squad her sister and brother helped her out every day all winter. Tryouts were in the spring and they wanted her to make the squad because it meant so much to her. They coached her, practiced with her, and put her on a training schedule that could have been designed by a pro. Everyone in the family took part, and they even modified their own diets to support her in eating right to increase her strength.

On the day of the tryouts two of Candy's siblings went with her, told her she was great and would do a good job, waited outside, and patted her on the back when she came out, even though she didn't know how she'd done.

Candy didn't make the cheerleading squad that year. But her family hugged her when she cried, distracted her by taking her to a movie, and told her they were proud of her because she tried. They vowed to help her again the next year *if* she wanted to and told her how much they had enjoyed helping her this year.

Derek's family is another story. When Derek didn't make the varsity team or even the starting lineup of the junior varsity team, his family quit going to games. They dropped him off before the game, didn't say much on the way there, and told him to call if he couldn't hitch a ride home. His dad said he was lazy and hadn't worked hard enough, and his mom just wasn't interested. His sister shrugged and said she didn't like to watch the games anyway and his older brother said, "Face it, Derek. You just don't have what it takes."

It's no wonder Derek started getting into trouble after the games when he didn't hurry to get home. Instead, he hung out at the corner to have a beer with the guys—the people who *would* accept him.

And then there's Gretchen's family.

"You're stupid!" yelled Gretchen's younger sister. "All you ever want to do is read. You'll never get a date to the prom that way. You'll probably never even get married. Mom says so. Everyone knows that you can't get anywhere by reading all the time."

In Gretchen's family anyone who was different from the way the mother or father thought they ought to be didn't have a chance. Boys were supposed to be smart, study a lot, go to college, and become professionals. Girls were supposed to look pretty, date someone who was studying to be a professional, and not appear too smart, much less read all the time.

The teens in Gretchen's family who fit that model were accepted and supported. Gretchen was an outcast because she read too much. Mack was also considered unacceptable because he loved music and wanted to be a musician. Even Hilda was in danger of being rejected, even though she was only nine, because she wanted to be an astronaut when she grew up. Her mother said outer space was no place for girls.

The children in this large family who believed exactly the way the parents believed were accepted. The others were not. Tension and stress were everywhere. Yet if differences could have been honored, no tension would have had to exist.

If you come together as a family and respect each individual member, you can alleviate a lot of stress. Fighting with and judging family members creates stress. It's really that simple.

Outside Assistance

A time may come when stress for your teen, yourself, or your family is severe enough that you need outside help. Here are signs that outside help is necessary:

- ▶ Stressful situations that do not de-stress with family meetings or one-on-one talking
- ▶ Stressful situations that increase in frequency and intensity
- ▶ Situations in which one or more family members becomes increasingly agitated, angry, depressed, or emotional with no resolution in sight
- ▶ Family fighting on a daily basis
- ▶ Situations in which a family member avoids the situation by running away from home, never being at home, using drugs or alcohol, developing other addictions, earning only failing grades in school, or missing work commitments

Several kinds of outside help may prove useful. If the problem is in any way school related, the school counselor might be helpful or refer you to a counselor who specializes in the kind of problem you're facing.

If your family regularly attends church or synagogue, you may find assistance with a clerical person who is trained in the kind of counseling you need. In addition, marriage and family counselors, psychotherapists, and counselors who work with youth and families can often assess a situation quickly and provide assistance in short order.

When addictions are involved, Alcoholics Anonymous or Narcotics Anonymous can be most useful. Alateen and Alanon also provide the kind of support and instruction that is a *must* for helping teens and family members deal with addictions.

If additional counseling is sought, it must be with someone familiar with addiction treatment. Do not fool yourself into thinking addiction or even problem drinking or drug use will *just go away* or that *all teens do it*. Get help right away before the problem gets any bigger.

Though stress is a normal part of life, it doesn't need to cripple your teen or family. You can find ways to cope with it. It can even be used to your family's advantage.

CHAPTER SEVEN

GUIDING AND DISCIPLINING YOUR ADD TEEN
What Works, What Doesn't

When you see the title of this chapter, some definite ideas about discipline probably come to mind. Whatever *you* visualize is likely to be quite different from what other readers think. That's because discipline is something we each tend to feel strongly about, with those ideas stemming from the way we were raised and our experiences as parents.

Let's start out by exploring four common concepts of discipline and then establish some general guidelines.

First, let's see what happened when Gary failed to clean up his room one Saturday morning.

Gary's father came home from work that afternoon, took one look around, and began screaming at Gary, calling him lazy and useless. "You know the rules of this house, and you will follow them!" he yelled. "And to make sure of that, I'll give you a lesson you'll never forget." Although Gary was sixteen, his father considered spanking a justified way to treat his son. He called it discipline.

He pulled off his belt and told Gary to lie down on the bed. Of course Gary refused and started screaming back—and that angered his father even more. His father started swinging at Gary with his belt and, even though Gary tried to protect himself, he was bruised on the arms, legs, and face. Eventually, his father left the room red in the face and almost hoarse, screaming at his son,

"And forget any plans you might have had about going to the prom! You're not going anywhere for the next month!"

Raquel's mom also expected her daughter's room to be cleaned on Saturday morning. It was a well-established house rule. When Raquel failed to do the job, her mom lectured her, saying that "a cluttered room leads to a cluttered mind." She scolded Raquel and moaned about her concerns that Raquel's lack of follow-through would leave her unprepared to be a responsible adult.

"You're sixteen now," her mother said. "You'll be graduating from high school in two years. How do you ever expect to get a job that pays anything if you can't even clean your room? You have to learn to be disciplined."

When that argument didn't work with Raquel, her mother switched tactics by saying, "I work so hard, the least you can do is clean your own room. Look at all I do for you. How can you do this to me? You go out all the time. And you don't even bring home good grades. I always did what my parents told me to do. If I hadn't, they'd have really gotten after me. I just don't know what's wrong with you."

When Raquel said, "But Mom, I don't want to clean my room. I will want to work at a job," Raquel's mom countered with, "But now is the time you have to get in the habit. You're grounded for this weekend. That will give you plenty of time to really get this room clean and think about how you treat me. That's my final decision."

Charlie's dad took a different approach when he found his sixteen-year-old's room still a mess after having reminded him that morning that Saturday was cleaning day. He called Charlie into the living room and asked, "What's up? You know Saturday mornings are the time we straighten things up around here. Why didn't you get the job done?"

He gave Charlie a chance to speak and then replied, "I consider keeping things straight a good habit to establish. Your room needs to be cleaned before you can go on with the rest of your activities for the weekend. You decide how long you want it to take. If you need help, let me know. But you're responsible for seeing that the job gets done. Let me know when you've finished. I bet you'll be out of here in no time."

Finally, let's look at Lorie's experience. Her mom talks about using Saturday mornings to clean up around the house, but Lorie never really follows through. On this Saturday, as Lorie's mom is leaving early to do the grocery shopping, she calls back, "Lorie, clean your room this morning. I'll be back at ten."

When ten o'clock comes and goes, Lorie may not even be out of bed. Her mom returns, notes the lack of any progress, and calls down the hallway, "Lorie, get going." No response.

Lorie spends that afternoon at the mall hanging out with friends. When she returns, her mom says, "Your room's still not clean." Lorie's reply? "Aw, Mom."

That evening Lorie calls to her mom on her way out the door to a friend's house, "See ya later." In response, her mom shakes her head helplessly as she passes Lorie's bedroom door. The room is still untouched. Lorie's mom goes in and begins straightening up the room.

The first three parents we discussed believe their forms of discipline are right or appropriate. Lorie's mom, on the other hand, hasn't disciplined her daughter at all.

In Gary's situation the father is abusive, venting his own inner anger on his son. He believes in physical punishment and physical force to get the results he wants. This is a man who has never been able to keep his own temper under control. He continues to try to control his son's behavior in the same way his parents tried to control him. But just as those methods did not help Gary's father develop self-control, neither will they help Gary develop it.

Gary will probably either become an abusive parent, like his dad, or possibly become helplessly passive and depressed, unable to exert any leadership with his own children.

Raquel's mom is not physically abusive. However, she uses verbal criticism to try to gain control over her daughter's behavior. When that doesn't yield results, she uses guilt in an attempt to get Raquel to do what she wants her to do.

Raquel's mom thinks Raquel should keep a clean room

because that's how she was raised. She really believes that Raquel's entire future depends on her cleaning her room on Saturday morning. And Raquel's mom takes everything her daughter does personally.

Actually, Raquel's lack of desire to clean her room does not reflect negatively on her mom. But because her mother's parents *made* her do things she didn't want to do, the mom thinks she must *make* Raquel do things Raquel doesn't want to do. Her weapons are guilt and criticism. She's not a bad mother, she just doesn't know any other way to talk with her daughter.

Charlie's Dad also wants Charlie to clean his room—enough so that he hooks consequences to the completion of the task. But he frames his remarks in a positive context rather than saying them as a threat: "You can go out as soon as your room is clean."

Charlie knows what the limits are. He knows what is expected. But his dad does not put him down, abuse him, criticize him, or try to control Charlie with guilt. Instead he respects Charlie's choices while still holding onto what he feels is important. He's trying to teach him, through the use of limits, to be orderly, conscientious, and responsible.

Charlie's dad was raised in that same matter-of-fact way. Business is business and simply needs to get done. Though Charlie may not like what he has to do, he doesn't suffer emotionally in the process, and he understands why his father thinks the task needs to be completed.

Finally, Lorie is left with a message that reaching goals is optional. Talk about completing a job is just talk. No good reasons are given, no explanations, and no consequences. Lorie is not being corrected and won't have any guidelines to direct her in the future. Nor will she know how to respond to others who may, in fact, *mean* what they say. And she will be surprised to find that some actions, or decisions not to act, have real consequences.

Lorie's mother doesn't mean to deprive her daughter of that necessary guidance, but she has no idea how to do it. She never received the guidance she needed from either her mother or father.

Consequently, she is still undisciplined herself and has no idea how to provide structure for her daughter.

All four of these parents really want what's best for their children. And each is doing the best he or she knows how to do.

WHAT DOES DISCIPLINE REALLY MEAN?

As you can see from the examples above, discipline has different meanings for different people.

Discipline to me must incorporate the steps a parent takes to help his or her teen learn behavior that will produce successful outcomes for everyone involved. Discipline used in this way teaches why a particular behavior is useful and important and the reasoning that led the parent to that conclusion. Discipline provides well-reasoned guidance to the teen. The goal of this type of discipline is to equip the teen to choose these success-producing behaviors *on his or her own* in the future and to develop *self*-control.

Think about it.

Discipline is not used here to mean any kind of repercussion or punishment because the teen *did not* do something the parent wanted, or *did* do something the parent didn't want. Discipline is different from punishment.

Discipline is also different from consequences. The natural consequences of an act are just that — the *natural* consequences of having done, or not done, something.

If you knock over a cup of coffee on your computer keyboard, it can short-circuit the computer and keep you from finishing your work. The natural consequence of putting coffee next to your computer is that it will ruin your computer if it spills. If you don't want this outcome, you will stop putting coffee on your computer work table. No outside form of discipline is involved nor is it necessary. You get the message without anyone telling you. And when you pay the bill for the computer repairs, you'll be paying for the consequences of your actions.

Similarly, if your teen spills a drink on her computer work table, the consequence should include her paying to have the computer fixed. You don't need to scold, discipline, punish, or do anything other than let the consequences occur.

If she doesn't pay to have her computer fixed, then she simply won't have a computer to work on. Don't let her take over your computer; there's no reason for you to be put out. You can allow her to use yours as long as you don't need it and as long as she treats it well and doesn't set drinks around it. But whenever you need it, you have priority. And if that means she doesn't get a good grade on her history paper because she has no access to a computer, that's part of the natural consequences of her keeping liquids near her computer and then choosing not to pay for repairs.

Punishment is never useful, as far as I'm concerned. It teaches nothing but fear and rage and does not accomplish the intended goals. Your goal is to help your teen learn to choose behaviors that will produce successful outcomes. In order to do that, your teen has to understand what her choices are and why choosing one particular behavior will be beneficial to her. Punishment will never give her that information.

Punishment usually accomplishes only one thing: It vents the anger of the person leveling it. And it's usually a replay of how that person was treated as a child. When an adult who was physically punished as a child thinks about that treatment, he or she usually comes to the conclusion, "I deserved it." To come to a different conclusion would require the person to feel the helplessness and fear he buried years before. Instead, that person, now a parent, perpetuates the belief that children need to be physically punished.

Forms of punishment other than physical punishment, though more humane, are archaic. Generally, they only teach that the parent is more powerful than the teen — something your teen already knows. Verbal scoldings, lengthy groundings, taking things away, assigning additional tasks of penance, such as cleaning the whole house or mowing the lawn "because you didn't do such-and-such" are examples of discipline that rarely reflect the principle of consequences for one's actions. As with other forms of punishment, they usually reflect parental frustration.

130

All parents do get frustrated periodically. In our society most parents have swatted their children on occasion or had a verbal outburst in a fit of frustration. There's a great deal of difference between this infrequent, stress-based behavior and routine abuse. When an occasional outburst occurs, rather than wasting time feeling guilty, you would do better to figure out where the stress came from and learn ways for each family member to get what he or she needs *at no one else's expense.*

When verbal, psychological, and physical abuse or near-abuse occur on a regular basis, the parent needs to get help. Even if you don't see yourself as a "child abuser," if you believe it's okay to routinely hit or verbally belittle your child, it's your responsibility to get some help. Your behavior is not healthy for your child or yourself. And don't try to fool yourself by labeling it "discipline."

THE PURPOSE OF DISCIPLINE

Guiding your child's behavior is probably the most difficult job you encounter as a parent. How can you do it in a healthy, constructive way?

Begin by asking yourself what you're trying to accomplish through discipline. What exactly are your ultimate goals?

To raise a youngster to be self-sufficient, self-controlled, and able to fit into society, you need to teach him how to get what he needs in socially acceptable ways. This includes everything from making a living to having fulfilling relationships, developing self-esteem to becoming a leader or teacher of others, and from using creativity to playing in fair, healthy ways. That *is* the goal of most parents—to raise their children to become responsible human beings who are self-supporting and self-responsible and make a contribution to the world while getting their own needs met.

What often confuses the issue is when the parents' needs become confused with the child's. For example, when Wade's dad pushes him to play baseball, practices with him every night, and constantly talks about Wade's innate talent, he may really be communicating that he wishes he had had Wade's talent because he yearned to play ball on a major league team when he was younger.

Wade's dad doesn't realize what he's doing, but he's probably trying to live vicariously through his son so he'll get what he needs. That's why he punishes his son by grounding him from social activities when his grades slip and endanger his eligibility for sports. Of course he wants his son to keep his grades up, but the real reason is his own need to have his son live out his unfulfilled dream. This type of punishment is not discipline. Wade's dad isn't trying to teach Wade how to make good choices; he's simply trying to make sure Wade can play out his own dreams.

Another misapplication of discipline occurs when a parent, such as Gary's, uses his son to act out his own rage. Unaware of what he is doing, this type of parent looks for opportunities to badger, beat, scold, and punish his children—any opportunity to release his own pent-up emotions. Such applications of "discipline" have absolutely nothing to do with the child's guidance.

Not only will the child not learn anything constructive from these situations, but there's no way he can do anything right. That's because the goal in this case is not to correct or guide the youth. The parent's goal, whether he recognizes and admits it or not, is to discharge his own rage.

DISCIPLINARY GOALS FOR YOUR ADD TEEN

Many disciplinary goals for ADD teens are similar to those for any teen. But one major difference often confuses parents: Many parents mistakenly believe their goal should be to help their ADD teen become *less* ADD. So let's be very clear about this. Your goal is to help your teen—as *herself*, as the person she is—learn to make behavior choices that will lead to positive outcomes for herself and others.

If you believe that you can use discipline to turn your ADD teen into a non-ADD teen, *you're on the wrong track*.

Consider Monica. When Monica failed to make the honor roll at school, her parents grounded her and demanded she give up her after-school job, which she loved, so she could study more. Being on the honor roll was not Monica's goal. She was willing to do enough to pass all her classes, but she wasn't willing to do more, and she didn't want to go to college. Monica's dream was to become a fashion designer. And her after-school job in retail sales was a good place to begin to learn about the field she hoped to work in.

Her parents, though, would not hear of her desire to skip college. They failed to understand how difficult school was for Monica and how well her natural creative talents fit the line of work she had chosen.

Because she didn't make the honor roll, her parents told her she was lazy. But Monica *wasn't* lazy. She always arrived at work on time. And she put her math to good use to balance her sales figures at the end of the day because she liked what she was doing.

Monica needed her parents to honor her goals. To punish her because she wasn't reaching her parents' goals would only lead to heartache. Her parents wanted to make Monica into an honor-roll student. And they wanted her to be just like many of her non-ADD peers. Their ultimate motivation was certainly their love and concern for Monica. But their lack of knowledge about Monica and their lack of respect for her goals led them to make disciplinary decisions that were counter-productive to Monica's needs.

By discussing Monica's needs and goals I am not saying that ADD teens are somehow so different that they should never be disciplined. *Not at all.* Every teenager needs guidance to learn how to make good choices and become successful.

For example, an ADD teen who doesn't want to go to college must have some alternative goal in mind. Lying around the house and spending his parents' money are clearly not acceptable options. If the rules of the house and set limits are not met, then natural consequences result — no work, no spending money.

Or, if an ADD teen is impulsive and unwilling to take medication that has been prescribed to help curb his over-reactions in certain situations, then one logical repercussion would be to take away the car keys. Discipline could be applied by requiring him

133

to take a defensive driving course that he pays for. He might also be required to volunteer at a local hospital where auto accident victims are recovering.

These are all logical consequences to this teen's lack of cooperation. Driving is an activity that carries a tremendous amount of responsibility with it. If you are legitimately worried that your teen might not be able to live up to that responsibility, then you wouldn't want him to endanger his life, or anyone else's, by allowing him to drive. It's just that simple.

Parents of ADD youngsters have a lot of experience intervening for their children because of their ADD. However, as the preteen and teen years unfold, the youth must increasingly take over self-management. Disciplining an ADD teenager to *make* her do her homework is not constructive. Rather, as you'll see in chapter 9, the teen simply must experience the consequences of not doing that homework. She has no other way to learn to be an independent person.

Life-threatening situations in which you *should* intervene would include drug and alcohol abuse, at least at first. If your teen continues destructive behavior after you intervene, you may need to let go of this one, hard as it may be. Hurting others, being promiscuous, or flirting with pregnancy (this applies to boys as well as girls) and engaging in law-breaking behavior all call for parental involvement. Otherwise, you need to let your teen take on increasing responsibility for herself. Continuing to discipline your teen's everyday behavioral choices only delays the inevitable learning process she must go through.

For you to know when and how to discipline your teen, you must be clear about the goals you want to achieve. The discipline must be in the best interest of your son or daughter as well as the rest of the family.

When your teen's behavior creates problems for others, then the goal is to help each person involved to get what he or she needs. There should not be winners and losers.

When your teen's behavior creates problems for him, then the goal is to try to guide him along a safe path so he can avoid trouble. Allowing him to experience the consequences of his behavior usually works best.

Physical discipline is never appropriate. It is disrespectful and teaches children that violence is an acceptable way for people to solve their problems. It is also not a deterrent to undesirable behavior, though it may shut it down temporarily. Physical punishment teaches sneakiness. As soon as the child is out of range of the person doing the disciplining, he'll return to the undesirable behavior. In addition, the child, angered by the indignity of physical punishment, is likely to take out that anger on an innocent victim. For similar reasons, verbal or psychological put-downs, scoldings, guilt-producing remarks, or threats also are not appropriate.

The key is to handle discipline in a matter-of-fact way that respects everyone involved. That does not mean your teen is allowed to "get away with" unhealthy or hurtful behavior. Rather, you must establish clear expectations for both your teen and yourself; clear, down-to-earth guidelines for living in harmony; and clear, logical consequences for unacceptable behavior.

HOW ADD TEENS "GET INTO TROUBLE"— AND HOW TO GUIDE THEM

The problems that get ADD teens into trouble are similar to those of other teens, but they may occur more frequently. They also tend to cluster in areas particularly affected by the ADD style of wiring. These include issues related to attention, hypersensitivity, activity level, impulsivity, temper, organizational ability, creativity, and being a kinesthetic learner.

With each of these main characteristics of ADD, your teen has a lot of learning to do. Your job is to help your teen learn to be responsible and effective more than to discipline him for apparent inabilities or inadequacies. True discipline only enters the picture when your teen refuses to participate in a learning situation to overcome the effects of his ADD characteristics; then logical consequences for his actions are very much in order.

135

Let's look at appropriate guidance and consequences for each of the ADD characteristics.

Difficulties with Attention

To help your teen learn to keep her attention focused on what she's doing, consider following these steps.

Step one: Tell your teen what you need from her. Calmly sit down with her at a quiet time and say, "I need you to work on improving your attention. This is very important."

Step two: Tell your teen how you will help her accomplish what you want. You could say, "When I ask you to do something, I'll make sure you clearly understand my request. Would you rather have me ask you or leave you a note?" (Teens often have a distinct preference for verbal or written instructions.)

In Elizabeth's case, her mother might ask her to repeat the request to be sure Elizabeth heard correctly. She might also ask for a time commitment: "Elizabeth, when will you be home with the cookies for your sister's meeting at school?" Or, "Where are you planning to shop for the cookies? I need them here by 7:00 this evening."

Step three: Tell her that you expect her to let you know if she's having any trouble understanding what you want or getting it done. You might say, "If you don't understand what I want or how to get the job done, you need to ask me. I'll clarify what I want. We may need to break the job down into small tasks that are more manageable for you."

Step four: Talk with your teen about using "prompts" such as notes — like a note attached to the dashboard of the car or a bathroom mirror — or a verbal reminder from you or someone else, or an alarm that sounds at a designated time. There are many watches and buzzers that are specially made to alert people to remember to do things. Your teen simply needs to commit to get in the habit of using one or more of these methods as reminders.

Step five: In the early training phase of learning to pay attention, many teens do a lot better working side by side with a parent. If you are willing to do this, say, "Would you like me to help you with the job? Just let me know. I'll need to plan a time that's convenient for me, but I'm willing to give you a hand."

Step six: Summarize the importance of learning to attend to business, and clarify consequences if your teen doesn't comply with the training program. Say, "I know that with practice you'll get better at paying attention. Remember, this is very important. If you're unwilling to work on this, then I'll have to restrict you from doing other things until you finish the job you need to do."

Hypersensitivity

Because your ADD teen is so sensitive, he feels everything that goes on around him, including your feelings, wishes, and desires. When your teen's hypersensitivity sets him up to make commitments he can't live up to, your job is to help him learn to be responsible and truthful, or to reap the consequences of not staying in control of himself. Here are some steps to guide him.

Step one: Affirm your teen's intuition and sensitivity to what others feel or want. You might say, "I notice that you often know what I'm feeling, sometimes before I know it. You just sense what others need. That's a real skill."

Step two: Set limits on what you expect from your teen: "But you must also be very sensitive to what *you* want and need. It's very important that you take responsibility for yourself."

Step three: Give your teen information. Say, "When any of us commits to something that another person wants but it's not good for us, we jeopardize our own well-being. We also set ourselves up to fail, so, in the long run, we let both ourselves and the other person down."

Step four: Give your teen permission to do what is best for him. "I expect you to say 'no' when someone wants you to do something that's not in your best interest. That includes a drug pusher telling you to use drugs, a friend trying to get you to spend the evening doing something you don't want to do, or me urging you to take a course you don't feel good about or don't want to put the effort into. I'd rather you be honest with me than tell me something that will make me feel good temporarily. Sooner or later we'll both end up feeling bad if you do what I want against your better judgment."

Step five: Tell your teen you expect *him to be honest about what he feels.* "I must insist that you take responsibility to be honest about what you feel, want to do, and are willing to do."

Step six: Offer assistance while your teen builds his emotional power so he can be honest. You may want to tell him, "Feel free to talk over the challenges you face. I won't argue with you. I'll try to help you figure out how to protect yourself, even if it's with me."

Step seven: Explain the repercussions you plan if he does not work on taking responsibility for his hypersensitivity. "If you commit to something another person wants more than you want, I expect you to follow through on your commitment until another plan can be mapped out. You'll need to let me know as soon as you realize you've gotten in over your head. You can call me if you're out somewhere and realize you're in trouble. I'll come, no questions asked.

"If you make a commitment to me and realize you didn't really want to, tell me right away and we'll try to figure out a way for you to get out of the situation in a responsible manner. It's very important to leave a situation responsibly so others don't pay for your misjudgment. If you run off or just don't do what you committed to, you'll have to come back and work out an alternative plan."

In Craig's situation, he might need to finish the semester, even if it means making poor grades. Then the next semester his obligation is to decline taking honors classes unless he wants to put in the work. That may be a difficult decision for him if he's taken advanced classes to "please" a parent or someone else, but he needs to learn to make responsible judgments and choices about his own desires and abilities.

As a parent you must allow your teen to use his judgment even if it means he makes choices you prefer he not make. It is in your teen's best interest that you honor his right to learn to be in charge of his life and take responsibility for his commitments.

Activity Level

Physical and verbal hyperactivity and restlessness are usually a part of ADD. Realizing that the ADD style of brain wiring drives your teen's activity level enables you to plan the steps needed to help your teen gain control. Here are some steps to guide you.

Step one: Consult with a professional about the use of medication. Often hyperactivity responds especially well to its use and greatly helps a teen.

Step two: Provide your teen with a structured environment that is consistent. This means having a similar schedule every day, which may not be easy for an ADD parent to manage. But do your best. Set consistent times for getting up and going to bed, meals, homework, chores, and fun activities. Though you don't need to be rigid about these, do try to be consistent.

Step three: Set limits on activities that get your teen "wound up." Too much television watching may precede hyperactive wrestling or fighting between siblings. Too much freedom to talk on the telephone may lead to late-night calls and inconsistent routines. Watch the patterns of your teen's behavior and then point them out along with the limit you are setting in place.

For example, you might say, "I've noticed that you talk on the phone late at night. Then you don't get enough sleep and are grouchy the next day. So I'm imposing a limit of 10:00 for phone use. Tell your friends not to call after that. If you use the phone later than ten o'clock, you won't get to use it at all the next night. I'm sure you'll get this under control and end up feeling better in the long run."

Step four: Instigate a quiet time prior to bedtime so that your teen has a better chance of winding down. Activities like listening to music, watching television (if he hasn't been watching it all night), and reading help many active ADD teens quiet down so they can go to sleep. Do realize, though, that some teens need help from medication if the quiet time doesn't settle them down.

Step five: Teach your teen acceptable ways to express her energy. Encourage sports and other physical activities for a physically hyperactive teen. Encourage your hyperverbal teen to take part in entertainment outlets such as radio broadcasting and song and dance activities or debate. Perhaps your teen needs to become a salesperson who can use her verbal skills to advantage. Your job is to insist that the appropriate outlet be found for the hyperactive behavior.

Impulsivity

Speaking and acting without thinking about the consequences is typical of people with ADD. As one mother said, "If my daughter thinks it, she says it before she's even finished the thought. I used to be just like her, but I've worked hard to engage my brain before I open my mouth so I don't get into so much trouble."

There are two basic steps to controlling impulsivity. First your teen must become aware of what he was feeling when he acted impulsively. Then he must learn alternative ways to handle his feelings. Both verbal and physical impulsivity follow the same pattern. Here are some steps to help manage impulsivity.

Step one: The next time your teen acts or speaks impulsively, stop him and ask what he was feeling right before. At first you'll probably have to help him discover what he was feeling. For example, Matthew always spent his money as soon as he got it. He might be feeling big and powerful because of the money and want to spend it to prove just how great he is. Or maybe he's feeling very, very fortunate and wants to celebrate.

Step two: Once the feeling is identified, you can help your teen find alternative ways to express it. Matthew's parent might say, "Matthew, I think it's fine that having money makes you feel powerful, but you need to know that you can be powerful even if you don't spend all your money. Let's talk about some other ways you can get that feeling."

Brainstorm together. Maybe starting a bank account that he contributes to regularly will do the trick. (As a kinesthetic learner he needs to go to the bank and open the account himself. Though you may need to accompany him, don't do it for him. That would make him feel like it's your account, not his.) Learning to save up for a big item by putting the money in a special place for several months may help him see how it can accumulate and benefit him down the road.

140

Step three: Set limits on the impulsivity in order to establish a new habit that delays action. You may say, "Son, I need you to learn to handle your impulses, so you may not spend all the money you make right away. It's yours, but you may spend only 50 percent of it immediately." (Set any percentage you want.) Then decide where to store the other 50 percent and let your teen decide what it's being saved for and how long it will take to reach the goal.

Be as concrete as possible. Reinforce the saving by keeping track of the saved money. When it's time to spend some or all of it, make a big deal of what a good job your teen did to accomplish his goal. Realize that in the process of saving, he's been establishing a habit he'll keep in the future.

With a verbally hyperactive teen, you may want to encourage her to make a note of something she wants to say so she doesn't forget it. Congratulate her every time she delays saying something even for a moment. Such reinforcement will slowly help her get her compulsive speaking under control.

When she does put her foot in her mouth, however, let her pay her own consequences, which may be embarrassment, frustration, or guilt about what she said. Say to her, "I'm sorry you're feeling bad, but you did speak up and volunteer to do the job before you thought about the amount of time you have to do it. I guess you'll lose some sleep doing what you agreed to do. I know you'll think about whether you have the time when a similar circumstance comes up in the future."

Temper

Telling people off, blowing up, stalking off, and having a temper tantrum are all problems many people with ADD must deal with. To help your teen deal with her temper, you must first check to see whether you or her other parent also have temper problems. Often a teen models the behavior of a parent. To handle this kind of temper problem the parent must also work on developing new skills and needs to tell the teen the truth: "I have a temper just like you do. We both need to get over this and learn new ways to behave. We'll do this together."

Next, consider whether or not you have given in to your teen's temper since her preschool years. If you have, you've unwittingly encouraged her to use her temper to get what she wants. To handle this kind of temper problem, say, "Ever since you were a baby, I found it was easier to give you what you wanted when you had a temper tantrum than to deal with your behavior. Frankly, I didn't know how to handle it so I just gave in. I'm sorry about that now because we've spent a lot of time out of control. I'm also sorry I was misled. It's like I trained you to have a temper tantrum to get what you want. Now we need to tackle this problem, and we'll do it together."

Step one: *Tell your teen the new rules by which you're going to operate.* "From now on, when you want something we'll try to figure out a way for you to get it unless what you want is not in your best interest or is hurtful to someone else."

Step two: *Set the limit you intend to enforce.* "If you whine, yell, or have a temper tantrum, I won't even talk to you about what you want. When you talk in a reasonable voice I'll try to work with you to get what you want. If you continue to yell or whine, you will also need to go to your room until you're willing to talk in a reasonable way."

Step three: *Reinforce positive steps your teen makes toward getting her temper under control.* You don't need or want to wait until she has her temper 100 percent under control; that's not realistic. But even if she lowers her voice a little, you might want to say, "I can hear that you're really trying to manage your temper. I appreciate that. So let's talk and see how we can get what you want."

If you must deny her something, though, and she "comes unglued" again, say, "Under no circumstances am I willing to listen to your temper tantrum. You need to go to your room until you get it under control." Then when she comes out, you can say, "I'll try the best I can to help you get what you need but sometimes I'll have to say 'no.' If you have a fit about that, then I won't even try to work with you on other things you want."

If your teen is feeling frustrated dealing with others outside your family you can say, "Look, I can't help you if you blow up at your friends. I suggest that you take a deep breath and count to ten before you do or say anything. I'd like you to walk away, then come home and tell me what the problem is. Maybe I can help you then." If your teen is feeling frustrated with other adults you might say, "Sometimes other adults don't treat teens fairly, but you can't do battle with them without getting into trouble. As another adult I may be able to intervene. I'll try to help you get what you need."

If your teen refuses to try to inhibit his temper, then you have to say, "I don't expect you to *want* to hold your temper, but I do expect you to *learn* to hold it. Even when you're treated unfairly, you'll only make matters worse by losing your temper. I hate seeing you make trouble for yourself, but if you won't work with me on this, then I can't help you." Stick to your guns and let your teen pay the consequences. That's discipline enough.

If temper training does not help your teen, you'll need to be sure that her temper is not physiologically based. Various seizure disorders and brain misfirings can result in temper outbursts and will not respond to the steps laid out here. A neuropsychological workup would be in order if this is the case.

Organizational Ability
Organizational ability may be the most difficult and far-reaching issue influenced by ADD, affecting the areas of time management, keeping track of details, and project management.

Disciplining a teen's inability to handle organizational tasks is rarely a good idea. Your emphasis needs to be on helping him accomplish the organization needed. Follow these steps and only consider repercussions if your teen is unwilling to work with you.

Step one: Determine whether the problem lies with time management, handling details and keeping track of things, or managing projects.

Step two: Work with your teen to develop the skills necessary to develop organizational ability in the area causing trouble. This work may cover many months or even years, so divide the learning of the skills into small segments that can be rewarded.

For example, the first step for Gerald as he tackles his time-management problems might be to get a watch that can be set with several alarms. Then he needs to choose one area of his life to work on. Suppose he chooses to work on taking his medication on time. Every morning at the breakfast table he could set the alarms on his watch for the times of day when he is to take his medication. He must agree to take it the moment the alarm goes off so he doesn't get distracted and forget. At first, you might need to remind him to set his alarm.

Perhaps he works only on this one time-management problem for a week or two. Each day that he succeeds in taking a dose of medication on time, he needs to congratulate himself and be congratulated. With no other time-management pressures on him, he is likely to be successful. After a couple of weeks he may have actually established the *habit* he needs to continue to successfully take his medication on time. Then another time management issue can be tackled.

Though it may seem like slow going at first, he'll accumulate successes and every single management problem will not need to be ponderously undertaken. Success will breed confidence, which will help him learn many other organizational skills once he believes he can do it.

A key to organizational management for ADD teens is finding what works for the individual. Many organizational management programs are designed by very linear, structured people and don't work for ADD people. Customization is absolutely necessary for success.

Creativity

Though creativity can be a great benefit in some cases, there are many situations in which it causes difficulties. For example, if the teacher gives an assignment but your child uses his creativity to do it in a completely different way, chances are he won't be rewarded. Deciding to tell a creative story about why the car has a dent in it is also not acceptable.

When your teen uses her creativity to fabricate stories or to make excuses for why she didn't do what was expected or to cover a mishap, it must be dealt with decisively. Follow these steps to get "creative lying" under control.

Step one: Express positive feeling about your teen's creativity. You might say, "I know you're a very creative thinker and you express yourself well."

Step two: Set a limit on the use of creativity. "However, you may not use your creativity to cover up for something you did that you weren't supposed to do. That's *lying*, even though you do it colorfully."

Step three: Make it safe for your teen to tell the truth. "Telling me the truth is extremely important. I need to be able to trust you. When you tell me the truth I can help you. Even if you did something that you weren't supposed to do, I will not punish you if you tell me the truth. You'll just need to fix the situation."

Step four: Explain the repercussions of telling a lie. "If you don't tell me the truth, you'll have to deal with the consequences of lying and you'll still have to fix the situation." An example of a reasonable repercussion for denting the car and lying about it would be to pull the car keys for several months until you feel your teen is ready to take responsibility for telling the truth. When he can act responsibly about telling the truth, he can also be expected to drive more responsibly.

Kinesthetic Learning

Perhaps this characteristic of ADD gets teens in trouble more than any other. Parents and teachers often think the teen is purposely refusing to listen to their advice and guidance. Instead, *learning by doing things in his own way* may be his only way to learn a lesson. The following steps will help you handle the consequences of your teen's kinesthetic behavior.

Step one: Assess the situation and tangible damage or problems that have resulted. Do this with your teen. React in a matter-of-fact, non-critical manner when your teen has a *learning* experience even though you may have told her what to expect and she "did it anyway."

Step two: *Make a plan with your teen for "fixing" the problem*—one in which she takes responsibility for the consequences of her action. For example, if she chose not to study before a crucial exam she thought she could ace, she may have flunked. Don't try to bail her out, even if it means she can't go to the college of her choice—the one where her friends are going. It's far better she learn right now to pay for the choices she makes than later when the stakes get higher.

Step three: *Tell your teen you know she'll learn from her experience.* You may even want to empathize with having to learn this way. "I know you really understand now about studying when the outcome is important. I'm sorry you're missing out on going to college where you want to go, but I know you'll make the most of your situation."

Under no circumstances scold or say, "I told you so." That turns the kinesthetic learning experience into a power struggle, which is not the issue at hand. Unless you've been trying to over-control your teen's life, you must remember that he learns by doing things firsthand, not from just doing what you say.

Guidance for Serious Offenses

Logical consequences and education are always the most effective, most constructive, and least damaging ways to change a teen's behavior. Punishment doesn't directly teach him more effective ways to get his needs met. Positive disciplinary guidance does two things: First, it allows your teen to take responsibility for the poor choices he made; second, it shows him how to get what he needs in more effective ways.

A reasonable repercussion of any serious drug, alcohol, or law-breaking offense would be counseling from someone outside the family who is trained to deal with such issues. This repercussion also would be reasonable for any situation not resolved in a family meeting or in a moderate amount of time, or one that is causing on-going trouble for another family member or the teen himself.

In this type of situation the teen's attendance in counseling must not be optional. You can say to your teen, "I don't know how to help you. And I don't know how or why you got into your situation. So I've found someone who knows about such things and can help us. I've made an appointment. I'll pick you up at school, and we'll go from there. We'll all learn some things that ought to help us avoid this kind of situation in the future."

Notice that I didn't say the counseling is *for the teen*. Nor is the emphasis solely on the teen's behavior. Teens never behave in isolation. When a teen is having trouble or acting unacceptably, the whole family (except young children) needs to take part in remedying the situation.

Your teen may be relieved to know that someone is going to help her. More commonly, however, she'll fight the situation. If you hear comments like, "I'm not going," or "I'm not crazy," or "You can't make me," don't be surprised. Don't make threats or get into an argument. First say, "You're right, you're not crazy or bad. But there is a reason why you made a choice that got you in trouble. We're going to find out together what the problem is." When you hear, "I'm not going, you can't make me," try saying, "I'm nervous, too, but I'm going to go anyway. I realize you don't want to go. Are you afraid that all the adults will gang up on you? A skilled counselor won't let that happen. And I won't let it happen. You're important and need to be heard. You can say what's on your mind, and I won't hold it against you or punish you for it."

Usually that does the trick. If it doesn't, you may need to say, "Look, I can't *make* you go. I'm not going to beat you or stop feeding you. But it's very important for you to go. You don't have to answer any questions you don't want to, and, if you want to, you can talk with the counselor in private."

Finally, you would have to say, "If you refuse to go, then I'll have to severely restrict you here at home. I don't like to make threats, but the situation has to change, and I believe counseling will help us. You only need to commit to going this one time. Then we can decide together whether or not to go back. But the bottom line is that *something* is so wrong that it has caused you to get in big trouble. That has to change."

Anytime your teen's behavior causes damage or loss, he must

immediately make a plan for reimbursing the person who suffered the loss. You must help him follow through on the plan.

Making the plan can be a problem for ADD teens and for their parents who may have organizational problems. Keeping the plan operating may be even more difficult because follow-through is a major weakness for people who are ADD. So keep the plan simple and keep track of the steps regularly.

What does the teen learn from this kind of process? She learns that her parents won't cover for her if she does something wrong. *She must be responsible for her actions.* And that is one of the most important lessons for any teen to learn, and one of the most significant goals of discipline. Though it may require a lot of effort on your part, you must let your teen take responsibility for righting a wrong situation.

GUIDANCE FOR DIFFERENT TYPES OF ADD

Outwardly Expressive ADD children often respond best to any intervention that settles them down, such as taking time out in a quiet place. Because of their tendency toward high activity levels, they often cannot stop themselves, so you are doing them a favor by stopping them.

Talking also works well with teens who have this form of ADD. Being talkers, they seem to understand the use of communication to solve problems. Of course, you don't want to be out-talked by your teen, but do listen to what he has to say. Let him say it once. Say what you have to say once. Then move on to the next step.

Trying to solve problems by using a "Let's suppose" format also works well for this type of ADD. "Let's suppose I let you continue to go out every night and not do your homework. What do you suppose would happen?" Or, "Let's suppose I don't make you pay for what you broke, what do you suppose would happen?"

If your teen can come up with an answer that lets you know he understands the problem and the solution, then you know you're on your way to having a better-controlled teen. If he can't solve the problem with you, then he may be in danger of doing the same thing again, which means you'll have to take a more active role in stopping him. He'll need more practice, and you can give it to him by setting limits on his behavior.

The most effective type of discipline for your teen with Inwardly Directed ADD is having the teen *fix* whatever is the matter. Not as verbal as their Outwardly Expressive counterparts, those who are Inwardly Directed often feel more comfortable and learn better when *doing* something. This type of teen is likely to quietly go about the job of fixing things without wanting to talk with you about it. Let him. Less talk and more action works well for these kids.

For example, when Jeffrey forgot, yet one more time, to put the yard tools away after he finished with the lawn, they rusted when it rained that night. His father said, "Jeffrey, you're having trouble remembering to put the tools away after you use them. They've rusted. You'll either need to get the rust off or earn the money to buy new ones. Think about what you want to do today and give me your decision this evening."

Though you are likely to have the least number of discipline problems with Highly Structured ADD teens, you will want to be precise and explicit about what you expect. You'll need to be equally precise about the ramifications of breaking the rules. Be sure to explain why you're doing what you're doing. Then follow through with the consequences. Highly Structured ADD teens understand structure and need it. Provide it.

When Caila, age seventeen, had trouble getting up on time in the morning and was falling asleep in school because she'd been staying up most of the night working on her computer, her mother told her they needed to talk at three o'clock that afternoon. Her mother said, "Caila, you need to get in control of your sleep so you can be fresh for school. I know you like to work on your computer, but you need to turn it off by 11:00 p.m. weekdays and 12:30 a.m. on Fridays and Saturdays. That will give you time to wind down before bed, and you'll be able to get enough sleep to get up on time in the morning and stay awake in school.

"Let's make a chart of the times for using the computer. We'll post it on the wall. Let's also make a list of your other obligations and see whether there are any times you can free up so you can use the computer then. We'll keep a close eye on how much sleep you need, and then you'll know what time you need to turn in. I'll meet with you in one week to see how the program is going. How does that sound?"

You'll notice that there's no negotiation about getting up on time or about falling asleep in class. Rather, the emphasis is on how to achieve these limits. And the method is very structured.

NOTICE HOW YOUR TEEN RESPONDS TO GUIDANCE

Most healthy teens will groan about being disciplined, but they'll go along with it without too much fuss *if you are reasonable*. If your family rules and expectations have stayed fairly consistent over the years, your teen knows what they are by now. So all you'll hear is a perfectly normal objection to being "guided."

If, however, you have lots of limits and rules so that your teen feels hemmed in, you are likely to get a lot of objections or just the opposite: sullen silence. With silence usually comes sneakiness, especially if you're an over-controlling parent. Your teen will not feel safe enough to be honest with you and will sneak around behind your back.

Anger and resentment will also erupt against controlling parents. This kind of anger and resentment doesn't result when discipline is moderate and truly intended to guide and teach rather than to punish. Teens who are appropriately disciplined will tend to brag about being grounded. They will dramatize their plight to their friends, saying, "You know what my mom did? She grounded me for next weekend, just because I didn't come in until after midnight. Can you believe it?" But if you watch the teen's face, you don't see anger and resentment. You see her watching the effect she's having on her friends, as she hopes to get sympathy. In a way, she's relieved that her mom is in control of the situation, and she knows she's safe and protected so she won't get too far out of control. Contrast that to the teen who is over-controlled. Seething, he may talk about how awful his mother is, call her names, and talk about getting even or getting out. Much of his energy will be used in plotting against his parents. He does not see them as members of his team.

With Outwardly Expressive ADD teens you are likely to get a lot of talk about your chosen discipline. But your teen will appreciate fair discipline, even if he doesn't sound appreciative when talking to his peers. The Outwardly Expressive ADD teen may make jokes and become the center of attention with his discipline as the subject matter. You are likely to hear plenty of mouthiness—"Aw, come on, Mom. You don't need to do that to me. I'm a good kid. Next time, I'll be sure to be home on time." Remember, this type of ADD teen can be a super salesman, winning friends and influencing people, including you.

If an Outwardly Expressive ADD teen is over-controlled, he is likely to run away or retaliate. Action oriented, this type of teen will fight back openly with huge uproars. No one is in doubt that there are differences of opinion in this kind of family.

When discipline is fair, Inwardly Directed ADD teens will do whatever they need to do to fix their situations. They usually don't talk a lot about what's happened. They just pay their price, burning off steam by *doing* something. But if the discipline is inappropriate and the parents are overly controlling, this type of teen may become quite depressed. They're not fighters, so they withdraw. They are more likely to drink or use drugs to numb their pain and get even with their parents by hurting themselves.

Highly Structured ADD teens usually will respond to fair discipline by correcting their action quickly and joining the belief system of their parents. They will tend to incorporate the behaviors needed to stay out of trouble into their repertoire of ways to behave. This type of ADD teen usually likes the structure that discipline offers.

If, however, the discipline is inappropriate, the Highly Structured ADD teen is likely to become very anxious and obsessive.

151

He may use alcohol to numb his anxiety. Frequently, this type of teen becomes a controlling, anxious adult who has major problems with compulsive and addictive behaviors.

Always remember your goal: As a healthy, responsible parent you are trying to guide your teen to becoming a healthy, responsible adult. Your motives are good. Besides, you love your kid, and you want the very best for him or her. And you want to spare him the problems you had. You don't want him to learn "the hard way."

But remember that ADD teens are kinesthetic learners. They learn by doing. All the discipline in the world isn't going to change that and, in fact, *can't* change that. No matter how right your discipline methods, you must realize you don't have total control. There will always be certain things your kids need to learn for themselves. They need to make their own mistakes. The important thing is how you, as a parent, react to the situation. You can turn it into a wonderful learning experience, or you can make matters worse.

When your child was little, you could stop him from doing something you didn't want him to do. But sooner or later you must teach your child to stop himself. That's *self*-control. And that's what guiding and disciplining your teen is all about.

CHAPTER EIGHT

TEACHING YOUR TEEN TO BE RESPONSIBLE
What Are the Goals?

Have you ever found yourself saying to your teen, "I'll give you more freedom when you show me you can be responsible," or "Prove to me you'll be responsible with the car and I'll let you take it out after dark"?

The battleground of adolescence is strewn with teens who want more freedom and parents who want those teens to take on more responsibility. How did the war start? It started because parents and teens have differing perspectives on how freedom and responsibility relate to one another.

A teen needs the freedom to make mistakes and learn how to correct them or bear the consequences. That's the only way he can really learn the meaning of responsibility.

As a parent, you fear for your child's safety and want to protect him above all. Since you are turning the reins of protection over to your teen you want to be absolutely sure he or she can do the job in your stead.

Unfortunately, the more you hold onto your teen, the more he will try to wrench freedom from your hand, often impulsively or in moments of high emotion. I would strongly advise giving your teen lots of opportunities to practice freedom—to practice developing responsibility—so that he can learn to be responsible over a period of time in a protected setting.

Gradually and cautiously let go of responsibility *for* your teen and watch him mature slowly but surely into an independent, self-sufficient adult. When he makes an error, uses poor judgment, or bites off more than he can chew, use that situation as a teachable moment. Your parenting job will take on increased importance at such times.

As I noted in the previous chapter, disciplining your teen for exhibiting poor judgment is much less important than educating your teen about how to do things differently the next time. That's how learning occurs. Do it for both of you.

WHAT RESPONSIBILITY LOOKS LIKE: MYTH VERSUS REALITY

Let's talk about what responsibility *looks* like. As a society, we perpetuate a lot of cultural myths about responsibility. Whether we're consciously aware of it or not, we believe we can discern whether or not a person is responsible just by looking at them. Adults often judge a teen to be responsible when the teen looks or acts in a way that is comfortable or familiar to the adult. In reality, you have to look deeper to determine if someone is performing in a responsible manner, especially in accordance with the values he holds. Being true to self requires an enormous amount of responsibility, though it may not fit the picture others have of responsibility.

What follows are ten culturally held myths about responsibility. Awareness of these myths will help you to look more accurately at your teen and the level of responsibility he has taken on.

Myth one: *A responsible teen has a paying job.* Parents often brag about their teens having paying jobs. But is it a good thing for all teens to have jobs? Would it be a good thing for your teen? There is a certain level of responsibility reflected in your teen showing up for work on a regular basis. But the motive may or may not have anything to do with responsibility. It may have to do with getting money to spend on who knows what. And the spending decisions may or may not be responsible. If the money buys alcohol or cigarettes, you'd probably want to question the situation.

If your teen spends his money as soon as he gets it, he may be trying to self-medicate the painful situations in his life by getting a "high" from spending. That doesn't do much to prove he's particularly responsible.

I'm not against a teen working for money, but having a job does not prove that a teen is acting responsibly. Your ADD teen may show better judgment and be more responsible by not working. Remember, at this stage of their lives, the primary away-from-home responsibility is to meet school commitments. Working for pay, going to school, keeping up on homework and studying, and having a social life is a schedule few teens can handle gracefully. It's especially difficult for ADD teens.

On the other hand, if your ADD teen is not having success at school, and he's becoming demoralized, he may get motivated by working a bit in a job he enjoys. But it doesn't necessarily prove that he's responsible.

Myth two: A responsible teen always works hard in school, studies his books and notes, and makes good grades. Parents and teachers often think they can tell when a teen is working hard by looking at whether or not she's studying her books and notes. And if she is, they expect it to be reflected in good grades.

Reality might be quite different, especially for ADD and learning-different teens. Sometimes just sitting in a seat for an hour without causing a major disruption can be an enormous task. And the way your teen learns may have little to do with traditional study methods. Even making good grades does not prove that an ADD teen is learning much that will last or be applicable in later life.

By the time an ADD teen reaches junior and senior high school, studying may have become so painful that the only responsible thing the teen can do is something else—anything else. Knowing the full story may change an outsider's perspective of your teen's actions.

Myth three: A responsible teen does his homework every night. Before deciding whether a teen doing his homework nightly reflects his level of responsibility, you may wish to consider how difficult schoolwork and homework are for him. Frankly, being trapped in a "job" all day that doesn't fit him (school), and which he cannot quit, makes him feel like a failure. The last thing your teen may want to do is more of the same.

It may be that the *responsible* thing for him to do—to make sure he doesn't burn out entirely—is to keep homework to a minimum. Your teen needs to determine how much schoolwork he can manage. Then he needs to set limits around it.

As one young man said, "It's not an option for me to study on weekends or more than an hour most nights. I can study four nights a week and before tests for a while, and that's it." He was very clear about what his emotional and physical system could stand. To me, that's being responsible.

Myth four: A responsible teen believes in the work ethic, "No pain, no gain." That's easy to say for anyone who's only moderately sensitive. But given the hypersensitive nature of the ADD teen, painful situations may feel overwhelming to them. In fact, painful situations may be so aversive that no gain is made. Reasonable effort is one thing, pain another.

Many creative people get the picture intuitively. Repetitive memorizing and tedious practice do not teach some kinds of people. For them, "pain" comes with no "gain." Rather, being relaxed and playful may actually provide a more effective environment for learning.

Myth five: A responsible teen goes to bed at a reasonable hour. Many forms of ADD are closely related to sleep disorders, making regulation of sleep patterns difficult. Even if no disorder exists, many teens who are ADD have discovered they can study better after others go to bed. Those teens may stay up half the night because they find they can focus better when the world is quiet and they feel more able to relax. For those teens, sleeping on a different schedule from the average person has little to do with responsibility. The responsible thing is listen to your body and decide the best time for *you* to sleep.

Myth six: A responsible teen accomplishes tasks ahead of time and in a systematic way. If an assignment is made at school a week before it's due, many people think there's only one responsible way to get the project done—break it down into equal segments and work on it every day, beginning the first day.

Along the same vein, most people think a person is being more responsible by performing any task in a systematic way. They envision a responsible teen constructing an outline or making a budget and following that framework step by step in a responsible way.

Most teens who are ADD do not see how they could benefit from trying to do a job a little at a time. By delaying the beginning of a project until closer to its due date, ADD teens receive the adrenaline charge they often need in order to focus. It often seems that they can use their time more efficiently this way. The responsible thing to do is to work in the way that fits best.

Similarly, many creative people do not work in a systematic manner. Rather, they follow their intuition, working with their flow of energy in the manner that feels right to them. Though it may appear to the outsider that the person is going from "Dallas" to "Miami" via "Chicago," so to speak, in reality some aspect of "Chicago" will prove important in the end. ADD teens and creative teens who are not ADD must follow their intuition if they are to act responsibly.

Myth seven: A responsible teen begins college or a trade school immediately after high school graduation. Many responsible ADD teens are not ready for college or any other schooling right after high school. Taking a break that buys time and experience may be the very best thing an ADD teen can do. The ADD teen is often "burned out" from schoolwork and isn't yet ready to choose a major to study in college. Being a kinesthetic learner, he needs to get some work experience that is satisfying and teaches him additional options about the world around him.

Myth eight: A responsible teen looks like a "preppy" or a "jock." If you have a teen who is creative, he or she may take on an eccentric look—colored hair, unique haircut, "way-out dress," leather motorcycle garb, or multiple earrings. Often adults judge a teen based on physical appearance without finding out anything about her values or attitudes. The truth is, the way a teen looks has nothing to do with her level of responsibility. Discounting a teen because of appearance shortchanges the teen's integrity.

Myth nine: A responsible teen is religious and attends religious services. Not all teens who are religious are responsible. Lowering one's head in prayer and exhibiting worshipful behavior may or may not carry over into responsible action outside of the religious setting. Many parents adamantly believe that if their teen attends religious services, he or she is living a moral or "good" life, one of responsibility. Unfortunately, wearing one's religion openly is no guarantee that inner thoughts, attitudes, and even behaviors emulate the deepest held beliefs of the teen's faith.

Adolescence is often a time of questioning, finding personal meaning in one's spiritual faith, and acting in a way that is different — at least on the surface — from their parents. But any time I've been in a serious discussion with teens, I've discovered some of the most thoughtful, spiritually sensitive, and thinking teens I've ever come across. These adolescents talk and think about religion even though no one is "making" them. They even choose to live in a respectful way with their peers.

Myth ten: A responsible teen does what his parents want. When a teen does what his parents want him to do, whether or not that behavior is right for him, he is frequently thought of as responsible. But going against his nature, even though his parents believe their suggestions are right, is being irresponsible to himself. Ultimately, the job of adolescence is to make the teen self-responsible, not forever responsible to his parents.

WHAT DOES RESPONSIBILITY *REALLY* MEAN?

Obviously you can't determine whether or not your teen is being responsible by looking at him or even looking at some of his behaviors. So how can you tell whether or not your teen is developing the responsibility he will need to manage his own life?

Fifteen-year-old Connie has green hair, wears six earrings, and doesn't always do her homework. Because of her ADD, school has always been very hard for her, but she hasn't quit and doesn't plan to. She wants very much to get an education so she can help her family and make a good life for herself.

Connie goes home immediately after school every afternoon so her younger brother and sister don't have to stay home alone for long. Before their mom gets home from work at about 6:30 or 7:00 p.m., Connie has fed the younger kids and helped them with their homework, which makes her feel good. She is truly a great asset to her third- and fourth-grade siblings. Whenever possible, Connie tries to straighten up the house a little before her mom gets in. She knows how hard her mom works and likes to help out.

When Connie thinks about her future, she wants to either work with little children or be a beautician or makeup artist. She's not sure which. These days, she's into experimenting with her own hair and makeup. She likes to decorate herself to see the effects. She learns better by seeing those effects than she would if someone told her how something would work out.

Connie, who knows she is ADD, is not against doing her homework; she does try, but sometimes she just can't get it. She doesn't like to ask her mom, who only went as far as the ninth grade. Connie has even wondered whether her mom is ADD.

ADD is a nuisance as far as Connie is concerned. Even when she can do her homework, she sometimes forgets to do it. She gets mad at herself for that and tries hard to figure out ways to remember it. So far, though, she's not been very successful.

Stepping back to look at Connie—to look at the *whole* picture—you see a teen who is taking on the responsibilities of many adult chores and doing it with a good attitude. She's loving, compassionate, and thoughtful. The minute you understand why her hair is green and why she wears six earrings, you realize this youngster is trying to develop skills she can use in the future. And with her creative, sensitive nature she's experimenting in a colorful way.

Connie will make it in life. She's a winner in my book. And whether she gets all her homework in or not, she's a very responsible girl. How sad that some of her teachers call her irresponsible! They haven't taken the time to get to know this student.

So how *do* you know whether or not your teen is developing into a responsible person? Let's look at some common areas that teens need to develop.

Self-Care

Self-care means taking responsibility for personal hygiene: bathing and washing, and caring for hair, clothes, and teeth. Your teen's concern about her appearance when she leaves the house falls into this category, too. However, responsible self-care doesn't mean your teen necessarily wears clothes that you like. It does mean that the clothes, though perhaps un-ironed, if that is the style, are clean.

When your daughter is thirteen, she will probably spend a lot of time on self-care and continue to do so throughout her teen years. If you are blessed with a son, though, you may need to continue to prompt him in the area of hygiene until he becomes enamored with a young lady. Suddenly, he'll know what to do to present himself in a good light. (He probably knew all along but waited until he felt prompted by a situation meaningful enough to him to apply the knowledge.)

All teens can be responsible for their clothes, though younger teens may not be ready to do the shopping for themselves. But once purchased, teens can certainly do their own wash, including their linens, and iron a shirt. Boys, too! This is a good area to begin to take responsibility.

School

Many ADD thirteen-year-olds still need a considerable amount of help with their schoolwork, especially if they are Outwardly Expressive or Inwardly Directed ADD. Organizing their materials is difficult for them—and at this age their ability to be successful in school is largely based on good organizational abilities.

Slowly, over the next four years, you will want to ease out of your teen's school business so that he's handling all of his school-work by the time he's a senior, or taking responsibility for seeking help, such as tutoring. (Obviously, there are a few exceptions, depending upon the capability level of the student.)

Part of teaching your teen responsibility means that you do not nag. You allow your teen to experience the consequences of his behavior, including his lack of cooperating with you. You don't do the work for him, but you can continue to help, though not at the price of being drained yourself. (We'll discuss this issue of schoolwork in great depth in the following chapter.)

Money

Learning to handle money responsibly can be a problem for almost all teens. For an ADD teen, keeping track of money, avoiding impulsive spending, and finding the time to work for money can be quite a challenge. You can help.

In the early teen years you may need to parcel out money in the form of an allowance, either once or twice a week. Slowly you can build up the time between payments so the teen can learn to spread out spending his money. Some teens may need their allowance placed in envelopes marked for spending a week at a time. Remember, breaking large segments down into small ones can be a major problem for people with ADD.

Some ADD teens can manage to work part-time while in school and others can't. By the time teens are fifteen or sixteen, it's good for them to get some work experience in the summer. This helps them understand the value of money and also gives them additional responsibility in a setting other than school. If it's a job they enjoy, they often find work quite refreshing. On the other hand, working at minimum wage in a fast-food environment or sacking groceries often makes school, including college, look a lot more inviting.

From ages thirteen to sixteen, teens need definite jobs around the house, such as mowing the lawn, housecleaning, and doing repair work and renovations. You can pay your teen the going wage for this work, but don't overpay so that he gets used to a pay scale he can't get anywhere else.

When your teen spends *your* money, you need to set clear concise guidelines. Though most teens don't have access to credit cards, they do have access to "900" numbers. You need to establish clear guidelines on the use of these phone services. Many families have received a phone bill many times more expensive than expected because a teen found a "900" number of interest. If that happens, your teen should pay the bill and agree to ask permission to use the "900" number in the future. Although blocks can be put on the use of a "900" number by the phone company, your teen will learn more by restricting himself.

If your teen cannot adequately take responsibility for his actions related to money, then you need to take steps to protect money you keep in the house, your credit cards, and your bank account until he proves he has matured in this area.

Driving

Though many teens take it for granted they will be able to drive at sixteen, an ADD teen must carefully evaluate her readiness to get behind the wheel. All teens are required to have driver's education now. In consultation with the driver's education instructor you can determine whether your teen seems ready to assume the responsibility of driving a car.

I would advise you to start talking about and observing impulse control in your teen at about age fourteen. Rather than threatening your teen, simply say, "I need to be sure you'll be ready to drive, because you're valuable to me. Some people are ready at fifteen or sixteen, and some need another year or two before they take on the responsibility of driving. I'm not going to let you do anything that will set you up to get hurt or hurt anyone else."

Many ADD teens opt to delay getting a driver's license when they understand the seriousness of the task at hand. Impulsivity and the tendency to do things fast are the biggest problems ADD teens need to overcome to become safe drivers.

In order to take adequate responsibility to drive safely, your teen must be able to regulate herself and her behavior — and that means on her own—without you telling her what to do. You can see how well your teen is doing with delayed gratification in other areas. Can your teen wait in line? Is she able to walk away from a fight? Does she recognize when she needs to relax and take a deep breath? Can your teen be angry without getting into trouble—hitting, punching holes in walls, pushing or shoving people or things, or becoming enraged? All these are signs that tell you how ready your teen is for driving.

Always remember that the issue of driving is one of safety. Giving your child permission to drive should not be based on rewarding her for good grades or punishing her for a messy room. Your decision about your child's readiness to handle a potentially lethal weapon should be based on her level of maturity, no matter what other circumstances—"Jennifer has *her* license," "David needs a ride somewhere"—cloud the issue in your child's mind.

Staying Out of Trouble

Impulsivity can be a major problem in areas other than driving. Although we will discuss sex, drugs, and alcohol in chapter 10, I do want to mention these issues briefly here.

Though there is considerable variation from culture to culture, sex in the early teens is likely to be a symptom that tells parents their son or daughter either has not been able to get nurturing in other ways or may have been sexually abused or stimulated at an earlier time.

By ages sixteen and seventeen, there's usually a lot of talk about sex, but more talk than action. With sex education and parental guidance, teens are not likely to develop serious interpersonal relationships that will culminate in sex until their late teens. By that time, parents cannot realistically control their teens' sexual behavior, as much as they might want to. Being responsible at this age means having safe sex, which hopefully has been taught since the preteen to early teen years.

I am not advocating that older teens have sex. In fact, teaching safe sex, including the ability to say no and the use of birth control does not make teens more likely to be sexually active.

It actually makes them less likely. What I'm saying is that it's more common for teens who do have premarital sex to have begun having sex in their later teen years rather than their early teen years. By that time they should be able to make responsible choices regarding safe sex and birth control.

If you clearly teach your family's values and preferences regarding sexual activity—*and live by those same principles*—and are open to your teen's questions, you are likely to have a responsible teen who respects the opposite sex and stays out of trouble.

You need to face the fact that alcohol and drug experimentation are likely to occur during the teen years. Unfortunately, use of chemicals is showing up at very young ages in many communities. As with sex, if you provide education about alcohol and drugs, model responsible behavior to your children, and clearly let them know what you expect, you are likely to raise kids who stay out of trouble.

That does not mean that your teen will never experiment. Trying alcohol (even getting drunk) a time or two, or smoking marijuana a time or two is what I mean by experimentation. More than that and a pattern of use is developing that can become a habit and, for some people, an abuse.

Some teens who are ADD try amphetamines and then begin to self-medicate regularly with them. If you notice repeated use or abuse of alcohol or drugs, reach out for help to a community resource such as the Council on Alcohol and Drug Abuse, and let them guide you and your family to curb a dangerous habit.

By the late teens many young people responsibly consume alcohol as they get out on their own in college or join the work force. This means they drink in moderation. They do not drink and drive, drink habitually, demonstrate unacceptable behavior when drinking, and do not drink to cover insecurities, pain, or fear.

The use of tobacco, smoking or chewing, is on the increase with young people. It is unhealthy and dangerous. Your best bet is to provide a smoke-free environment for your kids to grow up in along with solid, nonthreatening, accurate information about tobacco. Your best bet is to begin educating your children about tobacco when they are very young.

ADD teens who are struggling to fit in and looking for peer approval may be at greatest risk for using drugs, including tobacco and alcohol. If your child has a poor self-image and does not feel he is valuable, it will be easy for him to overlook and discount the self-destructive nature of these substances, even if he's been educated about them. Helping your teen feel valuable, and supporting a special interest that makes him feel special, is your best protection.

Living His Own Identity

The biggest job for a teen is to discover who he is becoming. That identity is what he will carry outside of the family. He'll build his life on it. To be a responsible person, he must learn about his innate gifts, talents, and interests. This goes far beyond what he's learning about himself in school and may even go beyond what he has learned about himself in the context of his family. Once he identifies his gifts, talents, and interests, he demonstrates that he is responsible by developing and protecting them. He makes sure he has enough time to do this, even if it means putting aside the expectations others have of him—including school and parental expectations.

In the process, of course, he must continue to refine his talents and abilities, not just talk about them. He must seek ways to use them in the world rather than only for his own amusement. Furthermore, he needs to decide whether he will use them totally or in part to make a living or will make enough money to live on from some other skill so that he can be free to pursue his special interests.

For example, if your child discovers he has a gift for music and, in particular, is a talented guitar player, being responsible means that he spends time developing that talent. If he is in his room playing quietly at 1:00 a.m., you might think he's acting irresponsibly because you think he should either be asleep or studying. But your child might be acting very responsibly by seriously working to develop his talents.

Fulfilling Commitments
One way to determine if your teen is acting responsibly is to see whether or not she follows through on commitments. Does your teen do what she says she will do—at home, at school, with friends, or on a job? Sometimes "Ms. Perfect Teen" makes grandiose promises, which she talks about but does not follow through on or leaves a lot of the work for others to complete.

Can your teen say no to you rather than having to say yes and then simply not following through? Do you have to nag to get things accomplished? Agreeing to do one small thing and actually completing it deserves, but rarely gets, a big pat on the back. Look for the completed tasks, despite their size, and measure your teen's level of responsibility on that.

RESPONSIBILITIES AND ISSUES
DIRECTLY RELATED TO ADD

Your teen will be going through all the normal issues related to responsibility and adolescence, but she will also have an additional set of issues directly related to her ADD. If you can understand those issues and how they affect her, you will be in a better position to judge her developing level of responsibility.

Making Honest Commitments
ADD teens may find it particularly difficult to consistently keep commitments. Often, sometimes for years, teens with ADD have failed to accomplish certain tasks. As a result, they've been punished, reprimanded, or shamed because they didn't do what they were supposed to do. This may have caused them to habitually protect themselves any way they can.

One way your teen can protect herself from shame or punishment is to lie or tell the other person what he wants to hear. That gets the person off the teen's back. Because the teen would *like* to keep the commitment, she will even delude herself into thinking she will do something she cannot accomplish in a timely manner.

Standing Up for Themselves

One of the best ways you can know if your teen is developing responsibility is to see her stand up for herself, even though this may mean going against something you or another authority suggests.

Of course, the manner in which she stands up for herself is important and also reflects her developing level of responsibility. The more matter-of-fact she is, the more responsibility you can assume she is developing. On the other hand whining, yelling, cajoling, or name-calling are all signs of weakness and fear.

If your teen can approach you in a forthright manner and "face you down," standing up for whatever she believes, take a deep breath and be glad.

The difficulty for ADD teens stems from years of being told to do things that don't fit them. In some ways the more they've forced themselves to fit into an ill-fitting mold — which usually means adults think they are doing a great job — the worse off they are with regard to developing true responsibility for themselves.

I know it seems ironic. But when your daughter stands up for herself, even if it's against something you've told her, she is developing responsibility for herself. And that's an asset.

Responsibility for Their Own Well-Being

When your teen has made good decisions and has handled situations all on his own, you know he is making fine progress. Perhaps he changed a class at school that was too difficult, without asking you. Or maybe he decided to stay home to study for a test rather than go out with the gang. You may not know about some of these decisions until afterwards, which is just fine. They belong to your teen, and that means your teen is taking responsibility for his own well-being.

You can expect to see increasing amounts of this kind of decision making as the teen years pass. Your thirteen-year-old will still be coming to you to ask your opinion. But you will notice that as he becomes fifteen and sixteen, you will only be consulted on rare occasions. By seventeen, eighteen, and nineteen, if your teen has developed appropriate levels of responsibility, he will be making most of his own decisions and will be taking care of his everyday living needs.

In today's world being responsible for all of his own finances is probably not realistic for most older teens. Career and job choices and majors in college will slowly come into line over the next few years. Beyond that, however, by the time he graduates from high school, he may be ready to go out into the world and take care of his personal needs.

Your ADD teen might not achieve these levels of responsibility or independence at the same ages as his non-ADD peers. After all, your teen has many issues and difficulties that his non-ADD peers do not have. So don't worry if your ADD teen is lagging some. What you are looking for is growth from year to year.

LETTING GO OF YOUR TEEN

The whole story of adolescence, whether your teen is ADD or not, can be summed up in this one phrase—"transferring responsibility for your child from you to her." No person *suddenly* becomes responsible at a specific age, such as eighteen or twenty-one. Your job as a parent is to slowly and consistently transfer the power and authority to her.

So let's be clear. There are two parts to this responsibility issue: (1) Your child must take on more responsibility for herself, and (2) You must give up, or transfer, an equal amount of responsibility from your control to your child's. Your teen cannot grow into a self-responsible and independent young adult unless both of these changes occur.

Up to this point we've been talking about your teen taking on more responsibility. Now, let's look at the flip side. What is your part of the bargain?

If you've already started this process, you are probably well aware that letting go of your end of the transfer is not as easy as someone on the outside might think. You've been accustomed to doing a lot for your child—everything when she was an infant, a lot as a young child, and some as a teen. Because letting go is such a hard job, let's talk about what it involves and what can block the transfer.

You must give your child permission to be independent and responsible. You do that by allowing him to show you what he can do, and that includes allowing him to try some things that maybe you, or even your child, aren't quite sure about. If you do things for your teen that he can do for himself, you are communicating that you don't think he's capable of doing those things for himself—at least not as well as you can do them.

The biggest obstacle teens face in becoming responsible is parents who do more for them than is necessary.

I realize that's a strong statement. And one that many parents—especially those who want to hold on to the belief that they always know what's best for their children—find difficult to accept. But it's the truth. This is called enabling; it's the inability to quit doing for your child that which he can do well enough for himself. No matter what you are *trying* to teach your child, the lesson he will *always* get from this is that he is inadequate and incapable of taking on this responsibility or that he shouldn't even bother to try.

When Doug, sixteen, started to change the oil in his car, his dad immediately ran outside and said, "Let me show you the right way to do that!" He didn't take time to see whether or not Doug knew what he was doing. Doug, who was ADD and was used to being told that he couldn't do anything right, backed off and shrugged. He didn't try to change his oil again.

The next time Doug's car needed an oil change, Doug muttered in passing, "My car needs an oil change." His father instantly got up and went to do the job, enabling Doug to stay helpless. Doug had a car that he couldn't take full responsibility for because he was being blocked from learning how to care for it. Even if Doug's father was only trying to help, his decision to do the job himself instead of letting his son give it a try kept his son from taking on that responsibility — something of which Doug would have been proud.

And then there's Tricia. Tricia, a sophomore who is ADD, continually left her homework at home. Her mother still ran up to school with forgotten assignments — something she had been doing for years — so that Tricia didn't lose credit. Tricia's grades were fine, and her mother was proud of that. But Tricia was not learning to become responsible. Her mother enabled her to stay helpless by not letting her experience the consequences of forgetting her work.

It would have been much better for Tricia to receive a poor grade for forgetting her homework. Eventually, that would have helped her learn to take responsibility for remembering to bring it to school herself.

Now let's look at how these two parents could have responded to their children's situations.

Suppose Doug's dad saw his son starting to change the oil. Most parents who didn't realize their son had learned how to change the oil would wonder whether or not he could do it satisfactorily. So, all Doug's dad had to do was question his son with genuine interest, not as an interrogation, questioning Doug's ability. He could say something like, "I didn't know you knew how to change the oil in your car. Where did you learn how to do it?"

With an air of camaraderie, Doug's father could observe his son and make a suggestion if he saw his son headed down a wrong path. For example, he could say, "When I change my oil, I've found that moving the car to an open space and draining the oil in a deeper pan works better for me. That way I don't get oil over everything. What do you think?"

If his dad finds that Doug actually knows very little about changing the oil but is attempting to do it anyway — a situation that is not uncommon for ADD teens — his dad might say, "Tell you what, Doug. How about letting me work with you. I can see you really want to learn how to do this, and I think that's a great idea. I'd be happy to show you what I know. If we work on it together once or twice, I think you'll be ready to tackle it on your own." This approach helps the teen save face, learn skills, and feel independent. And it won't be long until he *is* ready to take full responsibility for doing the job on his own.

In Tricia's case, I do not believe a parent should be absolutely forbidden from *ever* helping out a youngster who forgets something. Goodness knows we all need to help one another occasionally. The key word here is *occasionally*.

In general, Tricia's mom needs to help Tricia get used to the idea of being responsible for her own things. The best way to do this is to start early in elementary school with systematic training — not an easy job for an ADD parent. But it's never too late to start.

I would suggest that Tricia's mom begin by talking with Tricia about remembering her homework. I don't mean simply telling Tricia to remember her homework. Most likely, she would have been doing that for years with no effect. Rather, Tricia's mom could say, "Tricia, I realize we — not just you — are long overdue for this talk. I realize now that I've been enabling you to stay dependent upon me by running your homework to school every time you forget it. It's really time for me to back off and for you to take over. What do you say?" (Notice that Tricia's mother is taking responsibility for the part she has played in this situation.)

Tricia and her mother can discuss where Tricia needs to place her completed homework, maybe in a folder by the front door or on the front seat of the car if she's driven to school. Tricia might ask for a reminder for a while to get used to the new system, or her mom might ask her if she would like one. But either way they need to agree this is something Tricia wants. If her mother gives a reminder without Tricia's involvement in the decision, then enabling continues.

Next, they can talk about what to do *if*, not *when*, Tricia forgets her homework. The what-to-do needs to be different from what has been going on. Maybe they could agree that Tricia's mother would bring her homework to her *one more time*. Tricia could tell her teacher that she is learning to become more responsible, that she left her homework at home, and that, this one time, she'd like to call her mother to bring it. If the teacher agrees, she can make this one call. If the teacher doesn't, then that's the repercussion Tricia must experience. If she's allowed to call home, her mother can bring it, *but only this one time*. It's also important that the mother say nothing when bringing it — no complaining, no scolding, not even encouragement.

If Tricia forgets her homework again after that one time, it will be difficult for her mother not to bring it to her. Her mother may feel sorry for Tricia or may be so invested in Tricia making good grades that she wants to bring it again. At that point Tricia's mom would do well to have someone hold her hand, or better yet the car keys. If Tricia gets a poorer grade because of failed home-work assignments, then she gets a poorer grade. And she learns to become more responsible.

It's not always easy to know whether or not a parent is func-tioning as an enabler, especially if that someone is yourself. But here's a general rule of thumb: When you do anything for another person that the person can do for himself, you are enabling him. And when you are helping someone to stay weak or engage in self-destructive activities or behaviors, you are enabling him to remain irresponsible.

In extreme situations, enabling can be widespread in a fam-ily. Although parents *talk* about their children growing up to become responsible adults, some parents feel their lives have no meaning if they are not taking care of their children. They actually retard the growth of their children on the road to inde-pendence for fear of being out of a job. They may fear facing their own lack of direction without children. Usually, the par-ent is not aware of this and isn't meaning to hurt his child, but damage is done nevertheless. Family counseling or individual counseling for the parent to find a life agenda beyond children may be necessary.

More often, enabling happens innocently without deep-seated roots. It partly stems from habits established when your teen was a baby. Out of habit you continue to respond as you once did, taking care of your child.

If you think about your own history, you, too, started in the same way. You were unable to even roll over without your parent's help. But now you are a responsible grown-up and have been for some time. When did you become responsible? Chances are, you can't pinpoint an exact time. But you did become responsible, with or without your parents' help. Now it's your turn to pass independence on to your teen.

Once we learn about enabling, most of us want to avoid it. But it's difficult to spot in ourselves. It's especially difficult as a parent of an ADD teen, because there have been many times when your child legitimately needed your help with something his peers might have been able to do on their own by that time.

So how can you best make the transition from caregiver to consultant to peer with your adult child? To be sure, the completion of this cycle will go beyond the teen years, but not much. Here are some guidelines.

- ▶ Do I see my son or daughter as a small child?
- ▶ Do I fear that my teen has poor judgment?
- ▶ How much do I know about what my teen does when I'm not around?
- ▶ Do I regularly or constantly remind my teen of things?
- ▶ Do I do "a lot" for my teen?
- ▶ Do I scold my teen, trying to teach him, but still give in to him?
- ▶ Do I worry about what I will do when my teen leaves home and is on his own?
- ▶ Do I correct my teen's appearance, habits, or choices?
- ▶ Do I speak for my teen without consulting him?
- ▶ Do I make excuses for my teen's bad habits, such as drinking and spending money?
- ▶ Do I pay off my teen's debts?
- ▶ Do I fear my teen won't be able to recover from his mistakes?
- ▶ Do I rescue my teen when he makes mistakes?

173

► Do I feel so sorry for my teen when he's brought trouble on himself that I bail him out?

► Have I bailed my teen out of jail, paid off tickets, or covered up for my teen?

By answering these questions honestly, you should be able to get a picture of whether or not you have been an enabler for your child. If you have, try to step back and see the big picture. Focus on your goals and your teen's goals. How can you really work toward making it all happen?

LETTING YOUR CHILD "SUFFER"

Usually, adults talk about teens "suffering" the repercussions of their actions. I don't see suffering occurring in these circumstances. I see learning experiences from which the teen can find the limits of acceptable and unacceptable behavior. Bumping into the limits is a powerful way to learn what's okay and what's not. Consequently, I prefer to say that the teen "experiences" the repercussions of his or her actions.

And it isn't just a matter of semantics. No one wants to see his child suffer. So if we consider it "suffering" when Tricia receives a detention for not turning in five homework assignments, we are much more likely to want to rescue her. If we see that detention as a learning experience for her, we're more likely to give her the opportunity to learn that lesson.

The earlier and more consistently that limits are reinforced by parents, the easier the child's job of taking responsibility for his behavior. That's one of the reasons I'm so adamant about children being given learning experiences rather than punishment when they do something a parent doesn't like.

When your small child hit another child during the preschool years, you needed to remove him from that play situation. Isolated for a short time, he began to learn that hitting playmates is unacceptable. When he did that he had to be alone. In addition, hopefully, he was taught how to use words to get what he needed instead

174

of hitting. Children can learn much more quickly what *not to do* if they are taught what *to do* in order to get what they need or want.

As your child became older, he may have damaged someone else's property. The logical consequence of hurting something that didn't belong to him was that he had to pay for fixing or replacing the damaged object. And he may have needed to experience a reduction in his freedom until you were sure he could control himself without getting into that type of trouble again.

If, instead, you paid to have the object fixed, made excuses for why he did the damage, or made light of what he did, your child would not have learned the consequences of his irresponsible behavior. You were his teacher then just as you are now.

Now that your child is a teen, the stakes are higher. When he fails to let you know until a few days before the end of the semester that he's in trouble with his schoolwork, there's little you can do to help him out. He must learn that he has to alert you earlier if he wants your help. The consequence of waiting so long is the danger of failing.

Or maybe your teen has her first "old" car. She hears something different in the motor but is too busy to have it checked out and fails to say anything to you. The next week, you get a call that the car has broken down in the middle of the block. When you have it checked, it turns out the damage to the car was much more severe than it would have been if your daughter had alerted you earlier. The repercussion needs to be that she's on foot for a while.

Do not run right out, ruining the family budget in the process, and get her a new car right away. Neither punish her by *making* her travel on foot. Being without a car is just the natural repercussion of being irresponsible in caring for her car.

WHEN TO HELP YOUR ADD TEEN

Let's look at the following scenario. Your teen has a test in English that he's known about for a week. The test is the next day, but he has not yet started to study. A large part of his grade is in jeopardy if he doesn't pass the test.

Would you let him stay home the day of the test so he can study, writing a note that will allow him to take a make-up test? Or would you let him flunk the test and have the chance to learn that when you don't study in a timely manner, flunking is the natural consequence?

With a non-ADD teen who has a fairly well-developed sense of time, has success in school when he puts his mind to it, and has only recently become somewhat lax about hitting the books, you would want to seriously consider letting the consequences fall where they may without allowing him to stay home. If he did stay home, you would not write him a note. He'd be on his own with an unexcused absence.

With an ADD teen the decision is not always so simple. You would need to analyze how well your teen is doing with the areas of his life that are especially compromised by ADD. You'd want to see how much progress he's making over all. And you would want to assess how serious he is about taking responsibility for aspects of his schooling and life in general.

If, for example, he's doing better in school this year than ever before, has brought his grades up, is getting his homework done most nights, has a good attitude, and is starting to feel better about himself, you might make a different decision than you would if none of these were the case. Perhaps this is the first time he's even been willing to hit the books to prepare for something. And it may have taken the enormous pressure of the last minute, or of special accommodation—being able to stay home a day from school— in order to help him make this step.

If you did let him stay home, he would have to study or there would be no second chance. If you let him stay home to study, he would need to work at doing his pre-test studying earlier next time. In other words, being allowed to stay home from school to study is only an intermediary step, not an end in itself.

Ironically, being able to stay home the day before the test could help him retain the material. Even if the test was on Monday, he might experience studying on Sunday as a loss of free time, while studying on a school day would feel like a gain. The uniqueness might just be what was necessary to hold his attention. The purpose of staying home would be to give him the experience of studying for a long period of time for a test. Many youths with ADD are not able to study several days ahead and retain the information for the test. That kind of studying is not productive for them, and they know it. Also, taking the test alone may be an advantage over taking it with the whole class. Of course, he should not have to skip school in order to gain the accommodation to take his test in a less distracting setting.

The main point is that you need to evaluate what major step your ADD teen is ready to make and whether letting him stay home to study and take the test the next day helps him learn to take the step.

Because the ADD teen is more likely to be forgetful than non-ADD teens, you are not enabling your teen by sometimes filling in when she's forgotten something like her lunch or homework. But during the years between ages thirteen and twenty, you will see a lot of change in this area. If a nineteen-year-old is still forgetting a lot, and mama or daddy are still going behind him tucking his shirt in, then enabling may be going on. On the other hand, a thirteen- or fourteen-year-old ADD student trying to get used to the first year of junior high may have his hands very full and might legitimately need some help.

Teens with ADD often develop more slowly than their age-mates in areas associated with ADD—areas such as organization, impulsivity, and activity level. It's not unusual for teens to be a couple years behind their peers in these areas. And they might legitimately need some help in those areas on occasion, even if their peers do not.

Because teens with ADD are hypersensitive, they are likely to feel intensely their lack of ability to manage their lives. People with ADD suffer the same way as others who have learning differences. They are aware of the differences and aware they are not functioning at the same level as their friends and associates. They feel the pain of their inadequacy, which can hang on for the rest of their lives.

Parents of ADD teens have a fine line to walk in trying not to enable while supporting a child who generally intends to do better than he is able. You want to help your child take on responsibility as he is able, but you don't want to leave your teen stranded on his own prematurely.

Thirteen- to fifteen-year-olds with ADD are often very immature when it comes to dealing with the expectations placed upon them by society. As a parent you may feel during those years that your teen will never "get it."

Then, between fifteen and sixteen there is an almost magical change at which time you are likely to see a major developmental leap. Many behaviors will indicate that your teen is "getting it together." Suddenly your teen will be trying to do his homework or will volunteer to help around the house or will demonstrate care of his personal hygiene, clothes, or room. I don't mean the teen does these things perfectly. But he does seem to be getting the knack of self-control.

Though many teens who are ADD can use an extra year to manage the organizational chores of college and jobs after high school, they are often able to do fairly well, both interpersonally and creatively. You will also see another major developmental leap between ages twenty and twenty-one, when your teen develops a much greater ability to take on responsibility.

I've noticed that most teens with ADD do better when given one task at a time to conquer. So you might want to let your teen buy some of his own clothes at fifteen, but by eighteen let him be responsible for buying all his clothes while staying within his budget.

At sixteen, he might take on the task of driving. At seventeen, especially if he has a job, you might suggest he open a bank account. At eighteen, he can manage his graduation and get a summer job. At nineteen, he might manage to live away from you with other students in a dorm, get home on holidays, and care for all his personal needs separate from his family. And at twenty, he could get his own apartment. But you have to help him take it one step at a time.

Meanwhile, you, as a parent, can help in other areas he's not concentrating on. That way you don't need to worry about keeping him dependent by enabling him. Trust your feelings about what to do. If you feel put upon — like you're being used — then you may not need to do as much as you're doing. If, however, you see your teen trying and struggling, by all means help out.

If your teen keeps making the same mistake over and over, then she needs your help in solving that problem. If whatever you are doing isn't working, then you need to try something different. Also, since not all ADD teens are the same, you will need to vary your approach, depending on the makeup of your unique teen.

If you are the parent of an Outwardly Expressive ADD teen, you need to watch that you are not being conned into doing work your teen simply doesn't *want* to do. This type of teen hates paperwork, seated activities, and organization, and she may use her personality and salesmanship to try to talk you into doing things she could do but doesn't want to do.

In a situation like that, you might say, "I know you don't like to do paper-work, but I also know you *can* do it. I won't cheat you out of the opportunity to do the whole job yourself. And, you know what? I don't want to do it either. If I did your work and you didn't have to do it, I'd get pretty mad at you. I won't let myself set you up that way. You don't deserve it. But we'll celebrate when you finish. Let me know when that is."

On the other hand, as the parent of an Inwardly Directed ADD teen, you may find that your son or daughter may need extra motivation and cheerleading from you to tackle jobs that seem hard. More inwardly oriented, this type of teen needs to hear, "You can do it. I trust you. I'll be the first to congratulate you on your success." Then don't take over and do your teen's work, but maybe keep your teen company by doing a task of your own. Just watch to be sure she doesn't feel totally overwhelmed.

Parents with a Highly Structured ADD teen may not see obvious signs that they're enabling their teen, since the teens tend to have better success at school. The problem may show up outside of school, especially around the issues of money, curfew, or alcohol or drug use.

Because this type of teen usually does quite well in school, parents may not realize the teen doesn't "have it all together." Don't be blind to other areas that can be affected. Remember that the "good student" myth isn't all that makes up the teen. You don't need to become suspicious of everything your teen is doing. But don't close your eyes to telltale signs of irresponsible behavior just because your teen is a good student.

You might want to say, "I'm concerned that you're staying out late at night, and that's asking for trouble. I need to be sure you're in control of your time." Or you might say, "Even though you're doing a lot of right things, making good grades and planning your future, you still need to manage your finances. I won't be able to help you catch up. You need to earn money to get yourself out of debt. I know you'll do it."

THE IMPORTANCE OF COMMUNICATION

Don't stop talking to your teen. Even though both of your lives are very busy during the teen years, you need to find time to talk. Finding the time for an informal relaxed few minutes of conversation will pay rich dividends.

You don't need to make a big deal of the "talk time." It may be when you're driving somewhere together. Or you might sit down while your teen is relaxing and ask how things are going. Don't be surprised if you hear, "Fine." Don't give up. You might want to say, "What are you working on now that you enjoy most?" Rather than going over the list of school subjects or asking if there are problems, attempt to talk about something your teen likes.

When you know about something your teen is interested in, become more informed about it. Then ask questions that will tell you your teen is acting responsibly. Ask your teen for his or her advice.

Many times good communication revolves around a "problem." For example, I know one parent who was waiting to get an important phone call at home. It didn't come all afternoon. At about 4:00 p.m., she noticed her son, fourteen, on the phone. She motioned for him to cover the mouthpiece so she could tell him she was waiting for a call. He told her he thought someone had called at about 1:30 p.m. The teen had spoken briefly to the caller since the family had "call waiting" and had told the caller he'd have to call back later, because he was using the phone right then.

The teen's mother got angry and told him, "When you're on the phone and a call comes for me, do not tell them to call back. You tell your friend to hang up, and immediately tell the person waiting for me that I'll be right there. Then let me know I have a call." When he started to argue, she said, "Look, I pay the phone bill. I let you use the phone. If you want to save your money, get a job, and put in your own phone line, then you can have control of that phone. But not this one.

"This is very important to me. If you don't go along with what I'm asking, then you'll lose phone privileges altogether." He agreed and became instantly responsible about his phone behavior. They never had any other trouble about the phone.

When something like this comes up, be sure to talk in a matter-of-fact way to your teen about taking responsibility rather than in a scolding manner.

For example, if your teen's responsibilities include feeding the dog, but he consistently forgets to do the job, you might say, "The dog needs to be fed and given attention. I expect you to do that every day after school. If you don't want to do that, then we need to see about getting a home for the dog that can provide what he needs. I don't want to be responsible for feeding the dog, and I'm not willing for the dog to be neglected." This is a simple, clear statement that communicates the parent's limits regarding a family pet.

Be clear about which are negotiable and non-negotiable areas of responsibility within the family. Though you may wish your teen's room were clean, that can fall into a negotiable area of responsibility, since it doesn't hurt anyone else in the family. You can close the door and not look at it. Tell your teen, "I would prefer you keep your room neat and clean, but that's your private space. And I don't need to come into it, so it's up to you whether you decide to clean it."

In contrast, drinking and driving are totally non-negotiable. "You can call me to pick you up anywhere, anytime, if you've been drinking. I will consider you highly responsible for letting me know that you don't think you should be driving right then. But you may absolutely not drive if you've been drinking."

Learning to take responsibility for ourselves is a big task that took us many years to learn. Give your teen time to learn a little at a time about how to manage life. But expect more each year. Remember, every journey starts one step at a time.

∽⊖~⊖∾

CHAPTER NINE

MAKING THE GRADE
Helping Your Teen Succeed in School

When I sat down to write this chapter about school, I instantly felt tension in my throat and a knot in my stomach. I remember all too well the fears I faced about my ADD son getting an education. Stark terror may be a better description.

What lay beneath that terror? The answer comes quickly — a fear that, because my child was having trouble in school, he would never be able to make it in life. This terrible fear was one I learned early in my own life with my own school difficulties. Looking back, I believe that one of the reasons I stayed in school for so many, many years was so I could avoid putting myself to the test in the "real world."

Though formal education was hard and unpleasant for me, I felt I *had* to succeed, so I gave up everything else to stay in school. Because I had lost so much, I wanted something different for my ADD child. I knew he was smart, but I wanted him to feel smart. I wanted him to enjoy learning, something I had not experienced in school. I dreamed that he would become the person he naturally was meant to be, rather than an artificial combination of what others said he ought to be.

Yet, in spite of the difficulties I'd had, I still believed that schooling held the key to success — even though this belief ran counter to my desires for my son to avoid the struggles that school presents. I've spent a lot of time sorting through these discrepancies and I'd like to share with you what I've learned.

First I feared that my child would drop out of high school. Then I worried that he wouldn't be able to get into college. After that I worried that he wouldn't be able to graduate from college. Finally, I was concerned that if he didn't achieve certain grades, he would not be able to find a job that would provide financial security and self-esteem.

I wasted a lot of time and energy worrying.

What I realize now is that I really didn't need to worry so much. Here's why.

- ▶ ADD has nothing to do with intelligence.
- ▶ ADD has nothing to do with a person's desire to do well.
- ▶ Many people with ADD who do poorly in formal schooling learn easily and successfully in other ways.
- ▶ Many people with ADD do quite well in life, achieving success and satisfaction if they believe in themselves.

During the years I put so much energy into worrying about my son, I either didn't know or didn't allow myself to believe these comforting facts.

Consider the success story of Wilson, a forty-year-old doctor with ADD—primarily Highly Structured ADD with a component of Inwardly Directed ADD. Wilson came from a family of physicians. He was fortified throughout school with the belief that he could make the grade. His parents helped him study by quizzing him and they also served as models of academically successful people.

At times he found the going pretty tough. He was encouraged, though not forced, to stay in school. Now he's grateful. He loves medicine—especially the clinical part. He likes helping his patients and feels challenged and invigorated by the problem-solving that diagnosis demands.

Wilson uses his ADD traits in a positive way. He senses intuitively what's wrong with a patient and then uses his formal education to help him verify his diagnosis on empirical grounds. He then teaches his patients what he knows, translating the information into everyday language so they can know what's going on with their bodies.

His ADD still causes him some trouble, but he manages to overcome those difficulties by employing a great office manager who organizes his work environment for him. He loves computers, so he uses them to keep up with patient files and reports.

On the side Wilson lets his creative energies out by writing stories. All things considered, Wilson is a happy, successful man. It wasn't easy, but he made it through formal academic training.

Then there's Patricia. Patricia found school more than she could manage. By tenth grade she'd fallen so far behind that she figured she'd never catch up. She knew she could never pass algebra, thought she didn't have a prayer of learning a second language, and felt embarrassed by her seeming inability to learn *anything*. So she decided to drop out of school.

Patricia got a job in a day-care center because she had always enjoyed young children. At seventeen, she married her high school boyfriend and had two children over the next three years. By twenty-one, she ran a day-care program in her home and decided she wanted to take a class in child development at the local community college. She felt confident about her ability to understand children and figured she might be able to understand what was going on in class. She did.

Patricia's professor noticed that she seemed quite bright and was surprised that she didn't have a high school education. She immediately counseled Patricia to get her GED. But that was a daunting task for Patricia. She was so afraid of testing and education that she repeatedly put off taking the study course for the GED. Even though she made an A in her child-development class, she was afraid she wouldn't be able to study for the GED.

It took Patricia two years to face that GED study course. When she finally enrolled, she discovered that the material did not seem as hard as it had when she was in tenth grade. She passed the test on her first try and received her high-school equivalency certificate at the age of twenty-three.

She then took a deep breath and enrolled in freshman English at the community college. She received a B and continued in school. She took advantage of tutoring and worked with her special services adviser who helped her make course choices. Patricia earned her bachelor's degree in eight years.

Next, Patricia returned to school full time and earned a master's degree at age thirty-three. For five years she set up and managed child-development and early-childhood education programs, did in-service training, and consulted with local agencies. At thirty-eight she decided to go for broke and registered in a doctoral program. Five years later, her original community college child-development teacher was on hand to cheer when Patricia received her doctorate, wearing the robe of highest academic achievement. During a reception held in her honor, Patricia confided that she still didn't know how it all happened. "After all," she said, "I'm not really very smart. I've just been lucky and had some really good teachers."

As you can see, the tenth-grader still lives inside of Patricia, affecting her self-perception. But there's no doubt that Patricia *was* smart—smart enough to earn her doctorate. She simply needed support in specific areas affected by her ADD and the time to mature to accomplish her goals.

Let me tell you about Boyd, a photographer who is ADD. At age twenty-four, he already has his own photography business, which he loves, and is financially secure enough to consider marriage. Although he is successful now, academics were always very difficult for Boyd and he completed high school in the lower third of his graduating class. Fortunately, his parents supported his interest in photography from an early age. Even today, Boyd says he survived high school by being the photographer on the school newspaper. From the contacts he made at sporting events he was photographing, Boyd was able to get an internship with a local newspaper the summer before his senior year in high school. He didn't want to go to college, and doubted that he could be successful academically, so Boyd applied for a job at the newspaper before graduation and went right to work after graduating.

When he had three years of experience behind him, he decided he had enough business contacts to start his own business. He left the newspaper on good terms and has kept up his connections there. He now has two years of successful general photography behind him and is thinking about specializing in what he loves most—outdoor photography. He figures he can always fill in with free-lance work. Boyd is a success in a nonacademic career that uses his talents.

I hope you've taken the success of Wilson, Patricia, and Boyd seriously and not convinced yourself that they are the exception to the rule. Trust me when I tell you their stories are *not* unusual. I know that future success for your child might sound implausible to you right now, in the middle of these difficult academic years. But I assure you it is possible. It will happen when your child finds his own niche, his own fit.

Wilson, Patricia, and Boyd are ADD, and each has found a successful path in life that fits him or her. So can your teen. Remember how you identified your teen's strengths in chapter 5? Many different kinds of strengths can become the basis for a good career.

"Book learning" is *not* the only skill on which to base a career. But when I was at your stage of parenting, I didn't know that. And *that* is the reason I worried so much about my son. I was raised with the belief that formal education held the key to all doors in life. That is simply not true. No one intentionally meant to limit my vision of life, but that's what happened until I'd gained enough experience to see a different perspective.

Look around and you'll see that perspective, too. Stay focused on it. You'll find yourself able to relax a bit and look at your teen in a new perspective, too.

WHY *DOES* MY CHILD HAVE
SUCH A DIFFICULT TIME IN SCHOOL?

Before your child discovers his own path and is on his own, he does have several more years of school to get through. Because you'd like him to feel as good about himself as possible, you want him to experience as much academic success as he can.

But what is it about children who are ADD and their education that causes so much difficulty?

The most important thing to emphasize is that there are no bad guys here. Neither ADD children nor the education system is *at fault*. But the problems are created because the teaching methods used in most schools generally do not work for ADD children. Likewise, the teaching methods that do work well for ADD children are rarely used in most schools.

Most elementary and secondary schools rely heavily on teaching through reading. If a child is not a good reader, she becomes handicapped early on in this system. Unfortunately, many people with ADD have reading comprehension problems because of distractibility. Children who are ADD usually learn more effectively with hands-on activities. In school, however, students are more often taught *about* subjects, rather than being given an opportunity to experience what the subject is about.

Take math, for example. Most math concepts are taught and practiced using word problems, which require reading. The student must figure out what is supposed to be taking place. Then he must accurately turn those ideas into written numbers and remember to turn his paper in, preferably looking neat.

An ADD student would be able to better understand that same math concept if he was presented with a physical situation he could touch and see, not one he reads about. For example, if a student were building a table or buying supplies to stock a store, he would measure, weigh, or sort so that he could come up with the right combination to achieve his goal. Then he could show the teacher how he arrived at his answer, and she would know he understood the concept. With no distracting paper work involved,

188

no papers to lose or mess up, and the opportunity to walk through the problem, the ADD student might very well come up with the right answer.

The current American education system primarily favors children who can sit still in a seat, like to do paper work, learn visually first and auditorially second, read well, and learn well by practicing.

None of these teaching methods fits ADD children. Even Highly Structured ADD kids learn better kinesthetically. The most recent understanding into the way children learn shows that those who do not have ADD would also learn more and retain more with the hands-on approach that ADD learning requires.

Maybe one day our educational system will catch up to what your child already knows works best. In the meantime, let's look at several factors that make it difficult for your teen to succeed within the current system.

Boredom

Boredom is one of the most prevalent problems ADD teens face in school. Boredom is physiologically associated with a lack of attention. Once a student becomes bored and stops paying attention for even a few minutes, he's missed important information. If he does start paying attention again, what he hears may not make much sense because he's already missed too much.

This has nothing to do with whether or not the student is bright. If a child's learning method doesn't match up with the way the material is taught, he will get bored. If the student doesn't see the relevance of what's being taught, he will get bored.

Then there's the problem of the adult world's response to your teen's complaint of "I'm bored." The teacher's response might be to assign more work that your child finds boring. That doesn't do much to solve his problem.

So the student is confined to an endless cycle from which there seems to be no hope for rescue. Boredom, anxiety, and depression are suddenly on the increase. Motivation and grades are seriously on the decrease. Pretty dismal.

189

Difficulty Focusing Attention

An ADD student is easily distractible. The problem gets worse when she's supposed to be focusing on material that never interested her in the first place. At least when she's interested, she's more able to maintain a focus of attention for periods of time.

However, starting in elementary school, your child's teachers probably said to you, "Your child could do this if she just wanted to . . . if she would just pay attention." If this is said in a scolding manner, the child learns at a young age to feel guilty about not paying attention in all situations. Rather than acting as a motivator, the scolding and subsequent guilt is likely to cause her to lose even more focus of attention as she is distracted by her feelings.

No classroom, no matter how quiet it seems to the common observer, is really quiet. And in a classroom, which usually contains many students, there is no background noise such as a radio or TV to screen out the irregular and periodic noises that do occur. Other students might be able to focus on the history textbook in front of them. They might be able to block out the extraneous sights and sounds themselves. But because your ADD student is hypersensitive, she hears and sees everything.

She sees the dents in the walls, the scuff marks on the chairs, and every hair sticking out of every ponytail or braid in the room. She smells every smell. She feels every irregularity in her seatback. Her mind wanders to anything and everything that crosses her path. She cannot sit still and read her history text for a solid hour in study hall. But when that period is over, she'll be able to tell you the color and style of the bracelets worn by the girl two rows over and one seat ahead.

Difficulty Studying at Home

Students who are ADD are often burned out by the time they get home from school. Even though they may have accomplished little while in school, they have used an enormous amount of energy on what they did accomplish, on staying out of trouble or dealing with getting in trouble for things they have little control over.

The thought of doing homework is more than most ADD

teens can handle, and the prospect of studying for a test is even more dismal. At least homework is something tangible and finite. With tests, the ADD student will often complain, "The teacher wants me to know everything." That's such an overwhelming prospect for your teen that he may not even begin to study. He doesn't know *where* to begin studying.

In addition to these issues, people with ADD have a lot of trouble with organization, whether it's organizing time or materials. Just because they're spending time on something does not mean they're spending it wisely. Can you imagine doing all that studying and still not getting a good grade? It doesn't take many experiences like that to discourage even the best-intentioned student.

Difficulty Taking Tests

The setting in which a test is given may be the first problem ADD teens face. It goes back to the issue of distractibility: Every sight or sound imaginable disrupts the teen's thinking. A teacher pacing around the room, other students rustling papers, keys jangling, and bells ringing all distract the ADD test taker. Even birds flying by outside the classroom window and the feel of a blouse ruffle on a teen's neck may take her mind off the test. By the time she forces her mind to return to the test, valuable time has elapsed.

ADD students also lose time when they get distracted by the content of the test itself. They may begin thinking about something that has nothing to do with answering the question but was suggested by a test item.

For example, if the science test requires the student to describe a specific type of cloud, he might be reminded of the time he and his brother flew kites on a cloudy day several years ago. He remembers how the clouds looked, what the kite was made of, where they parked the car, and exactly how the wind felt as it whipped through his hair. He remembers what his brother wore and how fast he could run with that kite. That might remind him of his brother's recent bicycle accident. And then he might think about how well his leg is healing. By the time he remembers the test and gets his mind back on that, time has been lost.

For these reasons, ADD students could often use just a little bit more time on a test than other students. And there are some testing situations in which that can be arranged. It's not that they know less of the material, it's that they might not be able to produce answers as quickly as the other students.

Because the ADD mind is usually very creative, ADD students might come up with answers that are legitimately correct but different from the typical answers expected on tests—especially tests constructed by a teacher with a more traditionally organized linear mind. Given an opportunity to prove their point, their answers may make sense. But in fill-in-the-blank, true-false, and multiple-choice tests, this kind of creativity puts ADD students at a disadvantage. These kinds of tests usually measure details—a real weakness for ADD students. While Highly Structured ADD kids tend to handle tests of these kinds better than the other two types of kids with ADD, they still may perform less well than non-ADD kids, even if they fully understand the concept and its function. Essays, oral descriptions, and demonstrations of the function of the principles being tested will suit your teen much better.

Impulsivity also causes test-taking problems. In true-false quizzes and multiple-choice tests, the ADD student may impulsively answer something—anything—just to get the test over with. Even in fill-in-the-blank tests they may simply write a word rather than face an empty space on the paper and in their mind.

One of the watchwords of test taking is, "Go back and double-check your work." That's an almost impossible request for ADD students, especially those with Outwardly Expressive or Inwardly Directed ADD. Their goal is to get the pain of taking the test behind them as quickly as possible. The tedium of going back over their work can actually be physically painful to the student.

Attitudes About Test Taking
The type of ADD your teenager has will affect his attitude toward test taking. Students who have primarily Outwardly Expressive ADD tend to "blow off" tests after rushing to cram the night before

or even the hour before the exam. They will often spend more time trying to talk the teacher into changing the grade than they spent studying for the test. They believe that testing doesn't have much value, and they're not shy about telling you so.

Students who have Inwardly Directed ADD are likely to feel guilty about not preparing more thoroughly for the test. They feel they *should* study and will probably try to, although they may end up staring into space. If they do poorly on the test, they will feel depressed and guilty. Students with Highly Structured ADD usually do fairly well on tests. Their ADD-related problems surface when they work on long-term or group projects.

Hypersensitivity

By the time an ADD student is a teen, he may have suffered so much pain and, because of his hypersensitivity, felt it so keenly that he's averse to school. He doesn't want to be there and shields himself from more hurt by pretending he doesn't care. Even students who are "making it" often feel this way inside.

Students with Outwardly Expressive ADD often complain at length. It's good for them to get their feelings out. By the teen years, if they have become successful in an extracurricular area, one that is a good match with their abilities and needs, they may have developed positive self-esteem. They will be measuring themselves in an area that fits them.

Students with Inwardly Directed ADD are more likely to suffer depression and guilty feelings from their school difficulties. Equally hypersensitive, their bodies may be in the classroom, but their minds are often elsewhere. They will thrive if they have a special extracurricular interest that holds their attention. Students with Highly Structured ADD are equally hypersensitive, but an observer may not realize it. They can be very stubborn, which provides a shield of protection. It may seem as if they could do things but choose not to, almost as a matter of principle. But even though they often do well in school, underneath their emotional coat of armor they, too, may feel the challenge of low self-esteem. Although they may be able to perform well in school, they often have difficulty concentrating fully and *enjoying* learning.

Physical hypersensitivity makes sitting in classroom seats very difficult. Not only are these students distracted by every bump and pressure point caused by the seat, but the very process of sitting still for long periods of time is physically and emotionally painful.

Lack of movement or physical exercise also allows the "attention chemicals" in the brain to become even more sluggish than usual. As a result the student may fall asleep. This does not mean he didn't get enough sleep the night before. Nor is he trying to be rude to the teacher. He simply needs activity to "awaken" himself to a level of alertness that fits a classroom.

Often, a disruption in class serves this purpose. This type of student may hit or pinch a fellow student. Though he doesn't necessarily understand why he's "messing" with another student, this is often the reason underlying misbehavior in the classroom. It's an attempt to stay alert.

Doodling, taking notes, and being allowed to get up and move around during class activities and tests helps immensely. Also, listening to your teen complain, though you can set limits on the time you spend doing this, helps diffuse the tension and irritability caused by being so sensitive.

I know one eighteen-year-old with ADD who called his mom from college regularly. He always started the conversation by complaining. His mother responded by trying to help him think through ways to resolve his problems or issues. That wasn't really what he wanted. He told her, "No, Mom. I just need to get my feelings off my chest. I only want you to listen, not try to do anything."

His mother understood and appreciated what he needed. But it bothered her to listen to the complaints for very long, so she said, "Okay, I can listen for five minutes. After that, I need you to stop because I feel bad listening any longer and not being able to do anything about your situation." Her son agreed to the five-minute limit, and they both felt good about the deal they'd made.

Teachers and Administrators

Teachers and administrators add to the mix that creates difficulties for an ADD teen. Some teachers are not adequately trained, and many of those who are feel that the administration limits their autonomy and their ability to respond to the individual needs of their students. Then there are the inevitable personality clashes that can affect any student.

Teachers learn about teaching in college and from their own school experiences. Some teachers have a natural talent for teaching, while others learn from experience. Because teachers in training spend a lot of time in settings that are primarily based on visual learning, in their own education and research, the system of training favors people who are visual learners. The training also takes a linear approach to learning material systematically and in detail. Prospective teachers must be able to think and perform in a linear manner, teach students methodically, make lesson plans, do long-range planning, and test and re-test students in certain ways — and in certain ways only.

Numerous researchers and academicians have studied intelligence and agree there are many different types of intelligence. The current educational system speaks to only a few of those types. Many types of intelligence lie dormant within bright individuals who do not do particularly well in school.

Those people who have strong mathematical and verbal intelligence tend to do quite well in school. People who think systematically, have good recall, and are able to pay attention to detail do better in school than those who see the overview, pay attention to the function or processes of things, and generally work spontaneously and creatively in the moment. In general, teachers are trained to teach to the strengths of the former type of student.

A major communication difference between teacher and student can also cause frustration for both the ADD student and his teacher. If a teacher thinks in a linear fashion, but the student doesn't process information that way, the two are not likely to understand each other very well.

When Rodriquez's teacher asked him to turn in a plan for his chemistry project, she expected him to write an outline, list materials that he would use, and prepare a short summary of expected results. Instead, Rodriquez, who is ADD, turned in his list of materials and drew pictures of the results he thought he might get, although he didn't really have a systematic plan to achieve them. What he wanted to do was experiment with the materials and see what would happen. He couldn't understand how anyone could predict results if he hadn't done the project yet.

His teacher thought Rodriquez was not taking the project seriously. To the contrary, Rodriquez was intensely interested in the project and about learning how the chemicals worked with one another. He felt that his teacher was keeping him from learning what he wanted to know. The saddest part of this story is that the teacher realized Rodriquez was bright, but she just didn't understand why he "fooled around" so much instead of getting down to work.

The apprenticeship model of times past works well with people who are ADD. In this way the teaching is done incidentally with the process of doing. The student immediately understands why he needs to learn a particular thing and understands the application of it because he can see it in front of him and hold it in his hands. The ADD teen would learn beautifully this way.

Unfortunately, this method of teaching requires a lot of time and attention from a teacher—more time and attention than putting an outline on the board or handing out worksheets. Most teachers are not given the opportunity to provide hands-on teaching, even if they want to. Classes tend to be too big, and teachers have too many students to track and too much paper work. And in many districts teachers are expected to "teach to the test," that is, make sure their students perform as well as possible on district-wide or state-wide standardized tests. With the threat of being marked down if their students don't test "well," many teachers have to set aside creative teaching methods that would work for ADD students in order to save their own jobs.

Parents are often under the illusion that more work equals more learning, and, in some districts, will pressure teachers to give their children more work, usually more worksheets or assignments related to reading and writing. These parents are usually misguided. Stacks of paper have little to do with what or how students learn, especially ADD students.

Supplementary classroom activities have been cut to a minimum in many districts in recent years, due to budget problems. Travel, field trips, classroom speakers who bring in the materials of their trade, storytellers, and in some cases, music and physical education have been reduced. Yet ADD students usually learn more from these experiences than from reading books.

In addition, alternative education programs that allow teens to work while in school are usually relegated to students who are having severe problems in the classroom. If your teen is a fair student, she probably won't be recommended for this type of work/study program, even though she could greatly benefit from it. Technical programs have almost entirely been eliminated from our high schools, eliminating an excellent alternative for many ADD students. These programs tended to utilize teaching techniques that fit many ADD students. Some school districts do have magnet schools that specialize in technical areas of study. You will find many ADD students in some of these schools, such as the arts magnet, health professions magnet, etc. And the students, inspired by their heartfelt interests, do better in traditional academics as well.

The teachers in the alternative, technical, and magnet schools are often some of the most creative, dedicated teachers available, and they manage to reach students effectively.

All teachers deserve the opportunity to be able to teach this way, and ADD students deserve the opportunity to work with these teachers.

Grades
When Lynne, a high-school junior, received an assignment to write a paper about the American Revolution, she was excited. She immediately went to the library, checked out a stack of books, and read and read and read—jumping from one to another to find out

more about a specific aspect of the revolution when her interest was piqued.

Lynne began to talk about what she was reading to her parents. Every dinner-table conversation ended up on the subject. She told her little brother all about the Revolution, asked her parents if they were registered to vote, and asked how they made up their minds about which candidate to support.

She learned about colonialism and taxation without representation. She continued to question her parents about politics and may well have developed a lifelong dedication to the democratic process from this experience. She checked up on her parents to be sure they would vote in the next election, and she planned to vote as soon as she was old enough to register.

Lynne wrote her paper enthusiastically. She was so excited about her subject that she was sure she would get an A. Imagine her surprise when she got a C-, which was no different than the grade she'd received on previous papers she didn't care about.

When her parents examined the corrected paper they found misspelled words and inconsistencies in her footnotes and bibliography. Her thoughts had rambled. The paper was not tightly constructed.

The history teacher had made an assignment to write a paper about the American Revolution. What Lynne had understood from that assignment was that she was to *learn* about the American Revolution. In her mind the writing of the paper was secondary and not nearly so important as the subject matter. The teacher was required to grade the paper according to tight standards that had little or nothing to do with the amount of learning the student did about the Revolution.

Some teachers are very frustrated by this process and realize how frustrated the students can be, too. Some teachers compensate by giving two grades, one for creativity or content and one for grammar and presentation. But there are others who do not realize that many students, like Lynne, think and learn differently from the academic guidelines under which they are taught.

Let me emphasize again, because as parents of ADD students

we need to hear it again and again, *ADD has nothing to do with intelligence.* An ADD student can learn a tremendous amount that is not reflected by the grades she is given. And Lynne's situation is a perfect example. Given the public educational system that most of us deal with today, these students are often marked down and left behind. In reality, it is possible that Lynne learned more and incorporated more of what she learned into her life, than any other student in that class. That includes the students who earned A's by being meticulous with spelling and footnotes.

Given time and experience, most teachers will come to understand that it is not possible to teach all children in the same way or even in similar ways. In some cases, it might not be appropriate to grade all children in the same ways.

Personality Conflicts
Not all people get along well together. That is true for school personnel as well as for your teen. Often what we call personality conflicts are just differences in the way two people see the world. So your ADD teen may have trouble understanding someone who is not ADD or, at least, who is not appreciative of an ADD style. Moreover, that person might have trouble understanding your child.

Most people with ADD would have difficulty getting along with a teacher who is highly authoritarian. A teen with Outwardly Expressive ADD will "mouth off" and likely challenge the teacher.

An Inwardly Directed ADD teen, being more passive, may simply ignore the teacher, discounting what she says and does, or may use a subtle challenge, such as rolling his eyes, purposely turning in sloppy work that is difficult to read, or mumbling under his breath. A teen with Highly Structured ADD will often criticize the teacher by arguing and challenging her presentations.

Disorganized teachers cause great difficulty for all ADD teens. Critical teachers and those who use abusive tactics and putdowns to try to get a teen to accomplish something seriously abuse an ADD teen's sensitivity.

Cathy, a teen with Inwardly Directed ADD, moved to a new

city with her family when she was in tenth grade, and she became quite depressed. She missed her friends and found the new school confusing. It was bigger than she was used to, and everyone seemed *very* active, with a "go, go, go" mentality. Cathy preferred a small group of friends, enjoyed helping others, and liked to write poetry.

Cathy's English teacher recognized her talents and immediately wanted her to enter a writing competition. She also thought that Cathy would get used to the new school more quickly if she joined one of the clubs. So she tried to arrange a meeting for Cathy right away. When Cathy said she didn't want to enter the writing contest, her teacher assumed she was just shy and, in the name of encouragement, pressed her harder. But the harder she pushed, the more Cathy withdrew.

Cathy began to avoid the teacher and told her mother that she hated school. It took some real digging for Cathy's mom to discover what the real problem was. When she met Cathy's English teacher, she understood. There wasn't anything *wrong* with the woman. She was nice and well meaning, but she had a very different personality from her daughter.

This scenario could be turned into the *teachable moment* if Cathy's mom could sit down with her daughter and help her learn to communicate clearly with her teacher. One of the most important skills we all need to learn is how to deal with people who are different from us. You might as well start teaching your ADD teen now.

THE GREAT AMERICAN HONOR ROLL MYTH

The great American "honor roll" myth goes like this: Your child is a good person, which also means you have been a good parent, if he makes the honor roll. A corollary is that your child will be a success in life, which brings status to your family, if he makes the honor roll. And another part of the myth states that if any student *works hard enough*, he can earn honor roll grades.

No part of this myth is true. Of course there are some honor-roll students who are genuinely good people, who do work hard and will attain success in life, by anyone's standards. There are also honor roll students who are insensitive and friendless, who do not have to work particularly hard to earn good grades and who may not ever become successful in ways that you feel really count.

I'll never forget a bright fourth-grader who had ADD. He finally decided he was willing to do enough of his homework to make good grades. He managed to get all A's, except in one subject, handwriting. In that class he received a C. That C kept him off the honor roll. He didn't bother to try again. After all, what was the use? He couldn't control his fine motor coordination, no matter how hard he worked, so why try? By the way, that child later made straight A's in his junior high and high school years and went on to earn honors in college. By that time he was ready to learn in the way he was being taught, and he did all this work on a computer. He was not working hard just to try to make the honor roll.

Unfortunately, some children who do make the honor roll are in for a rude awakening. They may have made the honor roll consistently, only to find there is more to life than making good grades.

Even with top grades some high school and college students do not receive scholarships, get into the schools of their choice, or get hired for the jobs they'd like. Suddenly they find they also need to have lots of extracurricular activities and are expected to be an officer of school clubs, on the student council, and do volunteer work for the community.

Let's be honest. By adulthood, no one knows or cares who made the honor roll.

The main reason for you not to buy into this myth is because you could be doing your child a great disservice. The honor roll myth leads you to judge your teen by arbitrary standards instead of looking at your child as the wonderful, complex adolescent he is. Your teen is a real person, and there's no reason to hold him up in judgment to a meaningless, unattainable myth.

As parents we do feel drawn to the honor-roll myth, often as *proof* that our children are going to be successful, because we all want our children to do well and be successful. But in the long run we must support one another in turning our attention to the important values that truly guide our children to be all they can be. To do this I'd like to suggest several guidelines.

Recognize Your Teen's Value

The value of your child as a human being is *not* determined by the grades he makes in school. I know you know this in your heart. It's your mind and the pressure of other parents and of society that tells you differently.

If you go back to feeling with your heart, you will know that your teen is an inherently worthwhile and lovable person, regardless of the grades he makes. Your teenager needs your *unconditional* love and acceptance.

If it's hard for you to see your child in a positive light when he doesn't produce at a highly competitive standard, ask yourself how you were judged as a child. Making comparisons between your child and some arbitrary standard is learned behavior. Because it's so prevalent in our culture, it may seem to be an accepted fact of life.

The pressure can come from other parents. "How's Johnny doing in school?" your friend asks. "Gregory made the honor roll this semester." Then there are the bumper stickers that proclaim to all, "My child is an honor-roll student" or "I'm the proud parent of an honor-roll student." I'm hopeful that the parent who displays such a sticker doesn't replace it with, "I'm the disappointed parent of a student who didn't make the honor roll," when her child fails to make the grade.

Even though *you* may not buy into the myth, your teenager sees those bumper stickers, the display of honor-roll names in the school hallway, and the beaming parents and teachers who glow over the "honor roll" students during open house. You need to take the time to talk with your teen about this. I'm not saying that you should discourage your teen from making good grades. And if his friend does make the honor roll, he can be proud of his friend's accomplishment. But it's important to put those grades in proper perspective.

Good grades are expected and associated with hard work. Our society assumes that they are available to anyone who wants to work for them. You will want to recognize how hard it may have been for your ADD student to even stay in school for all these years, when he may only learn and retain one of every five bits of information that comes his way.

Value your child, unconditionally, for doing what he can. Provide a good model of self-discipline, have realistic expectations, and celebrate with your teen on what he does accomplish, no matter at what level.

Don't Judge Your Teen by His Homework

It's important for you to know that whether your child is or is not doing his homework isn't necessarily indicative of whether or not he is learning something, will get high test grades, or be successful in later life. Let's consider each of these points separately.

Some children do learn by doing homework. Some subjects appear to require homework in order for a student to master them. But homework is only one of many tools that can contribute to learning.

Homework may consist of practicing something that has just been taught in school. Some children don't learn from practice. I always recall a young man I knew who refused to do his math homework. One year he had a teacher who would allow his students to move to the next lesson if they could do five problems correctly based on the present day's work. The teen was ecstatic and progressed rapidly through the year's work.

This student, who had done a poor, sloppy job prior to having this teacher, suddenly responded with excitement and was motivated to see how far he could go. He still didn't do homework, because he would finish the problems assigned for the day before class was over. But he would thumb ahead in his math book and try out new problems. Compared to previous classrooms and the boredom that set in when he was required to repeat exercises he already knew how to do, he loved the mental challenge presented in this teacher's classroom.

Unfortunately, many an ADD student who has disciplined himself to do his homework and turn it in has still not done well on tests. Some of us with ADD simply don't carry over the results of repetitive work to test situations. (We may actually do better in some subjects if we react to the test situation spontaneously.) In these circumstances the one good thing about having done the homework is that the teacher may give credit for that, which can offset a poor test grade.

Finally, *whether your teen does well later in life has little to do with whether or not he does his homework now.* You might find that difficult to believe if your child has demonstrated a pattern of failure in school. But it's important that you do believe it. It is the truth, and it will enable you to let go of some fears, to relax a bit, and to enjoy your teen.

The bottom line is that your teen's success in life depends on the *type of work* he selects when he finishes school. If he is in a field that fits him, one that gives him an outlet for his talents and strengths and doesn't rely on his weakest areas, he will do well and enjoy success.

Even the selection of his major, if he goes to college, will determine how important it is that he be disciplined about doing homework. If he chooses a major that depends on spontaneity and creativity, then the discipline of doing homework may be minimal. On the other hand, if he goes into a line of work that requires a lot of continuous learning, doing homework may be important. But success in life, per se, is not dependent on successfully completing homework.

Focus on Your Teen's Learning Versus Grades
Your child may be learning important life skills in nonacademic areas—and they might be just the skills he needs, even though he isn't making great grades. Remember, your long-term goal is for your child to learn what he needs to have an independent and productive life. Achieving those goals may or may not have any-

thing to do with what happens in the classroom. You have to stay focused on your own child and his overall needs and abilities.

For example, some people think football is counterproductive to learning, even foolish and a waste of money. But I've got news for you. Football is a great training ground for some people. Team members must show up on time—an important skill to learn for teens who are ADD. They have to learn plays, which challenges their concentration in a subject in which they are motivated to work hard.

Football players have to learn to work with others, take orders, and inhibit their impulsivity. Playing some positions helps develop organization skills and memorization. Long-term planning is required when considering the whole season or the whole game. Timing during the game, and breaking it down into segments, is also important. You must notice details. All of these areas are challenging for teenagers affected by ADD.

Some students might not be motivated to work on these skills in history or biology class. But they might be motivated to make the football team and work hard to remain there.

I am not saying that football is more important than math, literature, or science and that teenagers should just play football and not worry about anything else. What I'm saying is that your unique child whom you love will learn more when he is excited and motivated about a topic. It's your job to realize that math, literature, and science are not the only areas in which he can learn important skills. So keep your eyes and ears open.

Let Your Teen Determine His Own Study Habits

Many people with ADD procrastinate. Contrary to what our society seems to believe, that isn't necessarily such a bad thing. In fact, for many people with ADD, it's the *best* way to accomplish things.

Many of us with ADD perform much better when we do an assignment under pressure at the last minute, because we're more focused and creative. The time crunch raises the level of the chemicals in our brains to help us focus our attention on a particular project. We become better able to identify the details that need attention. In this heightened state of focus even our internal organization improves. We become decisive.

No matter how guilty your child feels, no matter how much she intends to start studying early, most ADD students don't study for tests until the last minute. Parents and teachers continue to tell students that they have to study a little bit each night. And often teens believe they *should* be studying a little bit at a time, "like everyone else." But studying a little every night doesn't feel right to them. And it usually *isn't* best.

It's hard to see your teen, especially a young one, pulling an all-nighter. I know that. But nothing bad is going to happen because he or she stays up all night. The student will go to school the next day, take the test, and come home and crash. Sure, in the long run, this schedule is not conducive to all-around great health. But it's not going to hurt them every now and then.

You might want to let your teenager give this kind of schedule a chance, if he wants to, and see if it works for him. Let him be the judge on that one.

Since boredom is a factor for many students with ADD, they can become depressed if they feel a project will never end, and then they become easily distracted. A little procrastination helps a lot in these situations. And it's not because the teenager finally becomes fearful of the repercussions for not getting the job done, though that may be a factor from time to time. It's as simple as needing the pressure to focus attention and not become distracted.

As a parent your job is to help your student help himself. Help him learn to listen to what his body and mind tell him and help him run experiments to see what works best. You might want to help him learn from the pitfalls that a "wait until the last minute" system uncovers. For example, having a printer ink cartridge run out of ink at 3:00 a.m. may require that the student always learn to have an extra ink cartridge on hand. Or you might need to discover the nearest all-night store that sells poster board.

Parents often feel that they need to set limits on such "irregular behavior." Think twice before you do. Why do you need to set those limits? Is it because you always had a set bedtime when you were a teenager, and your parents would *never* have allowed you to stay up all night? Is it because you're worried about what the neighbors will think if they see your teenager drive off to the store at 3:00 a.m.? Don't let those types of issues bother you. Concentrate on whether or not this works for your teen. Your teen needs to do his work in whatever way is best for *him*—not what's best for you or your neighbor.

I have often heard: "If your teen wants to study in his own way, then he has to pay the consequences. If he messes up his last sheet of poster board at 2:00 a.m., then he'll just have to do without it."

But this attitude misses the point. We all have times when we need someone to help us out. A teenager who doesn't drive yet, or whose parents won't allow him to drive in the middle of the night, needs a parent to drive him to the store if he needs the poster board in the middle of the night. I'm not saying you should spend your nights running to the store. But if you have agreed to your child staying up through the night to work on this project, there's nothing wrong with helping him out.

As we discussed in the last chapter, your teen needs to take on more and more responsibility for himself as the teen years progress. But you are not enabling him by helping him out in a pinch when he is also working hard. If he were expecting you to do the entire project for him, then he would be acting irresponsibly. If you were to say okay and do it, then you would be enabling. But if your child is doing his best and putting forth an honest effort, don't worry about helping him out every now and then.

The "irregular" habits of a teen with ADD are based on how he works best. Each time he confronts a project or assignment, he is learning how to handle the next one. You will probably have to help with the preplanning stage during the early teen years. Slowly, your teen will take over that job. Both of you together need to track how he is progressing from semester to semester.

WHAT YOU CAN DO TO HELP YOUR TEEN
IN SCHOOL

Parenting an ADD teen is a full-time job. You are preparing your teen to be on his own in a world in which the buck stops at *his* door. Your teen *can* make it, though you may not see the full transition for another ten or more years. I cannot tell you how many people make a major step in maturity at age thirty, often finally coming into their own. Others of us, women especially, blossom at forty and fifty.

In this journey toward independence it is important for your child to take on more and more responsibility for himself. But there are many ways in which you can help him. Let's look at the ways you can help him in school.

Promote Long-Term Development

Every time your teen changes classes, schools, or you notice a development leap or change in his behavior, you would do well to reassess how you see your child. Without saying anything, watch how your teen solves problems, both those related to school and those that are not. When he's doing his schoolwork, sit down with him from time to time and ask him to explain what he's doing. Don't do it too often or he'll push you away.

If you are still helping your teen with his work, you can go over test papers and see what kinds of errors he's made and why. If you tell him you're genuinely interested in how he thinks and does his work, and that you might be able to help him figure out why he gets certain kinds of questions wrong, he'll probably let you see his work. Under no circumstances should you criticize, scold, or generalize by saying, "If you'd study harder, you wouldn't miss so many."

Remember, no one goes into a test planning to miss questions. Notice *how* he or she studies. For example, Becky, one ADD teen I know, spent all her time getting ready to study. An hour later she would be worn out before she actually started on any of her homework. Her mother had no idea what went on in her daughter's room until she began an assessment of her daughter's study habits.

Once her mother realized how Becky was spending her time, they talked about options that would allow her to get right down to work. Her mother suggested she might do better at the dining room table after it was cleared from dinner. That part of the house was out of the main pathway of traffic. However, it was near the kitchen where her mother could answer questions or they could talk from time to time about something in the homework.

That worked out well. Becky discovered that not only could she get right down to work, she could stay on the task at hand. Previously, when she came to something she didn't know how to do, her mind would wander. After moving to the dining room table, she simply asked her mom. And Becky also realized she had not liked the feeling of isolation when she worked in her room.

By supporting the study habits that work for your teen and letting her know you're on her side, you'll also be improving your relationship with her.

Work on Short-Term Goals

One way you can help your teen is by finding creative methods to accomplish short-term goals, and there are many tricks you can use. I particularly like the one I call having an organizational party. This is a good exercise to do during elementary school, but it's never too late to start. You can help your child during the early teen years, and then he can do it for himself.

Make the first night of every school semester organizational night. Have a special dinner that doesn't take much preparation, like pizza. If necessary, go to the store together to pick up school supplies. Then everyone in the family can sit down together and make out a calendar for the semester.

Pull out a calendar that covers the sixteen-week semester period; one with big squares works great. Fill in activities that are already planned for the family. Fill in school, work times, and any other obligations the teen has. Evaluate how much time the teen wants for leisure. Be sure to include recreational time on the calendar, including time for TV.

Help your teen set up a notebook, dividing it into category areas. Then insert tabs, place a calendar of the semester's holidays, and mark the dates of finals and any known test dates. Next, fill out a daily sheet if he or she would like. (One can be included in the notebook.) Mark the times of day your teen is in classes, times for homework, TV watching, telephone conversations, sports, or other practices. Mark bedtime and wake-up time. This doesn't need to be followed rigidly, but it's a good pattern to approximate.

An organized schedule will help your teen feel more relaxed when facing a brand-new semester. Finish off the evening with a favorite dessert for a treat.

Bridge the Gap to the "Linear World"

Throughout the teen years you must slowly help your child realize that he doesn't need to believe in the superior worth of the "linear culture," but he does need to learn to build a bridge to it. The linear culture is not *wrong* any more than being ADD is *wrong*, but it probably doesn't fit your child. Highly structured, tightly organized linear thinking is fine for people who are neurologically constructed to work that way. It's the basis for most of our culture and certainly the basis of our educational system.

So learning to build a bridge from your teen's ADD ways of thinking and working to the linear way of thinking and working is important. If your teen can learn to do that now, it will serve her well her whole life.

For example, if your teen leaves home and goes to college or a job, she will need to deal with this linear world on her own. If she can bridge that gap and make peace with it instead of fighting against it, she will be in a good position to utilize her strengths and talents, most of which result from her ADD wiring.

One thing you can do to help your child have all the opportunities she needs to develop her innate talents is to help alleviate some of the stress of requirements that just don't fit her.

Jason's father did this. When Jason was in eighth grade, he

hated school. He spent most of his time during class staring into the ozone. Then Jason went with his family to a dog show one night. He found that he was fascinated with the way the dogs had been trained and began to play around with training his own dog at home. His concentration was excellent while he was figuring out how to get his dog to obey certain commands and perform various tricks. His father noticed his interest and called the local obedience training school to find out whether they would be willing for Jason to hang out and learn some things about dog training. When they said yes, Jason was delighted.

Jason's father decided that it was okay for Jason to back off from some of his school work and spend time at the training center. It was a decision he felt was best for his son in the long run.

Jason became very disciplined and organized in his work with the dogs and training school. Slowly, as he learned to organize tasks, meet deadlines, think ahead, break projects down into smaller segments, keep track of details, and stay on task for his canine obedience work, his schoolwork began to improve. Jason's self-esteem jumped a "thousand percent" and he began to feel he had something valuable to offer.

Jason learned that he could be disciplined when he wanted to be and could accomplish goals of his choice, even when it meant doing something he didn't like in order to accomplish something he did like. And he realized he could apply these same skills to schoolwork.

The task for teens who are ADD is to learn some discipline, accomplish tasks in their own ways, and reach their goals. It's *not* okay for your ADD student to do nothing and be undisciplined all the time.

The challenge is to build the bridge between what's easy and natural and what's difficult and different. You can help by exposing your child to a variety of sports, arts, and music, and by encouraging him to try new activities. If he can use his ADD talents and skills and learn how to accomplish some of the more linear tasks, he will have expanded his capabilities greatly.

Be Supportive of Your Child's Capabilities

One of your jobs as a parent is to know enough about your child's capabilities to determine realistically in which areas he might be able to excel and in which ones he probably won't. For example, you might be able to expect him to earn a B in one class. However, in another subject area you might realistically expect just a passing grade.

I'm not talking about letting your teen "get away with everything" and not be accountable for making an effort. I'm talking about realistically evaluating your teen's strengths and weaknesses. If you force your teen all the time, you'll end up with a depressed or rebellious teen. True, there is a fine line. But remember ADD teens are kinesthetic learners, and you have to let them learn for themselves. They will figure out what works for them and what doesn't. You just have to give them some time.

Try watching your teen at work doing something he or she really loves to do. That's a good way to see her strengths and weaknesses. You'll notice certain areas of production she just zips through and others she finds difficult.

Watch how your teen tackles problems. Ask her to explain how she solves the problems, how her mind works. And tell her you are truly curious about how she approaches issues. Don't jump in too soon to correct the way she's doing something. You may miss an opportunity to see how *she* works.

Apply some of this information to school subjects. Together, you and she might be able to figure out how to use some of her strengths and apply those skills to mastering subjects that are much harder for her. I especially recommend this approach during the early teen years. Then you can practice together until your teen is ready to take over for himself by the late teens.

Set Ground Rules for Homework

You and your teen need to discuss where, when, and how he will do his homework. It's not a good idea to have this discussion when either of you is feeling stressed or frustrated. Certainly do not have it when you're upset about your child's work habits or grades.

212

In the early teen years the amount of time spent on homework should be minimal. It will increase as your teen gets older. You may want to begin by checking your teen's homework, with his permission. Together, you can track your teen's grades. Notice whether they are different when you help him. Later, talk with your teen about taking over a little more of the responsibility as the semesters progress.

Each year, back out more and more, even though your teen may stumble for a bit. Let him know you believe he can do homework on his own. However, be sure to tell him you're open to helping him anytime he asks for your help.

More than anything, you want to avoid power struggles during this time. Your teen has enough stress without that, and so do you. Tell your teen, "Getting your schoolwork done is your job, and I know you can do it. Let me know if you're having trouble in any particular areas and, of course, I'm always willing to help you out. But our job during junior and senior high is to get you ready to be completely on your own by the time you've graduated from high school."

You can't expect your teen—or anyone else's—to be delighted about doing homework. But you should expect him to do it with a bit of nudging.

If, however, your home has turned into a war zone, and your evenings are so miserable that you absolutely dread them, you may need to clarify with your teen what you will and will not tolerate.

You could say, "Look, I expect you to do your homework, and I'm willing to help you. But I'm not willing to fight about it. If you keep arguing with me, I will leave the whole homework business up to you. It's up to you to come to me. If you flunk because your homework is undone, I want you to know now that I will not pay for you to go to summer school. If you flunk, you'll have to redo this year."

It might be difficult, but your best bet is to say this in a matter-of-fact way. Let your teen know that you're not lashing out to punish him. You're just informing him of the facts. And then stick by your plan. Enjoy your evenings. Be there to help your teen if he comes to you. Otherwise, don't say anything to him about his homework. You told him it was his responsibility; now let him take it on.

You may want to talk with the school counselor about your child's homework situation. But remember, your teen is not a young child. You will need to work your way out of the picture. Unless he is willing to have you help, he will have to pay the consequences on his own. If he doesn't take responsibility for doing his homework and continues to flunk, at some point other arrangements will need to be made, such as an alternative public-school setting or possibly dropping out of school when he gets old enough.

Help Your Teen Study for Tests

When you know your teenager has a test to study for, your inclination might be to tell him to go in his room, shut the door, and get down to studying. But that is rarely a successful technique for ADD students. Instead, you can help him, especially during the early teen years, by participating in the study and review process. Remember, these students are kinesthetic learners; Make it fun, move around, talk out loud, and draw pictures.

Many ADD teens learn and review best by talking about the material at hand. You can help by being there to review questions and to listen while your teen explains the material out loud or makes up stories about the material—even silly ones.

I remember many evenings when my ADD teen and I sat around the living room for an hour or two discussing the subject matter on the next day's test. We told jokes, made fun of the material, did role playing, and diagrammed on big sheets of work paper taped to the back of a chair—anything to make the study time varied, interesting, and expressive. We laughed a lot. Invariably, my son earned at least one grade point higher on every test when we did this.

Teach Your Teen to Navigate the Administration

At some point you may find that you have to teach your child how to get the help he needs from teachers or other school officials, including how to ask for it. During the junior high years you may wish to accompany your teen to a meeting with the school counselor or teacher. I suggest a visit early in the semester to get acquainted *before* there are problems, to size up the willingness of the school personnel to help, and to reinforce with your teen that school is business and help is available.

When you accompany your child to such meetings, you will be modeling how to explain what ADD is, what your teen needs in the way of assistance and accommodation, and how to actually ask for that help. You might say, "My son has been diagnosed with Attention Deficit Disorder. I'm having the doctor's report sent to the school. You will find that he has particular problems keeping his mind on a task and benefits from gentle reminders to get back to work. He also does better if he sits in the front of the room.

"This semester we are particularly working on keeping track of his assignments, getting them home and back to school. We've found that he learns best by getting a daily reminder until he gets in the habit. I would appreciate you reminding him just before he leaves your class to put his assignments in his folder and then in his backpack. Even though you may remind the whole class, would you please remind him personally so you're sure you have his attention? Please let me know right away if there are any problems with this plan. I'd like to know what else works for you with him, too. If I don't hear from you, I'll check back with you in a month to see how everything is going. Will that work for you?"

After several of these meetings in the early teen years, your teen will be ready to take over the job. At first you'll do all the talking. Then the two of you will share the talking. Finally, he'll take over entirely. Then, when he goes to college or work, he'll be able to get what he needs and let others know how to make best use of his abilities.

When my ADD son was a young teen, I told him matter-of-factly that it was time for him to begin to learn to negotiate the system. "You and I will visit with the counselor to see how to get anything you might need during the semester," I told him. "This will give us a chance to size up the situation. During this first meeting I'll do most of the talking and you can watch and listen to how I talk with her. Afterwards we'll share our observations.

"During the visit, if you want some information, just speak up. If for any reason you need to talk with me in private during the meeting, just say, 'Mom, may I speak to you in private?' and we'll excuse ourselves and go outside for a minute."

Though you may meet with a little resistance initially, your teen will soon learn how valuable such a meeting can be. You may not see the result of his watching you until several years later, but I promise you that he's taking in everything you're doing. That's why it's so important to handle this meeting firmly, like any business meeting, in a warm, calm, matter-of-fact voice.

This is not the time to be emotional, even though your child's ADD is an extremely emotional issue in your life. I'd suggest that you and your child make a list ahead of time of the topics you want to cover. If you are a "gabber," be careful. Watch yourself; focus your comments and set a limit on how much time you spend talking.

If the counselor or official you are meeting with has an attitude that discounts your teen, or if the person seems to assume that all teens are irresponsible and try to get away with something or that the ADD teen is just using his ADD as an excuse, simply say in front of your teen, "I look at the situation differently." Then go on with the expectations you have. You might say, "I expect to work with you on this. I need you to ask my son's teacher (if you're dealing with a principal) to provide him with a quiet place to take his tests. I also need you to make sure my son is given a list of assignments in each class as he leaves the class—a list he brings home for me to initial and then takes back to the teacher for her initials. I also expect you to become familiar with ADD in teens and I'll see that you get some literature about it." Later evaluate the meeting with your teen. Talk honestly about what happened without putting the counselor down. But don't side with the counselor *just because she's an adult.* Your teen will appreciate your honesty and respect you for it.

Although you might meet some resistance, most counselors and many teachers will be delighted to work with you. I knew my son's ninth-grade English class might be quite a challenge, so we scheduled this type of meeting within the first two weeks of school. To my surprise, the teacher instantly made suggestions about how my son could manage the reading, introduced the use of *Cliff Notes*, and said she would stay in touch with both of us throughout the semester so things would not get out of hand.

My son, who greatly disliked the vast reading assignments associated with English class, found a teacher he liked who accepted him and guided him through his strengths to survive his weaknesses. She didn't let him get away with anything. She helped him achieve.

A counselor for the eleventh grade opened her own private office to a student with ADD so he could study for the Scholastic Aptitude Test (SAT) in a quiet setting. Later that year she again invited him there to fill out college application forms. She also established an application tutorial for students who had trouble with all the details involved in gaining admittance to college.

One ninth-grade algebra teacher I knew took extra time with students who were having trouble in her class. She personally invited them in to see her before and after school. By privately asking them to come in they felt special and were not embarrassed in front of the whole class. Then when they received a better test score the next week, she'd compliment them in private or slip them a congratulatory note. Needless to say, she didn't have much trouble getting her students to come in for tutoring.

By your teen's senior year in high school, he will probably be handling all his own classwork needs. However, you may get involved in issues such as transition to college or job, further training programs, and major areas of concentration beyond high school. You'll read more about this in the last chapter of this book.

I strongly recommend that you do not go behind your teen's back to deal with the school. Be up front with it. Even if he doesn't like your involvement, be honest. Tell him, "I realize you don't like me going to school, but I will not go behind your back.

You seem to be having some trouble—it's reflected in your grades—so I need to help figure out how you can get your situation turned around. I would like you to join me. I cannot force you, but your input is important."

One of the few *musts* in our household was that everyone went to parent-teacher conferences and open houses. I would say, "This is not optional. School is your responsibility and work place, so we will all go together. You don't have to like it but your input is important. I'll make the meetings as short as possible."

Every semester I ran into resistance from my sons about accompanying me to the conferences. But when we got there, I mostly received compliments or, at least, pleasantness. I don't know what the resistance was about other than the fact that teens, on general principle, don't want to go to such things.

Afterward we often went out for a snack and talked about all the teachers and subjects. It's amazing how accurately these teens can describe their teachers. They knew the ones who cared, the ones who were bored or irritated with their work, the ones who didn't much like teens, the ones who were bigots, lazy, or needed help with their own emotions. Even in the subjects they hated, they could spot a good teacher and respected that person.

I also made a point of meeting or getting to know the administrative personnel, because they were the ones who could open doors. My sons learned about school politics, interpersonal power, and how to get what you needed in a responsible way. We talked honestly about these things.

I recommend you do not assume that the adults are right and the teens are wrong in their assessment of situations. In fact, I usually found it to be the other way around.

I'll always remember a school principal whom my sons didn't like. I tend to give everyone the benefit of the doubt initially, and I had heard that this principal was sharp and cared about kids. So I told my teens to give her a chance. Unfortunately, they were right, although it took me a while to figure out what they knew immediately. In fact, it took me the better part of four years to learn what they had figured out in one semester.

They were right on target about not trusting her. She played politics to her advantage and to the disadvantage of the students, undercut faculty, favored factions that held the purse strings, and in my estimation misused power.

On the other hand, I saw them instantly like and work for a vice-principal who truly turned out to be on the student's team. He helped them learn to negotiate, encouraged them to be responsible, and helped them beyond the confines of school when they used poor judgment. Now a principal, some of the college seniors I know are planning to return to the district after graduation to find this man and show him how well they turned out.

Knowledge about people, institutions, and the negotiating it takes to get your needs met is the stuff of which real life is made. You *can* help your teen learn all about this during junior and senior high school.

BALANCING SCHOOL AND OTHER COMMITMENTS

Your teen can become overly stressed if she has too many responsibilities and commitments—classes, homework, a job, sports, clubs, socializing. Yet each of these areas is important in her life. You can help by emphasizing and modeling that everyone needs some unstructured down time and fun time.

Set limits on the amount of schoolwork you *allow* your teen to do. I'm serious. You can say, "I don't want you to spend more than (X) hours nightly doing homework." Obviously this amount will increase as your adolescent gets older. This approach helps you stay on your teen's side and relieves the overly-conscientious student of becoming compulsive about schoolwork.

On the other hand, you'll want to set limits on outside commitments that take too much time away from schoolwork. This includes the teen's job. It's a matter of balance between work and play. Obviously, if your teen is older and needs to make a transition from school to a job in order to find success and improve self-esteem, the job may take precedence over school.

SHOULD YOUR CHILD GO TO COLLEGE?

Students talk a lot about attending college, especially during the junior and senior high years. However, college might not be the right thing for your teen. Your attitude needs to be one that encourages college *if* it fits the needs, desires, skills, and talents of your teen. Don't discourage college if she seems interested in pursuing it. But you'll be doing her a great disservice if you make it seem that college is the only way to survive in this world.

College is not for everyone. And college immediately after high school may not be in your teen's best interest. Often a year of work or time in military service provides a foundation for returning to school later.

If your teen wants to try college, research your options: community college, colleges that favor learning-different students, small colleges, and large institutions — all must be considered. More and more colleges are responsive to the learning differences of students and often provide excellent special services. Check with your school counselors about what is available.

It's unrealistic to expect most ADD teens to sit down and browse through books describing colleges. They need to talk with people and see what goes on at the schools they're considering. Visit several colleges, if possible. Try to find alumnae to talk with. If your teen has a special interest, see if that can be supported at the schools she is considering.

Instead of attending a four-year institution right away, attending a community college often gives teens a good start in higher education. A community college will often have smaller classes and teachers who *want* to give individual attention to their students.

If you and your teen agree that she will continue to live at home, a community college provides a comfortable transition from high school into higher education. If she can handle college-level work, and enjoys it, she might want to continue working toward a bachelor's degree immediately after community college or in the future.

If, however, your teen is tired of school, you're better off

220

encouraging her to work for a while, especially in an area that interests her. Many ADD people return to school later, after they have a focus, and major in something they've come to love. When they find a subject area that thrills and motivates them, which can happen through work experience or even parenting, and they realize they need further education to get ahead in that field, they go and get it.

If you or a family member feels strongly that your teen *must* go to college, and an academically strong school at that, it may be a dream you really want for yourself. Ask yourself if college is realistic *for your child*. Maybe you're the one who needs to enroll in a strongly academic college, while allowing your teen to follow a path that fits *her* better. Examine your motives and emotions to see if your desire is for your own education.

The College Application Process

If your teen feels strongly that she wants to go to college immediately after high school, start preparations to do that. Getting ready for college isn't easy.

Preparation actually starts in the sophomore year of high school when students take the PSAT, the preliminary college entrance exam. In the junior year comes the SAT or ACT— college aptitude tests that are supposed to measure how well your teen is likely to do in an advanced academic setting. Many ADD students score lower on these tests than their innate intelligence and ability would indicate. However, they can be coached and can gain reasonable accommodation while taking them, which usually means an untimed test or a quiet setting.

Many college students have remarked that filling out a college application is harder than going to college. After studying the applications in recent years, I agree, especially if you're ADD. Applications are relentlessly boring and filled with detail, areas that are weak for people who are ADD. They require the teen to check details, write essays, organize letters of recommendation and complete and submit it *on time*.

You may be able to help your teen. It's okay to do this. You

221

can work with your teen, looking up information she might need and helping her go over her essay. However, don't do the whole thing while your teen goes out to a party. This is a "together" job, with your teen taking responsibility to request your help and the assistance of other people who are asked to write recommendations. You may want to make out a checklist of deadlines. And if you have never been to college and share your teen's feeling of being overwhelmed, or even if you have been to college and you're feeling overwhelmed because of your own ADD, you may want to ask for help from a relative, friend, or the school counselor. No one will think less of you. They'll probably be flattered that you asked for help. Anyone who has been to college knows that the application process is a "bear." You might find a parent who is especially good with this kind of task to set up an "application tutorial" after school for a few weeks. You, in turn, can send over "munchies" as your contribution.

Choosing a College

If your teen wants to go where all his friends are going, but you're fairly sure it's not a good choice for him, tell him why. You might say, "The college you want to attend is very large. It's known both as a "party" school and as competitive academically. You've tended to struggle with competitive learning situations. They don't show how smart you are. Add to that the way in which you get off track when there's a lot of stimulation around. You deserve to succeed at school. You'll make new friends wherever you attend."

After you point out your concerns, try to encourage your teen to make an alternate choice. If he insists, and the school is within your budget, you may wish to let him give it a try to find out for himself. If you do, don't say, "I told you so," if it doesn't work out. Remember, teens who are ADD learn by doing.

If your teen does poorly the first semester of college, don't continue to pour money down the drain. Figure out together what the problem is and be sure your teen has solved the problem before you continue to pay for school.

Too often I've seen college money used up to accumulate failing marks. The fear that their teen won't get an education often drives parents to continue to support such a losing process. But remember, many people return to school later, after finding direction, and they do quite well. There's no shame in realizing that college is not the right way for your teen to be spending his time right now.

One way to handle this is to tell your teen, "Get a job for a semester or a year so you can save money to pay for your own enrollment next time. Then I'll reimburse you for every passing grade you receive at the end of the semester."

CALLING IT QUITS: DROPPING OUT

When you hear the words, "I want to drop out of school," your blood probably turns ice cold. But it's not the end of the world. Trust me. And you really don't know why your teen has said this or what it means until you ask.

Rather than react and try to talk your teen into staying in school, or jumping to some conclusion, take the time find out what's going on. Say "I'm surprised," if you are. Then say, "I'd really like to know how you came to this conclusion."

As you listen to your teen, figure out whether the decision was made on the spur of the moment or whether it's something that has been brewing for a long time. Try to decide whether dropping out is the result of interpersonal and emotional problems or for academic reasons.

Is your teen's self-esteem low? Does she feel so far behind that she's overwhelmed and can't figure out how to get out of the pit she's in? Or is she just sick and tired of all the tedious work that never seems to end? Does she have something she'd rather be doing? Does she have a plan for returning to school or earning a GED?

Your job is to determine whether dropping out is what she *really* wants or is the only remedy she can think of to alleviate the stress she's feeling.

What you don't want to do is scold, be critical, or shame her in the hope of getting her to stay in school. That will only shut her down emotionally, and you won't learn what the real issues are. You can only help when you have an open line of communication with your teen.

If she really wants to drop out and you realize it might be for the best right now, you need to help her do it in a positive way so she doesn't feel like a failure.

Dropping out of high school is condemned in our society more than it needs to be. I'm not saying it's the right thing for every teen or even for most teens, but it's not the end of the world. And it's the right choice for *some* teens, especially teens with ADD who may never have fit well into the system and who mature more slowly than some of their peers. Some of these teens need to do something besides what *hasn't* been working for them.

Talk with your teen about these issues and convey respect for the thought she's given them. Your teen will know that you're really trying to understand her if you say, "You know, I realize you've been thinking about this for a long time. I respect that. And I realize, too, that you've been feeling awful for a long time. I'm glad you're trying to do something about that. You deserve to feel good." Your compassion will help her to be responsible about what she does next. You may even find that you're drawn closely together during this time of transition.

Now you must plan what comes next. And there definitely needs to be a plan. If your teen is legally required to be in school, you need to find alternative school opportunities. There are increasing numbers of alternative public school placements that allow a teen to work-while going to school. The teaching is often modified for teens who do not learn by studying in regular academic classrooms.

You may also want to look at magnet schools in your district to see if any would interest your teen. Talk with your school administrator and counselors to see what's available.

Home schooling is another option. It's often used with younger children, but you may discover it would work for your situation. Sometimes it's just a matter of joining your teen to find an alternative to help stop the treadmill he's been on. Adjustments at the present school may also be possible when the administrators understand how serious the problem is.

If your teen is old enough to be out of school legally, she needs to go to work immediately if she drops out. You may need to help her learn how to find a job. Don't assume she knows how. That's a whole set of skills in itself. And you can advance her real-life education by helping her find a job.

Before your teen drops out, no matter what she's going to do next, she must understand one thing. She is not dropping out to sit around the house and watch TV all day while you work to support her. Clearly state her options: to find an alternative educational environment or a job or a combination of both. Period.

Dropping out of college is somewhat different (no one is legally required to attend college). Unfortunately, it can happen without the parent even knowing about it for a while.

The biggest problem students who are ADD have is forgetting to withdraw from classes when they drop out. This produces failing marks on their transcript, which shows up later as a problem if they want to return to school. It's not an insurmountable problem. Many admissions departments understand this problem now, and a student can be provisionally admitted to prove himself at a later date. But there's no point in going through this needlessly.

If your teen makes the choice to drop out of college, then going to work or into the military *must* be the next step. You can help for a short period of time (two or three months) by providing room and board, but your young adult must spend all day every day finding his next step in life. No staying in bed all day and going out every night with friends.

Drugs and alcohol can be a problem with this scenario, and you don't want to enable the continued use of these substances. Talk with a chemical-dependency counselor if you see this behavior so you know how to handle the situation in a healthy manner.

SUCCESS STORIES

For many parents the area of academics is the most difficult one they face with their ADD child. It seems to go on forever and the same problems can continue to crop up year after year. It's difficult to see the proverbial light at the end of the tunnel on some days. I know.

That's why I want to leave this topic by sharing some success stories. I'm familiar with *many* of these young people. Your child will have his or her own success story one day.

First, let's look at Jackson. Jackson grew up in a tough neighborhood. He rarely did any homework, often dreamed about how to make big money, and had no one at home to support or encourage him to stay in school. Though smart, he found himself failing classes in ninth and tenth grade. He got so far behind that soon he would be nineteen years old before he graduated from high school. That was unacceptable to him. So he decided to drop out.

Jackson worked for a while in minimum-wage jobs and then answered an ad for a recreation assistant at a boys' club. He met a social worker there who hired and befriended him. That man saw Jackson's potential and began to tell him stories of his own life. He taught Jackson how to open a bank account and balance his checkbook. Soon he was having Jackson help him with paperwork. Then he told Jackson about taking the GED test to give him the equivalent of a high-school diploma. He found a study class for Jackson and encouraged him to attend.

As Jackson studied with his supervisor's support, he discovered he could understand things he'd missed before. Not only did he pass his GED test the first time he took it, he decided to try a class at the community college. He continued to work for two more years at the boys' club and took more classes until he was ready to transfer to a four-year institution.

By then, Jackson knew he wanted to get a degree in education. Though he quit working at the boys' club to go to school full time (his supervisor had helped him find some scholarship money and he took out a loan), he returned during the summers to work on special projects. After earning his degree in education, Jackson decided to get a master's degree in educational research right away. Then, after taking three more years off to work in that field, Jackson returned to school to get his doctorate. He specialized in field research in communities with high drop-out rates. He taught at the university and continued to drop in at the boys' club whenever he could.

Twenty-one-year-old Ellen, on the other hand, had managed to get thirty hours of college credit before giving up. She had worked hard to get that far, but she felt it would take her another six or eight years to finish her degree, and she just couldn't face that. She decided to get married. That was twelve years and three kids ago.

When her first and second children were diagnosed with ADD in the primary grades, she began to recognize some of the problems she had faced in school. She requested testing, was diagnosed with ADD, and decided to start medication. Instantly she was better organized around the house and even discovered that she could keep track of her checkbook and household files.

A year later, Ellen was feeling a lot better about herself. A friend wanted to start classes in interior design at the local college but was nervous about going alone. Ellen said she'd like to try school again and would join her friend.

Ellen whizzed through her first class. Before she knew it, she had a B+ grade average and was heading toward a degree in a lot less than six or eight years. She decided upon a marketing degree that would allow her to get a job with flexible hours until her children were older. She graduated in three years and is now happily employed part-time with a marketing firm. Her supervisors are so delighted with her work that they can hardly wait for her to join them full-time.

Ellen never thought she could do it, but now she knows she never was dumb. She's determined that her children will not go through the same agony she did. She knows that ADD kids can become successful adults. She's one.

YOUR CHILD'S FUTURE

Ellen's experience says it for all of us. ADD doesn't have to be a death sentence. In fact, its positive attributes far outweigh the negative. It's all a matter of finding a niche that fits.

ADD is not related to your child's intelligence or desire to be successful in school or the work place. ADD only means you need to help your teen find the path that fits him best with the timing that fits him best.

Believe in that teen of yours. Give him special encouragement that only you can provide. Say, "You can do it, but you'll do it in your own way. And that way is good."

CHAPTER TEN

SEX, DRUGS, AND ALCOHOL
ADD Teens at Risk

The big three—sex, drugs, and alcohol—make parents' hearts race and stomachs churn. Parents of all teens, ADD or not, worry about these issues. What they're really worrying about is the safety of their child. That's always the underlying issue. You want your child to stay out of trouble and remain healthy and able to live up to his potential. But between the media, talking with other parents, and your own recall of days gone by, you're likely to feel considerable anxiety for your teen during this time of growth and change—and experimentation.

CONCERNS ABOUT SAFETY

Sex, drugs, and alcohol are serious concerns. Not only can your teen hurt his own chances for a happy, successful future, he can physically hurt his own body or even kill himself with HIV exposure, drug overdoses, and drunk-driving accidents. He could also end up hurting or killing others or be imprisoned for crimes committed because of sex, drugs, and alcohol. It's no wonder parents worry a lot.

One of the things you need to realize is that inappropriate use of sex, drugs, or alcohol means that something else is wrong. Each is a symptom, a warning that your teen has a problem. You can learn to increase the odds that your teen won't be susceptible to these problems. You can learn to recognize the early warning signs and symptoms of such problems. Becoming an educated parent increases the probability that you can help your ADD teen weather this period successfully.

Since so much is at stake here, it's important to be really honest with yourself. So answer this one: In all your concerns about your child's safety, have you ever worried about how your child's behavior will reflect on you?

Remember when your toddler scooted down from her seat at a restaurant, crawled under the table, and trotted around the dining room to see what she could find because she was bored? My guess is you felt some (or a lot) of embarrassment. You probably wondered, at least for a second, what the other diners must be thinking of you and your parenting skills. You imagined them saying, "Just look at that child. Well, that's one mother who hasn't done a good job as a parent!" Probably they said nothing of the kind. But you *were* genuinely concerned about how your toddler's behavior would reflect on you.

If you are the parent of an ADD child, especially one who is hyperactive, this scenario probably sounds familiar—and not just for toddlers. But realize this: No matter how hard you tried, your child had needs and a mind of her own. Her behavior, though reflecting some of your training, belonged to her. You didn't create her hyperactivity and ADD behavior. And you found out you couldn't control it totally, either.

Now, during the teen years, you must face separating your teen's behavior from your own need to be seen as a good and effective parent. If you're more concerned about your teen's behavior because of how it reflects on you than you are about what it means about your teen, you need to shift your emphasis to this question: "What does this behavior mean *for my teen?*" However, to understand your teen's behavior, it's legitimate to ask, "What is my role in my son's behavior and the choices he's made?"

I would encourage you to join me in taking a long look at yourself, your thinking, and your real motivations.

HOW TO TELL IF YOUR CHILD HAS A PROBLEM

Drugs and Alcohol

Once you've done your own soul-searching, you're in a position to pay attention to your teen and recognize the warning signs. The following assessment can alert you to the likelihood of problems with drugs and alcohol. Give yourself a 1 for each "yes" answer, 2 for "somewhat" or "sometimes," and 3 for no.

____ Did you talk with your teen during the preteen years about drugs and alcohol?

____ Does your family talk openly about drugs and alcohol?

____ Have you ever experimented with drugs or alcohol and decided not to use them, or to use alcohol in moderation?

____ Has your teen told you that he/she tried drugs and alcohol?

____ Has your teen admitted to getting drunk?

____ Does your older teen assign a designated driver if drinking takes place?

____ Do you know where your teen is at night?

____ If your teen sleeps in, do you know why?

____ Are you in touch with other adults who are around your teen—teachers, other parents, coaches—who would let you know if they suspected a problem?

____ Do you know where your teen gets his/her spending money?

____ Do you know where your teen spends his/her money?

For the following questions, give yourself a 3 for "yes," 2 for "somewhat or sometimes," and 1 for "no."

____ Does anyone in your immediate family have a problem with drugs or alcohol?

____ Do you preach at your teen about drugs and alcohol, absolutely demanding that your child never have anything to do with them?

____ Does your teen stay out all night?

231

____ Do you see your teen up close when he/she comes in
at night?

____ Does your teen get drunk or seem spaced out often?

____ Has your teen's behavior recently changed drastically,
becoming more irritable, aggressive, or depressed?

____ Have your teen's grades dropped suddenly?

____ Has your teen changed friends lately?

____ Do you know who your teen hangs out with?

____ Does your teen often need money, but you don't
know what for?

____ Does your teen seem desperate at times for money, to
meet someone, or for no apparent reason?

Look back over your scoring of these questions. The more questions you answered with a 1, the less likely your teen is to have a problem. The more 3's, the greater the likelihood your teen may already have a problem with drugs or alcohol or be at increased risk.

Sex

Many parents want to believe their teens remain virgins until marriage, but statistics tell us that is not always the case. As your teen reaches age eighteen, it's possible that he or she is sexually active, although there is age variation from sub-culture to sub-culture within the United States.

The questions below might indicate whether or not your teen is at risk for engaging in promiscuous or dangerous sexual activity. Mark the questions with a 1 for "yes," a 2 for "somewhat" or "sometimes," and a 3 for "no."

____ Have you been able to talk to your preteen and teen
about sex and sexual activity?

____ Are you comfortable with your own sexuality?

____ Does your teen *talk* a lot about sex?

____ Can you listen to and affirm your teen's hopes for a
good sexual relationship in his or her life?

____ Have you talked about the potential consequences

SEX, DRUGS, AND ALCOHOL

connected with sexual activity? These can include
pregnancy, HIV and other sexually transmitted
diseases, the emotional impact for your teen and his or
her partner, the high cost of having and raising a child
in terms of money and time, and the difficulty of
stopping sexual activity once it has begun.
___ Has your teen been educated about unsafe sex?

Mark the questions below with a 3 for "yes," a 2 for "somewhat" or "sometimes," and a 1 for "no."

___ Do you dislike talking about or having anything to do
with sex or sexual issues?
___ Do you avoid sex?
___ Do you crave sex?
___ Have you had multiple sexual partners in or outside
of the home?
___ Has your teen been a victim of incest or sexual abuse?
___ Does your teen worry that he/she won't ever have a
satisfying relationship?
___ Does your teen see sexual activity as a conquest or as
"catching" the other person?
___ Does your teen have a different sexual partner every
weekend?

Look back over your scoring of these items. The more 1's you
have, the less likely your teen is to develop a problem with sex and
sexual relationships. The more 3's you have, the more likely it is
that your teen might need some help with issues around his or her
sexuality.

SEX, DRUGS, AND ALCOHOL

What's "Normal"?

Most of us would prefer that our teenagers *never* engage in premarital sex, *never* smoke marijuana, not even once, and *never* take
a drink of alcohol, not even one beer. But wishing doesn't neces-

sarily make it so. To get a better overall perspective in determining what's "normal," let's look at the role each of these plays in our lives.

Sex, as you know, is necessary for procreation and is the healthy physical expression of intimacy between husband and wife. Sex can be misused, but it can also be a normal, healthy part of life. Drugs and alcohol, on the other hand, modify a person's conscious state of awareness and are not a *necessary* part of daily living. (I am obviously not talking about therapeutic drugs to restore health.) In addition, the drugs we're talking about are generally illegal in the United States. Although the ingestion of alcohol is legal for adults, certain levels of alcohol in the blood are illegal if you plan to drive a car. And beyond legality, we must consider the effects of drugs and alcohol on the physical and emotional health and cognitive functioning of the person using them. Drugs and alcohol affect a person's quality of functioning.

When the use of any of these three — sex, drugs, or alcohol — fall outside the pattern of "normal" usage, either in amount or style of usage, your teen may be in trouble. Often the trouble is a symptom of some need that has not been met successfully, such as the need to feel good about himself, the need to escape from pain, or the need to feel powerful.

In general, if teens can get what they need from their parents and the home and school environment, and they are separating in a healthy manner from their parents, they do not need to turn to a substance or sexual behavior in order to feel fulfilled. This does not mean that a teen may not experiment anyway.

It's important to differentiate between behavior that is abusive or dangerous, and behavior that is typical for teens who want to test their limits or who want to find out for themselves what something is about.

Sex
With sex there is usually an innate resistance within the teen that holds him or her back from sexual expression until the early teen years. (The age varies from culture to culture but the sequence remains the same.) In the preteen and early teen years, children are

234

not interested in sex unless they have been prematurely stimulated through sexual activity, which is generally labeled as sexual abuse.

Often you will see eleven- to thirteen-year-olds wrinkling up their noses at the subject of sex or withdrawing to play in other ways. If thirteen- and fourteen-year-olds talk about sex or have "girlfriends" or "boyfriends," it's often mimicking what they think is expected of them. They don't necessarily desire or even find interest in sexual issues and intimacy.

Prior to age fourteen or fifteen, parents may experience their young teens as being very distant. Often the teens will pull away, close their bedroom doors, and only talk to their friends. At about age fifteen, however, don't be surprised if your teen suddenly comes back and asks for a hug, or several hugs, every day. There seems to be a resurgence of the need for touch and affection. If you're available as a parent to give it, your teen probably won't turn to others to get it.

If a parent is not available, it's not unusual for a teen to begin an intimate relationship with another needy young person. They cling together more because of a need for touch and affection than for sexual gratification.

At age sixteen and even seventeen, you may hear your teen talking a lot about sex, sexual desire, and the potential objects for their sexual gratification. If your teen's life is relatively satisfying and full, this is usually a time of more talk than action.

By age seventeen or eighteen, if your teen has been involved in a meaningful relationship for a period of time, it is possible that sexual activity is a part of that relationship. While you may have taught your child strong moral values and hope he will not be sexually active until marriage, you cannot rigidly control whether or not your older teen will choose to base his behavior on those values.

Be sure to teach your teen your own values and respect for other human beings. Even teen "babies" can have babies, which I promise you only complicates everyone's life. Pregnancy, no matter how it's handled, is disruptive and traumatic for a teen who's not ready for parenthood.

Let your teen know that even if he becomes involved sexually without your approval he can come to you with questions or just to talk in times of need. Sometimes teens have a sexual experience and desperately need someone to talk to about it but feel they can't go to a parent. Yet, who is better to approach for advice and counsel? You may not initially want to hear what your teen is telling you, but you have been presented with an opportunity to put the wisdom you've gained to good use. For all you know, your teen may actually be wanting you to say, "I don't want you to be sexually active. I'm going to ask you to stop, because I don't feel you are ready for that level of commitment in a relationship."

Some teens don't think realistically about sex until they have become sexually active. Only then does sex become real to them. Once they become sexually active, it's possible they feel overwhelmed and realize they're not ready to go any farther, but they might not know how to get out of the situation. Your teen *needs* you at this time—not to scold or criticize, but to reaffirm limits, share your opinions and values, and teach him or her how to terminate a sexual relationship.

Many a teen has tried to solve these issues alone or with others as inexperienced only to end up in a pattern of unhealthy relationships or a marriage that was wrong from the very first because he didn't feel he could go to his parents. That may or may not be because he knew you would "blow up" or become hysterical. All you can do is control your own behavior, leave the door open, and hope that your teen asks for your advice.

Drugs and Alcohol
Many teens will experiment a time or two with both drugs and alcohol. Even though you may have taught your child about drug and alcohol usage from the time she was very young, she may want to find out for herself what you were really talking about. It's not so much peer pressure that causes the experimentation, though that's part of it, but simply a need for firsthand experience. This is often especially true for teens with ADD.

Using a drug or alcohol once or twice, though potentially dangerous, does not mean your teen has a drug- or alcohol-abuse *problem*. The kind of experimentation I'm talking about is having a couple of beers, going to a party with an open bar and trying everything (and suffering the never-to-be-repeated result), or trying marijuana a time or two. I am *not* talking about your teen hitting your liquor cabinet every time you leave the house, drinking every weekend or night, or smoking marijuana several times a week on a regular basis, much less using other drugs.

Your teen could put his life in danger the very first time he uses anything, or get in trouble with the law from that one time of experimentation. As terrible as these consequences are, you must realize that you can no longer protect your teen against all bad things, as you have tried to do since childhood.

The best thing you can do is give matter-of-fact education early during childhood and preteen years. Learn about common drugs and their effects, talk about adverse drug reactions, watch and read the news with your child and be open to questions. Give examples from your own life of what you've learned.

What you don't want to do is lecture, rant on and on, threaten your teen if he ever touches anything, or say, "You'd better not let me catch you ever taking a drink (or using . . .)." And please don't waste your time saying, "You're not allowed to drink until you're grown up." That may just push your teen to prove to himself and you that he's already grown up. Trying to *control* either the problem or the teen will increase the likelihood he will rebel or discount everything you say.

Talk to your teen and, more importantly, *model* the behavior you want. After all, if you're sitting around every night with a cocktail in your hand, you're communicating much more strongly than any words you could use. And the message you are communicating is that alcohol is okay.

SIGNS OF REBELLION

If you feel as if you'd like to lock your teen in a closet to protect him, you're probably like a lot of other parents. But the whole business of adolescence involves beginning to turn the reins of control over to your son or daughter. You've given your teen a lot of training, modeled the kind of behavior you'd like to see from her, and set limits on her behavior when you thought it was necessary.

Your teen needs to learn to handle herself independently of you. While you can continue to dialogue with your teen and influence her, you can't *control* your teen's behavior. If you try to control your teen, you're setting up a power struggle that may lead to rebellion, whether active or passive. If you insist on more control than your teen needs, you create a need for that teen to push against you and the limits you've set. And there's no more common area of power struggle than sex, drugs, and alcohol. If you feel that your teen is constantly rebellious, remember this: It takes two people to create a power struggle and subsequent rebellion.

Whenever I think about this problem, I remember Marci. Marci's mother insisted she be home every night by 7:00 p.m and not make or receive phone calls after 9:00 p.m. She was never to mention the word *sex*. She must call her mom at work every day after school.

In response to such rigid requirements, Marci, age sixteen, went wild. She started sneaking out of the house in the middle of the night, sleeping with any boy she could, lying about where she was when she called her mom after school, and drinking at friends' houses rather than doing her homework at home.

Marci's mother thought she had *control* over her daughter. But Marci went behind her mother's back and took "control" of her own life.

That's how it works. And that's how it happens.

I'm not saying that a teen ought to "rule the roost." You are the parent, you pay the rent, and you buy the food. You make the rules at your house. But parents and teens must negotiate reasonable control based on *mutual respect* for each other's capability to make decisions and live responsibly. When that's what the house rules are based on, everyone is happier.

Thad didn't need to rebel. When he was fifteen he felt old enough to set his own hours. He told his parents what he wanted.

They listened carefully and then gave him their response. They told him he would be responsible for getting enough rest so that he could keep up with his schoolwork and get to school on time.

When Thad started to drive at sixteen, his parents told him they wanted to know where he was going and the approximate time they could expect him home. They began to talk to him about drinking and driving. They felt he was too young to drink; legally, he couldn't buy or be served alcohol until he was twenty-one. But they also realized he could get alcohol if he chose to.

Thad's parents absolutely insisted that he not drive if he'd had a drink. They made a deal that if he had the car and he decided to drink, he would call home, no matter where he was or what time it was. They would come and get him.

Thad's parents told him they believed he would honor their request. But they made it clear that if he did not honor that request, for any reason, they would immediately take the car keys back, and he would not be able to drive until they felt he could be trusted. They all shook on the deal, and Thad and his parents honored the agreement the one time he called them.

ADD TEENS AT RISK

Teens who are ADD are first and foremost teens. Everything I've said so far applies equally to ADD teens. If your teen has not learned self-responsibility or if his emotional background was fairly unstable, he may have some emotional problems in addition to being ADD. In that case, counseling assistance for the whole family is indicated to tackle both the ADD and the emotional problems.

In addition to just being a teenager, there are some factors that make weathering the sex, drugs, and alcohol territory more difficult for ADD teens. If your teen has had to struggle in school, at home, or to make friends, he's at an increased risk to have problems with drugs or alcohol. If his self-esteem is poor, he may think that sex at an early age will make him feel more powerful or better about himself.

Sex, drugs, and alcohol function in two major ways that cause ADD teens to be at increased risk.

First, many ADD teens self-medicate by using drugs such as amphetamines or cocaine, which actually do help them focus better. Sex and other addictive behaviors—such as gambling, risk-taking, and spending—also produce a high. If your teen seeks this kind of high, it's not only to pick up his spirits but to enable him to become clearheaded and focused on a goal, at least for a short period of time. The goal may be to play the gambling game or get the clarity that can come after sex. Or it may be the wonderful feeling that comes when he buys something new or has survived a risk.

Your job as a parent is to teach your teen about the physiological needs of his body. There's nothing wrong with wanting to feel good, even great. But taking a death-defying chance to get that good feeling is a bad idea.

You can say, "When you sit still too long, your brain becomes sluggish. It's natural for you to need to do something shocking or very active in order to stimulate it. The trick is to find something that won't endanger you or hurt others."

Talk with your teen about using appropriate ADD medication rather than self-medicating with street drugs. Set the limit on illegal drug use with an atmosphere of zero tolerance. You can say, "If you decide to use drugs to self-medicate or for any other reason, our whole family, including you, will immediately seek education and counseling with someone trained in drug-abuse treatment." This must be a non-negotiable issue.

Explain to your teen that, although sex produces a natural, normal "high," getting that high is not the purpose of having sex. That's taking without giving, mutually, to the other person. Cigarette smoking is another frequently used form of self-medication for people who are ADD. More and more research is showing that nicotine is one of the most, if not *the* most, addictive drugs known. As many people who have smoked can tell you, nicotine is a drug to which it is very easy to become addicted, and it is a habit that is very, very tough to break. Many

ADD youths begin smoking early and apparently are soothed or medicated in the process.

The other reason that addictive usage of sex, drugs, and alcohol appears to be higher in the ADD population is the felt need by ADD teens to numb the pain of being ADD in a non-ADD culture or environment. Years of being forced to learn in ways that are not natural, having their sensitivity bombarded and abused, feeling unacceptable, inadequate, and judged have left their mark on many ADD teens. Even in the best of family situations a teen will have sustained a lot of hurt.

Mental activity that never stops drains an ADD teen of energy. Physical hyperactivity that denies the ability to rest leaves your teen exhausted. Traumatized emotions endlessly wound your teen's psyche. So, your teen may be quite wounded, through no fault of yours.

Is it any wonder he seeks some respite? Alcohol and marijuana are two major ways people with ADD relax and cover pain. Sex, too, can temporarily make your teen forget the pain as the good feelings wash over him.

The problem with using this type of *self*-medication to get rid of pain is the low success rate. The results don't last, so your teen must use drugs again before too long, drink again, or have sex again for the wrong reasons. Self-medication is inefficient and can cause a lot of secondary trouble. And for too many teens, a previously unrealized problem arises when they find they are particularly susceptible to the addictive aspect of alcohol and drugs and even sex.

Some teens are said to have a dual diagnosis, that is, they have two things that are causing them trouble: drinking *and* ADD, drugs *and* ADD, or sexual addiction *and* ADD.

The trick is to help your teen find acceptable ways to respond to the pain and obtain medication or treatment for his ADD that really does the job. You'll find information about medication in chapter 11.

Identity Issues and Peer Pressure
Because kids with ADD have often been trained to think they *shouldn't* be who they naturally are, they may have difficulty trying to find out who they are.

241

There's nothing more frightening to a teen than not knowing who she is. If a teen can't be acceptable or identify with the "good guys," he may turn to being a "bad guy." Many ADD children enter adolescence detached from their identity and feel hopeless about being one of the "good guys." Terrified of being "nobody," they are prime candidates for becoming a "bad guy," or at least ending up on the fringes of what's acceptable.

Invariably, the teen who has not developed a solid identity has low self-esteem. That's because feeling like a nobody makes it hard to build self-esteem. Poor self-esteem is one of the biggest problems faced in early adolescence by our ADD teens.

As your teen searches for others like herself, she is highly susceptible to peer pressure. All anyone has to do is show interest in her and she's likely to join them and take on their behaviors. This is one of the reasons it's so important to help your young teen find and develop special interests. Then she can find others like herself and behaviors that are centered on an activity. She can feel good about herself in that context, and she has a social group that helps build her self-esteem.

For example, Lonnie found it through music. He was able to join the band and find other kids like himself. Patsy, who loved to write, made her way to the journalism room at school where she got involved with the production of the yearbook. She spent many nights on special projects with other yearbook staffers. Afterward they would go out to get pizza and talk about what they had been doing all evening and about their dreams for the future.

T.S. is an ADD teen who loved rodeoing. When his parents finally said okay to pursuing his interest, he found a place where he fit in and made a group of friends that made him feel good about himself. He loved winning but was even more happy about being a part of something. And he felt great when one of his new-found friends won. T.S. finally fit in.

Amber wasn't so lucky. She just didn't seem able to find what she liked. She had no clue who she was nor did she have any special interests. She would hang around the school steps after classes were over. Pretty soon she began to smoke so she had something to do and didn't feel so lost and embarrassed just standing there. It didn't take long for other kids like her to find her. They clustered as a group and moaned about their lot in life. They were a pretty unhappy lot.

Before long a local drug dealer spotted this group of misfits. After just a few flattering remarks, Amber tried marijuana. It really made her feel better. The pusher encouraged her, saying, "You deserve to feel good. I've got some other things that will really make you feel great." Amber started with the two most common entry-level drugs: cigarettes and marijuana. But, like many teens, she didn't stop there. Soon she was using several kinds of drugs. Though she felt good and accepted within the group at first, the drugs soon took hold of her. She was no longer in control of herself, the drugs were in charge. And she didn't feel well a lot of the time.

Amber got caught in the cycle of drug use and had to do something to get more drugs, so she began to peddle them herself. Initially, she told herself she would only sell a few to kids who were already using. Living in a twilight haze, she soon forgot that promise. Her group of supposed friends was gone, too, drifting on their own lost paths. It took a scrape with the law, a drug rehab program, Narcotics Anonymous, and counseling to help Amber find out who she really was and what she was truly interested in. Only then could she kick the habit.

Once Amber got excited about having something to offer herself and the world, her self-esteem began to improve. Finding her way back wasn't easy, but she made it. Now Amber counsels other kids who have nothing to do after school and nowhere to go. She's turned into an excellent counselor and wants to become a social worker.

There's one simple thing you must remember about identity and your teen. She *must* see herself as identifying with one group or another. If your teen can fit into a group with a style of behavior that is considered acceptable, then you can breathe a sigh of relief. But if your teen can't succeed at something that's considered acceptable, she's likely to go to the opposite extreme. Not only will she not go out for sports if she can't make the team, she'll make fun of or taunt the "jocks." Or she'll purposely refuse to study at all rather than try and fail to do well. That way she'll be the "dumbest" in the class. She'll have an identity and a reason for making poor grades.

Many teens who get in trouble with gangs and the law actually have strong leadership capability. But for one reason or another they did not identify with the law-abiding part of the population. Since they couldn't be one of the "good" guys, they became one of the "bad" guys. The most important thing to your teen is to be part of *something*.

Outwardly Expressive ADD and Risk Taking

If your teen likes to take risks, you've probably been dealing with breathtaking experiences since he was a young child. You may even have had more than your share of accidents to contend with. When working with teens, I learned long ago to ask *how* he broke his arm when he was seven. Invariably, if he had Outwardly Expressive ADD, he did something like fall off the roof or jump a culvert that was wider than he was tall.

As your child becomes a teen, the stakes get higher. Your teen with Outwardly Expressive ADD may be attracted to bungie jumping, aerial skiing, or even stealing cars or "playing chicken." Whether your teen is admired for his acts of daring depends a lot on his identity. If he identifies with law-abiding people or those who are doing an "in" thing that is socially acceptable, he will be admired, or at least tolerated.

For example, the teen who takes exorbitant risks, squeezing the last few seconds out of a downhill ski run while practicing for the Olympic ski team is considered a hero.

On the other hand, if your teen identifies with those who are outside the mainstream, he may choose an activity that breaks the law or is considered unacceptable. He may steal cars just for kicks or play "chicken," risking his life and others' by racing his car down the road at high speed at night with no lights. Within limits there is nothing wrong with taking risks. It's a matter of choosing the right type of risk. The high that comes from gambling with danger is a tendency that needs to be curbed with ADD teens. This, too, can be a form of self-medication as much as the use of drugs or alcohol.

On a more mundane level, the teen who is Outwardly Expressive may display his identity for all to see by sporting a purple mohawk hairstyle. Or your daughter might wear black fingernail polish, black lipstick, and all black clothing for months on end. These outward expressions are not necessarily unhealthy. Their intent is to shock adults and impress peers. The bigger fuss adults make, the more likely the teen will be to continue to dress or cut or color their hair in unusual ways.

Outwardly Expressive teens are likely to pretend and brag loudly about having sex, drinking, or using drugs when, in reality, they might not be doing any of those things. You don't want to close your eyes to the possibility that your teen is involved with harmful behavior, but don't automatically judge him based on his flamboyance and expressiveness.

Besides alcohol, other drugs of choice for Outwardly Expressive teens are amphetamines and cocaine. As a parent, you might be used to your teen's high activity level, but watch to see whether she also "crashes" more than she used to or exhibits erratic behavior. Are her mood swings broader? Does she have more frequent outbursts of temper? Is she extremely active but completing fewer projects than previously? Has she dropped out of groups where students are engaged in school-related activities? These are all signs that your teen may be using chemicals.

Inwardly Directed ADD and the Search for Identity

This group of teens is at the highest risk for trouble with sex, drugs, and alcohol. That's because teens with Inwardly Directed ADD have the highest occurrence of depression and low self-esteem. It's imperative that these teens have some interest that captivates them and helps them feel good about themselves.

Ironically, many adults see teens with Inwardly Directed ADD as much less of a problem than their Outwardly Expressive, boisterous counterparts, because they are usually easier to be around. But don't be naive. Just because you're not seeing a display of rebellious or revolutionary behavior doesn't mean the teen is making good, sensible choices.

When a teen is busy talking about having sex, chances are pretty good that he's not having sex. That's not to say that a quiet teen is automatically sexually active. But you cannot assume he isn't. The sounds of a teen trying to numb his pain can be pretty soft. You must keep your eyes and ears open.

The Inwardly Directed teen may rebel by doing something as simple as untying his shoelaces and slopping around with his shoes half off. Or he may spend a lot of time drawing comic-strip pictures that display heroes perpetrating violent acts. He may work endlessly on the engine of his car and refuse to clean the grease off before coming to the dinner table.

These behaviors are simply an expression of his individuality. He's saying, "I'm someone different from you. I'm showing you that by refusing to tie my shoes the way I'm supposed to." Or, "I'm someone who can draw pictures that kids admire and adults hate." Or, "I'm someone whose badge of identity is the grease I wear proudly on my clothes and hands. So there!"

All of these are benign ways for a teen to express a chosen identity. If you can't actually admire his actions, you'd do best to leave him alone. Of course, you can ask the greasy teen to throw an old towel over the dining room chair so the grease doesn't ruin it. Otherwise, don't make a big deal over his behaviors. Let your teen quietly affirm his identity.

If leaving his shoelaces untied doesn't feel like enough of an identity to him, a teen with Inwardly Directed ADD can get into a lot of trouble with sex, drugs, or alcohol. Unfortunately, they don't draw a lot of attention to themselves. Frequently, marijuana and alcohol are the drugs of choice of this group, and they are used alone or quietly with one or two other people.

You may not realize your teen has this kind of problem unless you pay close attention. So watch for signs of deterioration of physical health, lack of motivation, and irregular sleep habits. Also, pay attention to what your teen is doing with his time. Is he involved in any activities that preclude chemical use? Or does his life seem to be a mystery to you?

It's important for you to know as much as you can about this type of teen. And that often means joining him in his area of interest.

Highly Structured ADD and the Need for Relief

Teens with Highly Structured ADD may have stayed out of trouble prior to the teen years. But even though they can be very successful as students, the pressure can be great, and these teens need relief. There's a great tendency to turn to substances to relieve that pressure. Many teens with Highly Structured ADD turn to alcohol. And they can become fairly controlling drunks, loudly telling everyone what to do and how to do it.

Given the high levels of frustration and anger sometimes associated with this type of ADD, this teen can be demanding of a girlfriend or boyfriend. Bossiness, put-downs, and scolding behaviors are exacerbated by alcohol use. And rowdiness and brawling may result when the teen with Highly Structured ADD "enjoys" the party scene.

In addition to alcohol, cocaine and amphetamines often become the drugs of choice with Highly Structured ADD teens. Ask yourself whether your teen still talks a good story but follows through less in the completion of tasks than he did at a younger age. Do you know how your teen is using his time? Is your teen more secretive than before? Have his sleep habits changed? Who are his friends? Where does he go on weekend nights?

Boundary Problems

Another ADD trait that makes your teen susceptible to addictive behavior is difficulty knowing her boundaries. When a teen is clear about her identity, able to undertake tasks and remain focused on their completion, and able to set limits on others, including saying no, she is said to have good boundaries. But ADD teens often do not have good boundaries.

This tendency makes teens susceptible to suggestion. Unable

247

to organize and focus clearly, they scatter their attention, their actions, and their goals. They react to whatever stimuli is around. For example, Geri, on her way to study for the next day's algebra test, is swayed off track when her friend comes along and suggests she go by another friend's house. Geri's friend explains that no one is at home at the house, and they can relax a little, have a drink, and then get their work done. Geri, eager for friendship and discouraged about algebra anyway, doesn't think twice. Off she goes!

One positive aspect of the boundary issue, if the teen learns to maintain control, is empathy and sensitivity. However, until your teen learns to control these, she may feel *everything* too acutely and be continuously hurt, even traumatized because of her hypersensitivity. Or, she may be drawn to teens who are the underdogs.

When Don was kicked out of his house by his stepdad, he had nowhere to go. He managed to stay in school while sleeping at friends' houses until their parents said, "No more." Not knowing what to do, he talked to Celia, a very sensitive, empathetic fellow student with ADD. She felt Don's desperation and dropped everything she was doing to try to solve his problem. Because he was feeling so down, Celia was afraid of what he might do. So she stayed with him all the time.

That meant Celia stopped going to her own classes, sneaked him into her bedroom to sleep, fed him, and gave him money. By the time her parents found out, she had jeopardized her grades and used up all the money she'd saved. And she had not really been able to make a difference for Don. In addition, her own physical health was beginning to show the stress of taking on a job that was beyond her. She had become so enmeshed with Don that she'd lost track of her own goals and needs.

If you have a teen like Celia, you need to help her figure out what to do to *really* help her friend. You might say, "Honey, neither you nor I can help Don. It's a bigger job than we can handle. But let's call the crisis hot line for teens and see what they have to say. We can check with the school counselor and the Department of Human Resources. I'll help you find a good referral. And that will put Don in touch with people who might really be able to help him."

Another side of suggestibility makes it easy for someone to talk the teen into "just trying" the drug or having just "one drink."

"Everyone's doing it" becomes the reason for doing whatever "it" is. For this reason, it's imperative early on that you work to empower your child to say no and stick by what she likes or needs for herself. This includes saying no to you.

Girls, especially, can be talked into becoming sexually active, because someone needs them or others will see them as special because they are "doing it" with someone who has status. Start talking with your daughter as early as possible so that she doesn't have sex for approval. If she's already involved with someone who is getting her to do things that are not constructive for her, rather than trying to talk her out of it, support her in doing what is best for her.

You might say, "In your relationship with Mike, be true to yourself and your own values. Don't let him or anyone else take advantage of your kind heart. You are valuable." Empowering her will do more to break an unhealthy relationship than threatening or trying to force her out of the relationship.

Impulsivity

Because a teen with ADD is more likely to act impulsively than his non-ADD peer, a frank and thorough discussion about sexual issues may save your child's life. This might be difficult for you to face. But, once again, it's important that you deal with the reality of your child's situation.

Studies have been done which show that educating kids about sex and its potential consequences actually increases the likelihood that they will behave responsibly. The best way to encourage responsibility is to instill clear values and boundaries in your child from an early age. But because ADD teens are often highly impulsive, their values may go out the window when faced with sudden temptation.

Remember, even if you have encouraged your teen to remain celibate, you need to maintain an attentive, realistic posture. You cannot have total control over whether or not your teen becomes sexually active.

If you know for certain that your teen and his girlfriend are sexually active, you might jointly visit a physician or family planning center to get advice about birth control. That makes your teen more responsible for his behavior than if you, the parent, take him in for birth-control advice. By encouraging your teen to get that information, you will not be condoning his choice to be sexually active, and you have every right to make that clear to him. But you could be saving his life or preventing the tragedy of an unwanted pregnancy.

Learning by Doing
Because ADD teens are kinesthetic learners, they learn best by doing. Unfortunately, this means you can have conversations with your teens about sex, drugs, and alcohol, but they may not *really* get the message until they try them out for themselves. This makes educating your teen and stressing potential consequences for "experimental" behavior all the more crucial.

Tell your child the truth, which is that trying drugs even one time can be highly dangerous for some people. Tell her that there's no way to know in advance who will have a severe reaction. Explain to her that marijuana and cigarettes are "gateway drugs" for stronger, more dangerous drug habits. Tell her, "I don't want that for you. You don't deserve it."

If you are an approachable parent, your teen will probably be honest with you if she does experiment. If you tend to rant and rave, go into hysterics, or severely criticize your teen, you probably won't ever hear about it. That doesn't mean it didn't happen. In all likelihood (based on what adults say about their own teen years) teens who keep their drug use a secret tend to use more than teens who later shared information with their parents.

Experimenting with drugs once or twice does not make a teen a "druggie." But you must firmly explain to your teen that all drug use is dangerous. If your teen happens to get picked up for an "experimental" use of drugs or alcohol, let the chips fall where they may. Most law-enforcement departments have programs for first-time offenders.

Part of the logical consequence of trying a substance that is against the law is that the person may get caught. Remind your teen about that when you do discuss drugs. If your teen is caught, do not just pay a lawyer to get your kid off. Rather, stick by your teen and get involved with whatever program is available to reinforce both your support of the law and your teen. You will all learn from the experience and can turn it into something positive.

GETTING THROUGH TO YOUR TEEN
ABOUT SEX, DRUGS, AND ALCOHOL

When you talk to your teen about sex, drugs, and alcohol, you are aware of the importance of the information you're trying to get across. But to your teen, this might be just one more conversation (or lecture, depending on your tone) he has to sit through. It's crucial to make sure your child *hears* the information you have to offer. It can be a life-and-death matter.

Here are some guidelines to help make sure your ADD teen will pay attention and think about what you are saying.

Don't Get Hysterical

An hysterical parent is a parent who is out of control. Though you may feel hysterical inside, deal with your own feelings before you deal with your teen.

Your job is to communicate in a way that allows your teen to listen to what you are saying and respect what you decide to do in a situation.

If you've tended to become hysterical about every issue in the past—which, unfortunately, may be the norm for a reactive ADD parent—then your child may long since have tuned you out. I'm talking about getting upset over hairstyles, dress choices, grades, friends, how her room is picked up, and things like that.

251

You *must* make a distinction between these issues and the potentially life-or-death issues of HIV, drinking, driving, and pregnancy.

If you realize you've been in the habit of making mountains out of molehills, you can correct it. Be honest with your teen. Tell him you realize you've overreacted in the past. Tell him, *and mean it*, that you will try harder to control your reactions in the future.

When you do talk to your teen about alcohol, sex, or drugs, choose only one topic. If you try to cover all the issues at the same time, you'll overwhelm your teen and he'll tune out again. You can come back later to another issue. Remember, one at a time.

Don't Condescend

The fastest way to get your teen to either tune you out or discount what you are saying is to couch it in preachy terms.

I'll always remember the college student whose parents preached relentlessly against alcohol and sex. As soon as she left home and was living in a dormitory at college, this girl turned into a wild woman. With no previous experience and never having been encouraged to think for herself or be self-responsible, she took advantage of every opportunity that crossed her path. She did whatever was available without any thought to the consequences.

By mid-year, she was getting drunk five out of every seven nights, was pregnant because she didn't have much knowledge about birth control, and was flunking all her subjects.

I'm not saying that you shouldn't teach your family values. Of course you do that. But it's all in how you say things.

Listen to the difference between these sentences: "Drinking is bad and you are bad if you drink," or "I don't want you to drink. It can be dangerous, and I don't want anything bad to happen to you. You are precious to us, and you deserve to stay healthy." Or you could say, "Our belief system disapproves of drinking. You will have to make your own choices, but I'd rather you not drink."

When you give information to your teen, also talk about how *you* feel, and let him know what you would like. That way, you stand the best chance of being heard.

Involve Both Parents

If both parents are available to your teen, whether you're married or not, it's a good idea for each to talk to your teen separately, and more than once. Men and women have very different approaches to these important issues. Both boys and girls need to hear them.

In the teen years it's a good idea for boys to learn some things about females from their mothers and girls to learn about males from their fathers. With both parents participating, you can help your teen begin to understand the opposite sex or at least understand how different they are. And your teen will hear more than one viewpoint on sex, drugs, and alcohol.

Choose Your Battles

If you haven't made a federal case out of everything else that has come along, chances are better that your child will realize how seriously concerned you are about these particular issues. And you are more likely to be heard.

Right now, before you have this discussion with your teen, think about which activities are non-negotiable and which are negotiable. You might want to consider the following activities as non-negotiable: promiscuous and unprotected sex, drinking and driving, problem drinking, drug use, any type of abuse (including verbal, psychological, physical, and sexual abuse) of other people or property, lying, stealing, and breaking the law. You may think of another few, but there won't be too many that are absolutely non-negotiable.

Explain Potential Consequences

You do need to talk to your teen about the realistic consequences of behavior. Educate your teen about HIV and AIDS and explain clearly what can happen to them if they have unsafe sex. Talk about teen pregnancy and what it would mean in your teen's life and the life of the other parent. Be specific in terms of daily care. This is true whether your teen is a girl or a boy.

Visiting a child-care program or baby-sitting a young child for a day or two can help drive the reality home. If you introduce

253

this kind of personal experience, you need to do it in a matter-of-fact way, not as a threat.

You might say, "It's hard to imagine what it's really like to have a child. I know I had no idea what it would be like. I'm very glad I have you, but I'm also glad I waited (if, in fact, that is the case) until I'd finished my education and could earn enough money to support a family."

If your experience was different, you might say, "I had you when I was young," or "I had you before I could support a family adequately, and it was tough. I don't want you to have to go through that. You deserve the chance to give your child what you'd like and to have the time to enjoy your child. That's why I want you to wait."

Talk about the consequences of doing drugs. Teach how both cigarette and marijuana smoking often introduce teens to other drugs and to a way of life that often leads to drug abuse. Explain the cycle of drug dependency and how hard it is physiologically and psychologically to get "unhooked." Explain that overcoming pain is important but that using drugs to numb pain is not a way to eliminate problems or change feelings. Rather, offer to help your teen find other ways to feel better.

If your teen is suggestible and needs approval from peers or has no other way to feel important and special, offer to help her find these good feelings at the same time you set a limit about drug use.

Educate your teen about alcohol use and how it affects his or her ability to drive a car, work, attend school, and sustain good health. Get some statistics from your local Council on Alcohol and Drug Abuse. Share stories from the newspaper, TV, and radio that pinpoint what you feel is important for your teen to know. Do this in a matter-of-fact way, without threats.

One of the most powerful lessons for people in my community came when an eighteen-month-old downed an eight-ounce glass of whiskey. Encouraged by adults who were having a party and who thought it was "cute" the way he was "getting drunk," the child drank himself to death without having any idea of what he was doing.

After the story hit the media, teens and adults across the city began to talk and plan for better education among all people who drink. Private citizens joined law enforcement and juvenile personnel to try to prevent such a thing from happening again. Though a tragedy, the result was an enormous heightening of awareness for many young people who simply didn't know the power of alcohol. And no one who heard the story has forgotten that little boy to this day.

Hopefully your child will not have to experience severe consequences in order to learn how to deal with sex, drugs, and alcohol responsibly. There is a great deal you can do to help your teen avoid the inherent dangers of these temptations.

Be responsible yourself. Stay involved. Talk. Listen. Love. Model for your child what it means to develop strong values and behave accordingly.

﹏❁﹏

CHAPTER ELEVEN

MEDICATION FOR ADD TEENS
Sorting Through the Options

No other aspect of ADD is as controversial as the use of medication. And that's something I'm sure you've already run across, whether or not your child has ever been on ADD medication. You've probably heard parents discussing the issue, wondering what to do and who to turn to for advice.

Some parents automatically assume that medication is "bad," and they are firm in their decision that their child will never use it. Others are more openminded but don't know how to make the decision about whether or not to try it for their child. There are a lot of opinions—and quite a few myths—floating around out there.

Though ADD medications have been used for decades with young children who were hyperactive and unable to focus their attention for even short periods of time, physicians have tended to take the children off medication as they enter adolescence. What we know now is that adolescence may be the very time medication can be most useful for the young adult. Medication may help a teen to focus more effectively, think more clearly, and behave in a more organized manner as he makes the complex transition to adulthood.

Let's review briefly some current information about ADD and its treatment with regard to medication.

▶ ADD is a neurobiochemical style of brain wiring you are born with, retain through puberty, and have when you die.

▶ *Acquired* ADD can result from illness, head trauma, drug use, fetal alcohol syndrome, and the use of crack (cocaine) by the child's mother. But these conditions are not what this book is about. They are not affected by the traditional ADD medications.

▶ ADD is not the result of poor parenting. It is not a mental disorder. It does not mean something *wrong* needs to be *cured*.

▶ Damage to self-esteem often results from ADD because the individual learns and behaves in ways that are different from the mainstream culture. The educational system tends to teach non-ADD children more effectively than ADD children. Behavioral and relationship expectations and job requirements frequently do not fit the ADD-style person. The result of that lack of fit causes low self-esteem and emotional problems, such as anxiety and depression.

▶ Medication is one of several ways to assist people with ADD to become more effective in the culture in which they live. But it must never be used alone. The teen must have training and education to assist the development of behaviors and skills that give him the ability to be in control of his life. Psychotherapy and counseling can assist with healing the damage that results from the mistreatment of someone who is ADD.

▶ No single way of treating ADD is useful for all people. Some individuals do not need or want to use medication. Some use it for a finite period of time. And some choose to use it indefinitely.

WHAT MEDICATION CAN AND CANNOT DO

ADD medications physiologically add chemicals to the brain that assist a person to achieve the skills that a non-ADD person does naturally. For example, the ADD teen's brain is low in the chemicals that assist in focusing attention on a task. By taking stimulants, the teen is better able to focus, pay attention to details, and deal with tasks requiring organization.

In addition, stimulants often help reduce hyperactivity. Some antidepressants and other medications that affect mood can assist with temper control, impulsivity, and hypersensitivity. What must be understood with regard to the use of medications for ADD is that they are not mind-altering drugs. Rather, much like the use of insulin injections in diabetics, they help a person access non-ADD skills.

Medication can buy focused time for a teen to learn behaviors and skills until they become habits. Many teens find their lives much easier during the early teen years with the help of medication. They can keep up at school, learn to inhibit their impulses, and develop interpersonal skills that will last a lifetime.

I've seen miracles with the use of medication. Stephen spent time in the principal's office every day for the first six weeks of seventh grade. He simply couldn't keep his mouth shut in class, he messed with other kid's things, and he continually got up out of his seat without permission. His parents, though not pleased at the prospect of having to put their son on medication, decided the damage being done without medication was probably worse than their fears about using medication.

With medication Stephen passed algebra, which he had been flunking prior to medication. Visits to the principal's office ceased. In addition, he received an award at the end of the year for most improved citizenship. Sadly, no one recognized that Stephen was the same child with or without medication. Only his behavior changed. But that's the system in which he found himself, and he needed help to fit in.

I've also seen what happens when parents or children expect medication to solve all their problems. Lisa also did better with medication during school, but as soon as the medication wore off she became a terror. She had refused to take part in training classes to manage her temper and impulsivity, and it showed. It's no surprise, then, that after a year on medication her temper and impulsivity were no better than before. She was fine at school, but at home she was out of control. By not doing her part in remedying the impact of ADD on others, Lisa is setting herself up for a rough ride. She will probably have difficulty in her personal relationships because others will not be as accepting of her inappropriate behavior as her parents have been.

Thomas has been using medication since the upper grades of elementary school. It helped him get his behavior under control, bought him time to develop interpersonal skills as a preteen and teenager, and helped him not lose too much information as he progressed through each school year.

During his last two years of high school, he used his medication less often. He no longer needed it for behavioral control. Rather, he only seemed to benefit from medication when he had to spend a lot of time studying. Because he felt confident in school, had developed good study skills, and generally had a good grasp of much of the material with which he was being presented, he backed off from taking his medication.

When he went to college, he started back on it to help him cope with the more complex learning situations in which he found himself. And he definitely needed it to be able to put in time at the library. Again, as he moved into more familiar areas of study as a college junior and senior, he found that he could reduce the amount of medication he took and only used it his last year for two heavy-duty library projects.

In the work place Thomas has found that if he selects jobs that don't involve large, intense amounts of detail or paperwork and he places himself in situations that reflect his strengths rather than his weaknesses, he no longer needs any medication. He's doing just fine without it.

My own position regarding the use of medication is open. I'm neither always for it nor always against it. It is an individual decision made initially by the parents and teen together and eventually by the teen himself.

There are times when medication can make all the difference for a teen, helping him to get on his feet so he can find his potential and use it more fully. There are other times when medication becomes a crutch, and the teen feels he doesn't have to do anything to help himself except "pop a pill." That attitude will always leave behind a path of helplessness and frustration as the teen finds out that a pill doesn't do it all.

I am also supportive of work done by the alternative and holistic healing community. Some professionals are adamantly against this form of intervention, disclaiming *any* effectiveness. If you, as a parent or family, are drawn in this direction, pursue it. You may be breaking new ground to share with others.

You may find that you can integrate both traditional medical treatment of ADD with alternative methods. Or you will choose to use one for a period of time and then another. Don't feel that you have to choose between the two systems. Make your own judgments in conjunction with your teen. See what works.

I would advise against refusing to try medication because you fear "drugging" your teen, while he struggles to sit in his seat or pay attention in class. On the other hand, to refuse to consider alternatives from which some people are gaining benefit, just because "the literature" and research journals have not yet been able to *prove* the effectiveness of the technique or natural substance makes no sense to me. Your best bet is to stay flexible and open-minded and then make your own decisions.

Unfortunately, once your teen has been diagnosed as being ADD and has been given medication, your insurance company will probably consider your teen to have a "preexisting condition." As of this time, people taking medication for ADD cannot fly airplanes. That's how the law reads.

There also seems to be a lot of confusion around the status of ADD medication usage and the armed forces. All of this will need sorting out over the next few years, but it's something to make your teen aware of, so he doesn't rush into a situation uninformed and potentially ruin his chance for something that's important to him.

261

MYTHS ABOUT ADD MEDICATION

There are a lot of myths about ADD medication. Here are a few you've probably come across.

Myth one: *ADD medication is habit-forming or "dopes up" your teen.*

Neither is true. ADD medication does not alter your child's state of mind.

Myth two: *ADD medication leads to addiction.*

In fact, just the opposite is true. Many youths self-medicate either to achieve the ability to focus better or to numb the pain of being out of synch with the world around them. But they do not misuse ADD medication. In fact, the bigger problem is getting an ADD teen to remember to take her medication when the previous dosage has worn off. Any misuse tends to be by people who are not ADD and manage to get the medication on the street.

Myth three: *Taking ADD medications for long periods of time is dangerous.*

This is not true, so far as we know. Each medication has been carefully researched and the contra-indications and side effects are liberally described in the *Physician's Desk Reference.* Several of the more commonly used medications such as Ritalin have been used safely for decades.

Myth four: *ADD medications make teens aggressive.*

This is simply not true. ADD can coexist with other conditions, everything from seizure disorders to psychosis. These other conditions could possibly have an aggressive component. But no evidence has been found to blame aggressive behavior on ADD medication.

Myth five: *Your teen will feel or act drugged if she takes ADD medication.*

Actually, your teen is more likely to be alert and focused toward constructive action when on ADD medication. A hyperactive teen who immediately falls asleep on the couch, the proverbial "couch potato," will find that his mood and activity level will even out when taking medication.

Myth six: Your teen's creativity will be compromised if he takes ADD medication.

Medication apparently has no effect on creativity. The ability to harness creative production increases with the use of medication.

Myth seven: Teachers are recommending the use of medication simply to quiet lively children.

Rarely is this true. First of all, teachers are not allowed to recommend treatment for children. And, although an occasional teacher may wish to squelch a young child's disruptive behavior, teachers are generally well aware of the developmental norms for children's and teen's activity levels.

If they think that your teen might be ADD, that opinion is probably based on observing your child over a long period of time. The teacher might recommend having your child evaluated for ADD. But she or he knows that any treatment would be decided by a professional team trained to handle ADD.

Myth eight: Physicians over-prescribe ADD medication to teens.

Just the opposite is true. Many are reluctant to prescribe such medication. Often, still believing that ADD goes away at puberty, many physicians either take children off the medication at adolescence or do not want to aggressively provide stimulants to teens. Be sure you work with someone who is knowledgeable about the *most recent* findings about ADD and its treatment.

Myth nine: Teens who are being treated for chemical dependency will compromise their sobriety if they take stimulant medication.

Again, not true. Many health-care professionals protected sobriety at all cost in the early days after recognizing that ADD continues into adolescence and adulthood. We have since learned that ADD medication presents no problem *if* the individual is actively engaged in chemical-dependency treatment.

Obviously, no ADD medication is to be used while a person is actively abusing alcohol or using drugs. But once the commitment to recovery is implemented, ADD medication can actually help those people who are ADD and chemically dependent to successfully go through treatment. ADD medication reduces the risk of relapse and makes the road more bearable, especially if self-medication of ADD was one of the factors in drug or alcohol use.

MEDICATION OPTIONS

There are several categories of medication available for use with teens who are ADD. Unfortunately, it's not possible at this time to tell which medication will work best for which person.

As you may have noticed, the behaviors and difficulties associated with ADD vary greatly. For example, if you have two children with ADD, your daughter may be having trouble focusing her attention while your son is primarily hyperactive and impulsive. A teen with Highly Structured ADD may have more problems with anxiety, perfectionism, and temper.

It doesn't take long to figure out that the same medication probably won't work well for everyone.

You also need to realize that some physicians have their own drug of choice. They feel more or less comfortable with one than another. So everyone who goes to that physician is started on that particular drug. Unfortunately, *that* particular drug may not be effective for your teen.

One teen I know struggled for a whole year with a physician who insisted on adjusting and readjusting a particular medication. Finally, in frustration, the parents sought a second opinion. The teen was given a different stimulant and almost immediately had favorable results. His struggles with medication adjustment ceased, and he began to perform more effectively.

The drug most often prescribed for ADD, and the one that has the longest track record of use with people of all ages is the stimulant Ritalin. Other stimulants include Dexadrine, Cylert, Adderall, and Desoxyn. (Brand names are used throughout this section because those are the labels parents and teens are most likely to hear.)

Stimulants generally help a teen focus attention better and tend to curb hyperactivity. Concentration improves with less distractibility and mental fatigue, and forgetfulness decreases. Often, the teen is able to think things through more thoroughly, which aids in the control of impulsivity.

Unfortunately, many physicians do not realize that the same drugs that have been used to treat children are equally effective with teens and adults. Often they avoid prescribing stimulants when they could help the most prevalent symptoms associated with ADD. Another problem is the fact that stimulants are classified as a Class II drug, which requires a triplicate prescription. With a paper trail following the physician's use of this drug, many become nervous about being seen as over-prescribing them. You must also fill triplicate prescriptions immediately and go to the doctor's office to obtain the prescription. It cannot be phoned in.

Antidepressants are frequently used to treat ADD in teens. Many physicians are more familiar with these drugs than stimulants, because they've used them to treat depression. Unlike stimulants, antidepressants do not require a complicated paper-tracking system.

Some of the more commonly prescribed antidepressants are Prozac, Zoloft, Tofranil, Paxil, and Wellbutrin. These medications seem to provide the most help with temper control, including irritability and anger outbursts, and with mood swings. Clinically, other than Wellbutrin, they do not aid the primary ADD symptoms of distractibility and concentration problems.

The antidepressants may be especially helpful *in conjunction with* a stimulant medication, rounding off the uneven effect of the stimulant throughout the day. They definitely can be an asset with teens who are experiencing mood-related discomfort and difficulties with temper, anger, and depression.

It's beginning to appear that different forms of ADD require different medication regimens. The Highly Structured form of ADD has many characteristics in common with Obsessive-Compulsive Disorder and anxiety. Other medications, such as Luvox, Buspar, and Anafranil, are being tried effectively with some teens who have this form of ADD.

Other common medications that seem to do well for some teens who have tantrums, rage reactions, or violent behavior include Tegretol and Depakote. They may be combined with a stimulant to get the best possible benefit for the teen.

For those teens who suffer from considerable edginess and tension, Beta Blockers such as Klonopin, Corgard, and Inderal can be effective and may be used in conjunction with stimulant medication. They also have been reported to be helpful in reducing temper tantrums and explosiveness in some hyperactive teens.

As you can see, there are many medications and combinations of medications from which to choose. As a parent, what you need to remember is that every ADD teen is different. Your job is to find a knowledgeable physician who will *work* with you and your teen—not one who is set on *one* way of prescribing ADD medication for all teens—and one who respects input from the person being treated. Each medication has some side effects which your physician needs to tell you about. If you see any of them, especially tics and any undesirable or uncomfortable reactions to the medication, contact your physician *immediately*. Do not hesitate or feel you are bothering the doctor. That's what the doctor is there for.

New information about the medical treatment of ADD is becoming available every year. The best place to obtain much of this is through your local self-help chapters and through national organizations dedicated to ADD. (See Appendix.) Talk to other parents about their experiences and remember to use a physician who is knowledgeable about ADD in teens and adults and who is willing to work *in partnership* with you.

WHO DECIDES IF YOUR TEEN SHOULD USE MEDICATION?

Even when you are dealing with a teen who is at the younger end of adolescence, you don't just lay things on her—especially not something like a long-term medication she will be responsible for taking. If you are considering starting your child on medication, I would suggest that you first become knowledgeable about ADD medication yourself, consider the pros and cons, and synthesize that information for your teen.

If your teen's ADD has only recently been discovered, then you can expect the person doing the ADD evaluation to be a part of your team. You, your teen, and the evaluator will discuss options, including medication, after a diagnosis is made. After the evaluation, go home and talk about what has happened. Share any information you have gained or make plans to get more information. Then have a family meeting.

Be sure to give your teen plenty of time to air her feelings. If she says, "No way am I taking any drugs," don't worry. That tells you that the drug-education program at school and through the media is having an effect. That's great, and don't argue with her.

You can say, "I'm really glad you feel that way about drugs. You'll stay a lot healthier that way." Then take a breath and continue, "You know, ADD medication is not like the drugs that can hurt you. It's medicine. It's more like wearing glasses if you don't see the blackboard clearly." Or, "You know how some people have to take insulin because their body doesn't produce enough? Well, ADD medication basically gives the part of your brain a boost that is sluggish about producing the chemical that helps you concentrate and sit still. But I don't want you to make up your mind until we get more information."

Then decide together whether to go to a support group meeting, talk more to the evaluator, or visit with your physician about options. If your teen is even remotely willing to give medication a try, and your research has led you to believe it could be a good thing for her, you can say, "Just give it a try. Let's see how it works. We'll keep a close eye on how you feel and how it affects you. Let me know the minute you feel anything, good or bad. And we'll keep a list of questions, okay?"

If your teen absolutely refuses to try medication, and you feel you'd like for her to, you really have no way to force her. But what you can say is, "I feel strongly that medication may help you a lot. But there's no way I can force you to try it." You might as well admit it. Then continue, saying, "You are, however, responsible for your grades and behavior. And I don't want to hear any excuses, because I feel you are not doing all you can to help yourself." You can say the same type of thing when your teen comes to you and says she doesn't want to take her medication any longer. Don't argue, just say, "I'm glad you're looking closely at your situation. But you need to be clear about the fact that you're responsible for your grades and behavior. If you find that you're having trouble without your medication, you can always start it again. I'm glad you're giving it a try. You'll find out for yourself what is right for you now."

At any rate, if you and your teen decide to try medication now, that doesn't mean she will or won't use it in the future. Even if it serves your child well as a teen, she may decide not to continue its use as an adult. And that's fine. The decision to try medication is a decision for *now*. There's no reason to go into it with any long-term goals, such as definitely continuing it in the future or definitely stopping it. But because teens often don't have a long-term perspective, yours may think that whatever she decides today is the way it will always be. Clarify with her how things change. And by doing that, you'll be teaching her a lesson that applies in many areas of her life.

Next, make plans to meet with your teen and doctor together. Ask your child how much she wants you to talk and how much she wants to do the talking herself. This will vary with age and temperament of your teen. Don't try to push a shy teen to speak up for herself. Encourage her, but don't push her.

Suggest that your teen make a list of questions for the doctor. You may want to consider the following, plus add a few of your own:

- ► What does the medication do?
- ► What options do I have?
- ► What are the side effects?
- ► What will I feel like when I'm on the medication?
- ► How will it change me?
- ► When should I call you with a question?

▶ How long will it take to work?
▶ What if it doesn't work?
▶ How should I take it?
▶ What if the other kids make fun of me?
▶ When can I stop taking it if I want?
▶ Can I become addicted to it?
▶ Can I use it when I need to study a lot and then not use it at other times?

Your Teen's Role
Your teen's first job is to decide whether or not she will take her medication. You cannot *give it to her*, as you did when she was a little girl. You certainly do not need to get into a battle, threatening to ground her or deprive her of things if she doesn't take it. From the very beginning she needs to be willing to cooperate, or you don't have a deal. She knows that already. And you need to realize it, too.

Then there's the completely separate issue of whether or not she can *remember* to take it, even if she wants to. One of the major symptoms of ADD is getting distracted or off task. And as the medication wears off, she's likely to become more distractible and forget that it's time to take the next dose. This is one of the reasons time-release medications and those that are longer lasting can be effective with teens. Ask your doctor about them.

You and your teen can work out ways to help her remember to take her next dose. It's all right for her to ask you to remind her. That's a form of taking responsibility for herself. Of course, you are not obligated to play that role, but in the beginning you could probably be a great help to her. Some teens choose to use a watch that has more than one alarm. The alarms can be set at the beginning of the day for the time each dose is taken.

After an initial period of forgetfulness, many teens form the habit of taking their medication, and reminders are not necessary. So your teen needs to know she's facing a two-phase training program. Phase one involves getting used to taking medication and phase two involves having become used to taking it.

As your teen approaches age twenty, she will generally be in charge of her own life. She will decide whether or not she wants to keep taking her medicine, and she will take the responsibility to remember her doses. She'll know by then what it does for her and how she benefits from taking it.

The Doctor's Role

Your family physician may not have the latest information about ADD or ADD medications. Don't be afraid to ask your family doctor what her experience is with ADD in teens and whether or not she would be comfortable working with your teen.

However, be prepared. If your doctor informs you that ADD disappears at puberty or that it is being grossly over-diagnosed or doesn't really exist at all, you know you'd better find someone else for this part of your teen's care.

On the other extreme you'll also know that you need to find another doctor if your physician sees your teen for only a few minutes and immediately makes a diagnosis of ADD. ADD cannot be diagnosed on the basis of a few minutes of conversation and "body language."

If your teen has already been diagnosed by a professional familiar with ADD and your physician insists on re-diagnosing her, you can offer to have a report sent to your doctor. But explain that you really aren't willing to pay a second fee for work already done to your satisfaction. In this case your physician may be uncomfortable treating ADD with a team approach, or he may feel anxious about prescribing Class II drugs. Whatever the issues, you are in charge. I would suggest finding a physician who is a team player and comfortable with treating ADD.

No one specialty of medicine is trained specifically to treat ADD. Often a family doctor or general practitioner who is familiar with your teen knows or is willing to find out about what this member of your family needs. Sometimes you will find a physician who is interested in ADD in internal medicine, psychiatry, or neurology. A number of pediatricians also have taken on teen and even adult ADD patients. Your local ADD support group will generally know the names of physicians who are responsive to treating ADD with medication. You must, however, work with a *medical* doctor who can write prescriptions, since the medications used, typically, require a prescription.

Your doctor's job is to build a liaison with your teen and you. As a team member, her specific role is to find the medication that fits your teen. Together you can talk about the type of results you would most like to achieve—for example, help with concentration, temper, distractibility or mood swings. Once the physician decides on the medication to start with, she needs to share that information and the reasons she chose it with you and your teen.

Next, you can expect to check back within a week. You can expect to make several visits during the early phase of medication management. Later, they will taper off with occasional visits to update the needs and response of your teen. Expect the physician to be available for questions and willing to listen to feedback from both your teen and yourself. You two live with the results day in and day out. You will know how behavior, attitude, and moods are being affected.

Remember, if your physician isn't available for feedback or is too busy to listen, you need to find someone who is more able to play the role you need.

In addition to medication management your physician needs to encourage your teen to obtain training and education about ADD. With managed health care and insurance practices of today, coverage for the treatment of ADD may fall under the auspices of the physician. Hopefully, if you belong to a health-care system, someone there knows about ADD and the most efficient, effective ways to treat it and give you training and education about it.

You can most likely obtain the services you need at a modest cost. Unfortunately, much of the ADD medication is somewhat costly, and few resources are available for a cost break.

ADD has become a big business. Some people are paying many hundreds of dollars for a *complete* workup to determine whether ADD is present and whether other kinds of "conditions" are present. This over-testing syndrome has spread to ADD probably for two reasons: First, a lot of money can be made; second, there is a lot of litigation-based fear that causes professionals to over-test so they can't be found negligent.

I would suggest you use common sense and build a partnership with a professional you have come to trust who is moderate in her approach to ADD.

STARTING MEDICATION

What Can You Expect?

Most ADD medications work quickly. In fact, I cannot tell you how often the parent of a teen has said to me, "I could tell within thirty minutes of the first five-milligram dose of Ritalin that my teen had taken it." Even antidepressants that tend to take several months to build up to a therapeutic level for treatment of depression can be seen to have an affect on ADD within a few days.

Reports of "smoothing out," "calming down," "becoming focused," and "settling down" are common. Often the person taking the medication is less aware of the results than those who are around him. One young man told me after a week on a stimulant that he didn't feel anything. He guessed the medication wasn't working yet. A few minutes later he happened to mention that he'd read a newspaper from front to back for the first time in his life. Not until I called his name, raised my eyebrows, and said, "And the medication isn't working?" did he realize that it was the medication that had allowed him to concentrate on his reading.

The physician may need to adjust the dosage levels during the early phase of medication management. It's not uncommon to increase the dosage several times, especially because most physicians choose to start with a very low dose. Eventually the level stays constant. Once a good level is reached for your teen, she will not become habituated and require ever-increasing levels of medication. You don't need to worry about that.

If any side effects such as tics, sleeplessness, weight loss, irritability, headaches, increased blood pressure or heart rate or rebound effect occurs, consult your physician immediately. Your doctor will inform you of other precautionary indicators to watch for. For example, one drug requires periodic liver-function testing. Other needs will be monitored by the doctor.

Your feedback is very important during this period, since you may be more aware of changes than your teen. Actually, the person taking the medication often does not *feel* anything and must also rely on others' observation of their behaviors.

You might want to alert your teen to watch for these changes:

- ► Can think more clearly and is less confused.
- ► Can think on one track at a time instead of having a "central switching station" of twenty tracks going at once.
- ► Can sit in his seat at school.
- ► Can complete an assignment.
- ► Can leave an assignment and then go back to it and get started again.
- ► Gets into less trouble in school or elsewhere for "rinkydinky" behavior such as getting up out of his seat, talking out of turn, or messing with others' things.
- ► Follows through on commitments better.
- ► Can remember to turn work in.
- ► Listens better to what others are saying.
- ► Has more peaceful social relationships.
- ► Feels better about himself.
- ► Feels invigorated to try new things.

This is a partial list of responses to watch for. Your teen will have fun seeing how many others he can collect.

Teens with Outwardly Expressive ADD

Though still lively and vivacious, the activity level of an ADD teen who is Outwardly Expressive is likely to be more goal-directed when she is on medication. A willingness and ability to sit down and concentrate on a project may be possible for the first time. Verbal and physical impulsivity is likely to be reduced.

Teens with Inwardly Directed ADD

One of the biggest changes medication usually provides to a teen with Inwardly Directed ADD is the ability to "come in from outer space" and concentrate on a project. He'll often experience less restlessness and less mental irritation, too.

Because this type of teen is often depressed, an antidepressant is frequently a part of the ADD regimen. Though antidepressants take a little longer for visible results, you are likely to see a positive upturn in the teen's mood, more enthusiasm and motivation to do what he likes, and less frustration and irritability about life in general.

Teens with Highly Structured ADD

Medication can help the perfectionistic, controlling teen with Highly Structured ADD to enjoy a greater degree of flexibility. This will go a long way in improving various relationships. This teen, though highly focused, tends to become irate when interrupted and can't return to work very easily. Medication allows for a smoother flow between stopping and starting work. Medication also can assist if temper problems are a part of your teen's difficulties.

What you need to know about the use of medication with your teen is that each teen is different. For some teens medication makes the difference between night and day. Other teens do fine without it, or use it only as needed. All teens, however, must be trained to manage their ADD whether they are using medication or not. They need to build the skills that help them cope with the style of brain wiring they have. They must learn to make allowances for their weaknesses and take advantage of their strengths.

You also need to remember that your teen must have a say in his medication management and learn to communicate with the physician who is managing his treatment. Sometimes adjustments have to made before the right medication or combination of medications is found. This involves talking with the doctor and monitoring reactions and changes your teen experiences. Your son or daughter must be willing to cooperate in order for medication to do the job it can do. You will want to learn all you can about what is going on so you can be a source of information and feel comfortable that your teen is getting the best care possible.

CHAPTER TWELVE

WHEN YOUR ADD TEEN BECOMES AN ADULT
Supporting Him in the "Real World"

Just because your teenager has finished high school and is going on to college or about to get a job in the real world doesn't mean your job as a parent is finished. In fact, some of the most important work you have to do as a parent comes during this phase of your child's life. For some people with ADD, negotiating the transition from being a child to an independent, responsible adult goes on until he or she is near age thirty.

Making choices that honor their ADD is one of the primary tasks for young adults of this period. Discovering how their ADD will affect them as adults in the world beyond school is another. And revamping a life plan that got off to a bad start into one in which ADD is taken into account and used as an asset may be another reason your son or daughter returns home for advice and support. If you can make it through your child's teenage years by building a respectful and supportive relationship, you can expect that relationship to continue. Now, even when you give advice and support, it will be because your son or daughter has *asked* for it. You know not to try to control your teen's life, and you respect his independence and separateness. You have wisdom, but you know you can't make his choices for him.

One mother and son I know are a great example of how this can work. Though Jon and his mom had lived in separate towns

277

since he went to college, she had visited him every month or so during his senior year. She discovered that if she simply sat down by him for a few minutes, he'd begin to talk to her. Rather than her having to ask questions or supply answers, she found that her new job was to listen and, from time to time, make a comment.

When Jon weighed options for anything, she found herself saying, "What do you feel you'd like to do?" or "What feels best to you?" One of her strongest roles was supporting him in doing what he wanted, rather than what other people, both friends and other adults, told him to do.

Jon has known since he was in elementary school that he was ADD. Being predominantly an Outwardly Expressive ADD person, he needs plenty of opportunity to move about. A desk job is not for him. He also has a few of the characteristics of Highly Structured ADD and does very well in a structure to his liking. His experience as a member of a sports team since junior high years showed him he liked having a training program to follow and liked the structure of working with others toward a goal.

As he more clearly understands the ways in which his ADD impacts him, he is able to decide what route to take after college. He's strongly considering joining the military as an officer. Jon sees the military as a transition step. It provides the type of structure he likes, and he will seek an assignment that gives him the mobility he likes. Though not sure how long he may want to stay in, he realizes an initial commitment will give him time to mature and gain the experience he needs to get a job in the line of work he desires.

Neither ADD nor its effects ends miraculously when your child turns twenty-one. The issues and demands of ADD stay with even a well-trained, successful youth throughout life. But with your help, by the time your teen reaches twenty-one, he has begun to sort through choices and recognize and respect the choices he needs to make for his ADD.

I've experienced this myself as I've watched my son, Mendel, grow into his early twenties. His head is on straight, having done a lot of hard work during his elementary and early teen years. He's realistic about how his ADD affects him and doesn't consider it a disorder. In fact, he works with the assets.

In part, his attitude about ADD comes from having learned to deal with his impulsivity, temper, and extreme sensitivity as a preteen. As he progressed through junior high and high school, he developed organizational skills that he was able to carry forward to college and exercise on his own. He knew to seek accommodation for his ADD during his early college years and successfully got the help he needed. As an upperclassman, he turned the tables and helped younger students exercise the ADD resources they needed to succeed. Mendel found outlets for his hyperactivity in athletics. When he was required to do sedentary work, he was skillful at finding ways to get it done. He plans to maintain a high level of physical activity throughout his life, because he realizes it's important for him.

Mendel knows who he is and what he needs to feel good about himself. He knows what he needs and how to make good choices. And these are the keys to leading a successful life. I must say I wish I'd had the clarity and insight at his age that he has. I would have been able to avoid a lot of pain trying to do things I thought I *ought* to do that just didn't fit me.

As a parent, I'm really happy for my son. He'll be able to make contributions to the adult world that do not cost him an enormous price or discount his nature. He can have his cake and eat it, too.

GETTING STARTED IN THE "REAL" WORLD

Our job as parents is to help our children find and reflect their true identity, to help them find that special something they love. Obviously, that means they cannot be pushed and pressured into doing a "should."

"Shoulds" are those things that parents, authorities, and the culture in general tell us we ought to do in order to be acceptable or responsible.

"Shoulds" are often associated with respectability, prestige, and success. But if you do something because you "should," such as go to work for a corporation as an engineer when you want to start your own business as a mechanic, you are likely to feel a great deal of resentment and depression. You're trying to do something that *doesn't fit you*. And that will always backfire. If you *don't do* something you think you should do, then you will tend to feel guilty. That's a painful feeling, too, and it's likely to create a lot of anxiety. So either way, you're doomed to feeling bad.

Everyone must be who they are naturally and innately. And that includes you and your ADD teen.

It is crucial to sort out the "shoulds" from the "wants" during the teenage years. Your job is to help your child by giving him permission to follow his own sense of what's right for him. I realize this can be a scary process if you've lived your own life based on what you thought you *should* do. And if you always think things through based on logic or what others think is the right thing to the exclusion of listening to your heart, this may seem like frivolous advice.

Based on more than thirty years as a counselor as well as my own personal experience, I can promise you that many of the symptoms I saw in clients young and old resulted because the person followed "shoulds" rather than "wants."

Just as you can't try to train a marigold to become a rose, you can't take an artistically inclined teen and turn him into an accountant without exacting a price. And that price tends to be chronic depression, anxiety, or physical illness.

As I look back over my own transition time, I realize that my well-meaning parents didn't understand this principle. And I was totally oriented to "shoulds." I didn't have a clue who I was. The natural Lynn was buried early and replaced by the good student who worked all the time.

When it came time to graduate from high school it never occurred to me to do anything but go to college. So I did. It took me three college degrees and several decades of living until I began to discover the real Lynn underneath. The creative, multifaceted visionary had lain dormant for more than fifty years, afraid to be seen. It took all the strength and courage I could muster to face the truth within myself.

I'd had little signs along the way. For example, I used to do artwork as a child. I dreamed of being on the stage and listened to "There's No Business Like Show Business" for hours on my 78 RPM record player. I wrote some short stories and saw pictures in my mind constantly. But I realized none of this was acceptable in the world in which I was being raised. So I left it behind and did what I was supposed to do—become a *professional*.

Now I know why I was depressed and anxious for so many years. But I didn't know why then. I covered well, at least to the public, and underwent a lot of psychotherapy. Most of my behavior helped me survive, but ultimately I was able to acknowledge and accept who I truly am without feeling like I *should* be something different.

As high school ends and the transition years to full-fledged adulthood are negotiated, you and your teen have a chance to go for the real thing. Encourage your teen to *be who he is*, and he will be the architect of his future.

LIVING ARRANGEMENTS

Independent living requires a lot of organization, something an ADD teen often finds difficult. Hopefully, you started her training, one task at a time, beginning in the earlier teen years. Laundry is a good place to begin; that includes teaching boys to iron. Next you may have taught him to cook for himself rather than eating out all the time or snacking.

I vividly recall my own son the summer before his senior year in high school. I'd asked him what he'd like to do for lunches during the next school year. He said that he'd take care of them. I said I'd be happy to pack his lunch. I never expected the response I got, but it taught me a lot. "Mom, I need to get used to doing more things for myself so I'll be ready to go to college next year, so I'll take care of my own cooking this year."

I have to tell you I felt a tug at my heart. I *wanted* to pack his lunch because I knew all too well that this was the end of my nurturing, parenting role. But I took a deep breath, let a tear roll out of the corner of my eye, and said, "You bet."

I've also learned that I'm still an important person in his life. The job has just changed. Now I wait for him to ask me for advice.

If your teen goes directly to college after high school, one of the advantages is a slower transition to the responsibilities of daily living. Living in a dorm, for at least the first year, is an excellent idea. Learning the process of finding and renting living quarters is another job that takes time to master.

The first year at college is one simply to get used to being away from home, managing school (which includes learning to deal with asking for reasonable accommodation in relation to classes), maintaining a car, and keeping a bank account.

The second year is either dedicated to the same or, in some cases, adds living off campus. A lot depends on how well your student has settled in during the first year. If living off campus is the plan, I recommend the student start during the summer. Once school begins, there's no time for new lessons. The third year, in many cases, is an extension of the first two plus the addition of declaring a major, along with gaining more experience with roommates, telephones, rent, and car maintenance.

Depending upon whether your teen lives at home or in a dorm during college, he will be ready, more or less, to be on his own when he graduates. You will still be cosigning leases in most cases. But by the last year of college your youth may have become quite expert at moving and helping friends move. If not, it will be the first year after college when he learns these skills. It's a lot easier to learn this while still under your financial support and guidance than when he's on his own.

If you feel like your child doesn't need you for anything except money during this time of transition, you're not alone. That's a pretty common feeling. But it's important to realize that your financial support is a major cushion that buys time for your child to acquire additional skills.

Many ADD students take five years or more to complete a

four-year college program. It's often wise to plan on this from the very beginning so that she can take lighter academic loads. Some students do just fine when they keep the load light throughout college. Others can add a few hours later on, but usually a steady pace is preferable to one that bounces up and down.

The fourth and fifth years of college provide a time in which your ADD youth can level off in preparation for exiting from college to the next step. Much of the senior year, in fact, will be spent preparing for graduation and what comes next. Otherwise, you may have a student who has no idea what to do once the diploma is in her hands.

The steps I've mentioned here are similar for all youth. However, students who are ADD may have a harder time making changes. They may find that organizing the changes and adjusting to them as they come more difficult. So don't be surprised if your child flounders a bit. If your college student doesn't bound off as a special representative to a senator in Washington or win a scholarship for advanced study, don't fear that he will never be successful. Transition times create stress, and he will need a bit of extra time to get in the swing of things after college.

Moving Back Home

Returning home to live with parents happens more and more frequently. Young adults with ADD aren't any more or less likely to return home than their non-ADD peers, but this is a growing trend in general. Moving back home can be a very good idea if it's been carefully discussed as a family and viewed as a positive move. Sometimes financial reasons prompt the move. If a family is strapped, and the only way for the student to stay in school is for her to move home, then the family members consolidate their money so schooling can continue. Also, if the chaos or complexity of living at school—either on or off campus—disrupts the young adult's ability to study, returning home can be a good idea.

Moving back home is one thing; making it work is something else. It requires each family member to take personal responsibility in the home and respect the other family members. Just as parents should no longer watch over what time their twenty-year-old comes home, the twenty-year-old cannot expect mom to do the laundry. Household chores need to be divided as they would with roommates. Respect for others' sleeping and rest times, for quiet, and for their need for privacy is a given.

Let's face it. If mom just can't go to sleep until her twenty-year-old son is in for the night, the arrangement might not work out. That doesn't mean there are any "bad guys" in the relationship. It just means it's a mismatch.

If the parents do tend to treat their returned child as younger than he is, then it probably isn't a good idea for the ADD youth to live at home. That will just delay taking responsibility for himself. Neither is it a good idea for him to return to a lot of criticism, nagging, or chaos. You, as a parent, must evaluate your own ability to back off and let your young adult make his own decisions, even if that means he will fall down from time to time.

If your teen has a problem with drugs, alcohol, promiscuity, or any other addictive behavior, consult with a family counselor who knows about addiction treatment. It's hard to determine whether you would be enabling your youth by letting him move in.

Once moved in, you would need to be on guard not to get into old family patterns that would undermine any positive work you or your child had done. Perhaps you would need to continue family counseling or support through Alcoholics Anonymous and Al-Anon or a comparable group.

RELATIONSHIPS

Relationships are trying at any age, but just think back about how little you probably knew when you were a young adult. Most of us have been known to say or at least think, "If I'd known then what I know now. . . ." The bottom line is that you didn't know it then. The only way you learned it was by making the mistake.

One of the more prevalent and erroneous myths is that if children (of any age) would only listen to their parents and do what their parents told them, they would be saved a lot of trouble. But young adults *must* find out on their own what works and what doesn't work for them. Your job is to be available when and if your young person wants to talk with you. And you'll be surprised how often that will happen if you just settle down quietly in a warm, nurturing corner of the house. The kitchen table is often a great place. Later evening is often a good time.

You can bring up the subject, saying to your daughter, "How is Harry (your daughter's boyfriend)?" Regardless of how your daughter responds—which may range from nothing to "Okay" to "I never want to hear his name again"—keep still and listen. She'll probably tell you more if you don't start talking right away.

Don't make decisions for your adult children. You can say, "I trust your judgment" or "Listen to your heart" or something like "Just be sure you treat each other with respect and truly want to be together, not because you're afraid to be alone, but because you want each other."

Once in a while, I go into my "mother thing," a piece of experience that I want to pass on to my son. I always introduce it first with, "I need to do my 'mother thing.'" Then I keep the information or advice short, such as, "One thing I've learned is that staying with someone because of fear is the wrong reason. If I'm afraid I'll never find the right person or I'm afraid to be alone, I've come to know it's a set-up for a really poor relationship." Then I stop.

I neither require my son to answer, nor do I aim the comments directly at him as if that is what he's doing. In fact, he may or may not be doing that. I truly am just sharing what I've learned. By the time our children are in their late teens and early twenties, we are not going to know enough about their relationships to really know the whole story. And often we don't know that much about any part of our children's lives during this time of enormous change. Later, when they are closer to thirty and older, we may come to know them more thoroughly as adults. But right now, they hardly know themselves. So how can we know them?

One last piece of advice, even though you may want to say

something in your own young adult's behalf: Don't take sides in his relationships. If you talk against the other person, you can be sure the two will make up, and you will become the "bad guy" real fast. If you try to point out what your own child did that made things worse, you may be wounding an already wounded person who needs support. Whatever you say will probably be seen as criticism. When we are hurt, we see anything less than support as criticism, even though our brains may know better. Just say, "Uh-huh, I know, I'm sorry, it's tough," and let advice or criticism go for the time being. Never give it unless asked.

If you don't know what your offspring wants, ask. You might say, "Do you want me to support you and say the other person is all wrong?" There are times when we just need to hear this, even though we know it's a lie. "Or would you just like me to be quiet and be here with you?" Later, a person who is hurting can look at his or her role in the situation.

LOOKING FOR WORK

Seeking employment provides a great opportunity for you to become a mentor and teacher to your young adult. You might meet with resistance at first. But continue to make yourself available. You might ask, "Do you have a plan for looking for work? I'd appreciate your sharing it with me."

If this is the first time your youth has looked for a job, you might sit down with her and say, "Let's go over the steps to finding a job."

First, establish the kind of job she's seeking and its purpose. Is she looking for a job that's part time, full time, temporary? Is her goal to make spending money, to meet people, to fill in time, or build a career?

Then, depending upon the answers to these questions, tell her *one time* what you know about dress, appropriate ways to seek employment, sources of leads for jobs, applications, and networking. Watch her response. Don't fight to get her to listen. Ask whether the information you are giving is useful.

Even if your daughter or son has worked before, this time she may be looking for a more important job. Explain about networking and information interviewing and ask whether she would like some leads from you. And if you do have some leads, would she like you to speak with the person first.

I met someone at an ADD meeting in another state who was in the criminal justice business. My son was interested in that field, so I asked him if he wanted me to find out if the man would be willing to talk with him about that field of work. With an okay from my son, I asked the man and he agreed. I got his phone number and passed it on to my son. Then I got out of the picture.

It's not my business to get my son a job, to get him to make that phone call, or to find out what the results are. It's my business to help him learn to network and even to do networking for him, just as I would for anyone else I meet.

Next, talk with your child about what kind of person he is and what his needs and desires are from this job. By this age he may not want to talk about himself as someone who is ADD or has ADD. That's okay. He's just who he is, ADD or not. But you can, and probably should, talk about the ADD attributes it would be wise to accommodate.

For example, if your son hates paperwork, it would be wise to find out how much paperwork is required on a job he's considering, as well as how much clerical help is available to assist with the paperwork. Or maybe your ADD daughter is a true artist at heart and would feel like a butterfly with her wings clipped if she took a nine-to-five job. If she's a dreamer whose sense of time is practically nonexistent, she needs to be in a setting that honors her creativity.

It's important for you and your child to remember that people with ADD don't outgrow it. Having to stretch to accommodate it day in and day out is very stressful. Help your youth know what to look for as he seeks something that fits him well and his life will be a whole lot more pleasant.

At this stage of his life, it might be difficult for your child to talk or even think about his ADD. He's been making accommodations for so many years, he might not want to be reminded that he has to think about it again, and face those issues again, as he looks for work. Your young adult has come a long way and been through a lot of growth and maturing in the last few years. Remind him that *he can do it.*

Here are ten tips that will make it easier for your teen to feel good about himself and his ADD.

- ► Acknowledge and learn all you can about the way in which you are "wired."
- ► Put yourself in situations that benefit the way you are "wired."
- ► Be committed to making the most of your ADD.
- ► Find your "fit," which includes doing what you love and using your gifts and talents.
- ► Take responsibility for using the discipline necessary to make the most of your ADD.
- ► Team up with others who have the skills you lack.
- ► Communicate your needs and listen to the needs of others. Then negotiate so everyone can get his needs met.
- ► Be prepared to tell those in charge what you need so you can do a better job for them, whether in school or at work.
- ► Get your emotions and behavior under control.
- ► Remember that you are a valuable human being who has a lot to give to the world and a lot to gain from the world.

MONEY MANAGEMENT

Managing finances can be a major problem for most people who are ADD. One of the difficulties is breaking down large projects into smaller parts; another is keeping track of details. And, of course, it has a lot to do with impulsivity—which leads to impulsive buying. And let us not forget the high that comes from a new purchase!

Start out by not only showing your teen how to open a checking account but how to keep a running balance. Be sure to explain about check charges and extras. I know this isn't easy. In fact, even as I say this, I wince. I have enough trouble with this myself, much less trying to explain it to a young adult.

If you feel overwhelmed by the prospect of teaching your young adult about money management, you can let someone else do it—a friend or someone you know at your bank. I advise suggesting to your daughter that you add a buffer to the account that doesn't show up in the running balance. Obviously if your youth automatically uses that extra money, I wouldn't suggest continually replacing it. But it can be a good safety net for anyone really *trying* to be responsible.

Next, determine who will be responsible for reconciling your youth's checkbook, and when that person will do it. I say this because for some people with ADD—and I'm one of them—this is a task that just cannot be managed, no matter how hard they try. This has nothing to do with being conscientious and nothing to do with being lazy. And there is no shame in finding a friend who is willing to help you or, as your child gets older, maybe hiring a bookkeeper or an accountant. This is an important task to do accurately. But it doesn't really matter who does it, as long as it gets done.

Your job as a parent is to see how well your teens can manage. If your young adult is really trying and still failing, talk about options, including using cash only instead of checks, going over the checkbook weekly, using duplicate checks, or having someone else handle the finances.

Determine whether your teen is serious about managing money and whether she's making progress. If she's not willing to cooperate with you and is not ready to take responsibility for a checking account, don't continually bail her out. Bouncing a check can get to be a habit, and the more times *you* pay for them, the less quickly your teen will learn to manage money. All too often, a spending addiction develops when a young adult is not required to be responsible from the very beginning. Do not be an enabler.

Credit cards are another major difficulty for a lot of people with ADD. If your young adult is beginning to manage a checking account, even if he can't balance his statement, you may wish to consider a joint credit card with a limit on it. These are now available and give the youth an opportunity to practice with a safety net.

Your job is to sit down ahead of time and explain the limits. How is the card to be used? What kinds of purchases? Then explain the dangers: girlfriend/boyfriend presents, the holidays, a night on the town, the need to "feel better."

Next, go over the statement every month with your youth to see how the money is being spent. One girl I knew was buying food from a gasoline/convenience store. Her parents thought she was charging gasoline until they realized she wasn't driving that much. She really didn't mean to create a problem and didn't realize that she was spending more on each food item than she would at a regular grocery store. But when she ran out of money at the end of the month, it seemed like a good way to get food for a few days.

Her parents talked to her about letting them know of her problem. That way, they could help her decide if she needed more money each month or needed to cut back in some area of her spending. They worked this out together, the problem ceased, and she learned a lesson about smart shopping.

Sooner or later your young adult must face up to handling money — even if it means admitting that she can't handle it, or at least not yet. Then she can make responsible arrangements to get the help she needs to deal with her finances. But you must not bail out your son or daughter. You'll get tired of spending money that doesn't need to be spent, and your offspring won't learn for herself.

Remember, misspent money is only part of a learning process. If it doesn't yield results (if you don't come to the rescue), it will cease. And if she has a spending addiction, the sooner your youngster faces the need to get help for it the better. A responsible counselor or support group can assist her.

WHEN SHOULD A YOUNG ADULT
REVEAL HIS ADD?

During the course of your child's life there will be appropriate times to discuss her ADD with friends, bosses, colleagues, college professors, neighbors, your accountant, or bank personnel. Knowing when and how to discuss her ADD is not always easy. But there are guidelines.

Tell your young adult that when her ADD affects the kind of job she does or affects other people, she needs to let anyone involved know what to expect. That doesn't necessarily mean saying, "I am ADD."

In personal, committed relationships she will probably want to bring up the subject of ADD at some point. It's a good idea for a spouse or close adult to understand a lot about ADD, because it's going to surface often. However, the person with ADD has to carry her full responsibility. She cannot use her ADD as an excuse or the relationship simply will not work out.

For example, if she is communicating with her boyfriend, she might say, "I love you and I like to have you near. But when you run your fingertips over my skin, it makes me feel like I'll jump out of it. My skin has always been extremely sensitive to touch. If you touch me like this instead, it will feel much better." She may never have mentioned her ADD, but she talked about one of her ADD traits. On the job you need to suggest that your young adult follow his own feelings about whether to mention his ADD. You might suggest that he assess the type of person his boss is before he speaks up. If his boss is the kind of person who thinks people should "tough it out," then talking about ADD is probably a big mistake. On the other hand, if the boss is interested in what makes people tick and what can be done to make job performance more efficient, then your son might want to share some helpful hints. Whether he says he's ADD or simply talks about what will make work easier for him, it will be up to him. He'll learn from experience.

I've found that sharing with the people who assist me in my life, such as my agent, accountant, editors, banker, attorney, and others is important. Right at the beginning I come out and say, "I'm ADD." From then on, I don't say it, but rather tell them where and how I need their assistance. I don't need to prove to them that I'm ADD. What I need from them is help with my areas of weakness. If, because they are not ADD, they make a suggestion that doesn't fit, I explain why it doesn't fit, but I don't necessarily need to say it's because I'm ADD.

Recently I spoke with my agent. I was having trouble getting down to work on a manuscript. Her interpretation of the situation was that I needed more time to complete my current project so that I wouldn't get burned out. I thanked her for trying to help but explained that just the opposite was true. I had too much time. I needed a closer deadline so I would have to gear up and get the lengthy project done. She understood right away. And sure enough, as soon as time began to run out for me on the project, I was able to work just fine.

The point is, people who are not ADD don't always know what to do to help us. Your teen has to learn, as a part of becoming an adult, what he needs to be successful. And he must take the responsibility to guide any other person who is on his team as to the type of help he needs.

People who are ADD must realize that, although ADD causes many difficulties, it does not make them different from others in one important way: *Everyone has something or some things that create problems for him or her.* The person who is non-ADD may have just as much trouble being creative and intuitive as her ADD counterpart has being structured and linear. And it's very, very important that your child understand this.

Though it's wonderful that the world of ADD has been uncovered, your young adult must realize this is only the first step. The next step requires all differences and individuality to be respected, accommodated, and honored. Those of us who have discovered a reason for why we are the way we are feel relief and hope.

At first, sympathy and compassion came our way from those who have known us. But more and more I'm discovering a hesitancy or withdrawal of others who really don't want to hear more about ADD. That's not to say they don't care about those of us who are ADD. But, they, too, have difficulties and need understanding. They really get tired of hearing that we have a reason for our difficulties when they don't.

So I recommend caution. Life is more than ADD. I would advise your young adult to experiment with various ways to accommodate her ADD without necessarily saying a lot about it, unless she feels the other person is really interested. In this way ADD is like any other character trait. You don't reveal everything you know about yourself to every person you work with or date. You hold some things in reserve.

Your young adult definitely needs to keep ADD out of the picture when she's up against someone who doesn't respect human differences, unless she's willing to go all the way, including a possible legal confrontation. She'll know whether she's talking with a reasonable person or with someone who's single-minded and hardheaded. Then she needs to make her decisions accordingly.

SUCCESS STORIES

If I leave you with just one message from this whole book, this is it: Your child, turned young adult, can lead a very successful, fulfilling life — in spite of and because of ADD — if he or she finds the right "fit."

Your most important job is to stay on your child's team until he can learn to believe in himself. And that belief is learned from the way you feel about him. If *you* believe he can do it, he'll feel supported, no matter what. He will learn that he is a capable, talented, wonderful person. That's the gift you can give your child.

That doesn't mean enabling your child to stay undisciplined, ignorant, or hurtful to others or himself. It does not mean you do for him anything that he can do for himself. It does mean you support him to the degree that he genuinely needs help from time to time throughout the teen years and beyond.

Just as we adults need someone to lean on occasionally or someone to support or believe in us, your teen needs this support from you into adulthood. It's okay for your child to come home and get hope throughout the teen years and beyond, even if it's only for a moment here or there. "I believe in you," are the most powerful words you can share with your offspring.

Use them.

I'd like to tell you three stories of special people who have crossed my path over the last ten years. Each made a heartfelt impression on me and I want you to experience the hope they provide.

Denise's Story

Denise's grandmother read a story about ADD in her local newspaper and recognized in her granddaughter many of the characteristics mentioned. Twenty-one-year-old Denise was in an outpatient drug rehab program because of two DWIs. She had been in several foster homes while she was growing up and Denise's grandmother had lost track of her and her mother until about a year earlier.

As soon as she discovered Denise's whereabouts, she encouraged her granddaughter to come live with her until she could get on her feet. Denise had barely gotten through high school, hadn't learned much that she could transfer into the real world, had no apparent marketable skills, little self-discipline, and two DWIs. She also had no money and no place to stay.

Denise's grandmother didn't know where to start to help her granddaughter, but when she found the newspaper article it gave her hope. She was afraid, though, that it was too late. She lay awake nights and worried that Denise wouldn't make it through her rehab classes, be able to get a job, wake up on time to get there—and on and on and on.

The good news came when she was accepted into a special training program for adults suspected of being ADD who had run into trouble with the law because of drug or alcohol abuse.

Denise was properly evaluated and found to have Inwardly Directed ADD. She participated in an eight-week training program to learn about her ADD. She began to believe in herself when she realized there was a reason for some of the many problems she had faced while growing up.

She related well to the other group participants. She learned to keep up with medication that helped her focus and keep better track of time. She finished her rehab class, got a job, managed to get there on time, and finished the ADD group follow-up three months later with flying colors. Denise was intent on making a better life for herself.

Denise also had a dream. She loved little children and clothes and dreamed of having a resale shop for children's clothes. But she had never been able to get anywhere with her dream.

Several months after she finished her ADD follow-up group, Denise called me. She had started her business on her own. She didn't have a shop yet, but she had begun to scout garage sales. After a few weeks of doing that and refurbishing the clothing, she had her own sale and made money from it. Her hopes were high and she began to realize that she could make her dream come true.

Denise's grandmother gave her a chance, even though she was afraid Denise wouldn't make it. We're all very proud of Denise.

David's Story

David's parents realized he had a problem when he was in elementary school. He was extremely hyperactive, his attention span was very short and, though he was a good kid, his impulsivity left a trail of damage. Wherever he went, something was sure to break. David himself suffered a few accidents, but because he was athletic, he usually managed to escape with only minor injuries from his escapades.

His parents started him in martial arts training when David was nine years old, and he kept that up with other sports throughout high school and college.

Though he was bright, David didn't do especially well in school because of his inattentiveness. However, he slowly learned his lessons, and he and his parents began to build dreams.

David's parents supported him fully. No one overly criticized him. They just kept working with him and supporting him in his interests, and they provided solid limits for him to follow.

As he got older, if he broke something, he was required to earn the money to get it fixed or buy a replacement. They saw that he studied each night for a while, at least. This time increased as he got older and was able to sit still for a longer period.

When David showed a special interest in animals, his mother helped him set up cages in the backyard and his room. He owned a ferret, a snake, several guinea pigs, a dog, two cats, and an assortment of birds.

From his experiences with these animals David decided he wanted to become a veterinarian. He went to a state college, then worked for a while, then went back to school. He changed his major because he didn't think he could get into veterinary school. He went back and retook many of the science classes in which he'd gotten B's or C's and came out with A's. When finances became tight in the family, David went to work. But his parents never quit urging him to go after his dreams. They did all they could. And he did all he could.

David next thought about becoming a doctor or a medical assistant. Then he decided to try for dental school after reassessing his interest in helping people, his skills, and the practicality of finding a job later. He did some more make-up work at school and made out his dental school applications. Neither he nor his parents ever gave up.

Just a few weeks ago David was admitted to dental school and will begin next semester.

With persistence and desire and the support of his family, David has a good chance of reaching his dreams.

Mary Lou's Story
As a child Mary Lou was barely an average student in school. Though she never caused any real trouble, she could often be seen staring out the window when she was supposed to be doing worksheets. At recess, she spent all of her time with friends. Her classmates liked her. She was a helper and good listener.

Mary Lou had no special goals in life. She really only wanted to be with her friends. Sometimes her parents worried about her as she continued through high school and then took a course to become a manicurist. Shortly after Mary Lou finished the course, she met Bill, an easygoing country man who preferred to live in a small town. They married, moved back to the country, and had two children. Mary Lou is ADD. She still "spaces out," looking at the clouds and shifting from one activity to another. She may garden for a little while, tackle a few dishes in the sink, or make a phone call to schedule an overdue appointment at the dentist.

She's not winning any awards for housekeeping. She doesn't head any major community projects. Now that her kids are in school, she works a few hours a week doing nails so she can be home by the time they get home.

Mary Lou also spends a lot of time with her friends. She's still a good listener and will often be found dropping whatever she's doing, kids in tow, to go off to help a neighbor who needs something.

Mary Lou isn't organized enough to get recognized for her volunteerism. Her children do okay in school, but they are as distractible as she is when it comes to getting homework completed and back to school on time. She's sensitive to the needs of the environment and recycles aluminum and plastic, though she often carries this "trash" around in the trunk of her car for several weeks until she gets them to the recycling bins.

Fortunately, Bill doesn't mind a messy house. In fact, Bill considers himself very lucky to have found Mary Lou, because he knows how much she loves him. He feels supported and cared for by her. Mary Lou's children laugh a lot, play freely, and more or less get their chores and schoolwork done. Mary Lou's friends feel blessed that she's in their life. They feel her unconditional acceptance and willingness to give what she has, as well as let them help her out when she or her family need something.

Mary Lou does not work on *treating* her ADD. Mary Lou *lives with* her ADD. She has found her fit and has good self-esteem. She feels good about herself, her values, and her loyalty to those in her world.

To me Mary Lou is the picture of a truly successful human being who cares about herself, her family, her neighbors, and her community. And Mary Lou is happy, at least most of the time, as she lives honestly and with respect for the innate worth of all people. To be sure, Mary Lou wouldn't state her feeling in this way, but she lives her life by those principles.

I'm glad Mary Lou is exactly who and what she is. The world is a better place because of her.

The greatest gift you can give your teen is the gift of unconditional acceptance and belief in his or her goodness. With realistic, solid limits that allow your teen to increasingly take responsibility for his actions, you will guide and support him to become a responsible, caring adult who knows who he is and what he wants.

Your job is not to live your teen's life for him, but to be there for encouragement. Be glad that you are who you are and pass that model on to your sons and daughters so they can see what a successful human being is really about.

Do not lose sight of the wonderful variation with which life provides us. The animals, the flowers, and the rocks reflect enormous diversity. Each is beautiful and useful in its own right. So, too, are each of our children — a blessing to be protected, encouraged, and released to fly on his or her own.

Know that you've done a good job when your teen doesn't *need* you any more to get by in life but feels good about himself and is on his way to finding his own fit.

Appendix
ADD Organizations

National ADDA (Adult Attention Deficit Disorder Association)
P.O. Box 972
Mentor, OH 44061
(800) 487-2282

AIEN (Adult Information Exchange Network)
P.O. Box 1701
Ann Arbor, MI 48106
(313) 426-1659

CHADD (Children and Adults with ADD)
499 NW 70th Avenue, Suite 308
Plantation, FL 33317
(305) 587-3700

LDA (Learning Disabilities Association of America)
4156 Library Road
Pittsburgh, PA 15234
(412) 341-1515

AUTHOR

A nationally recognized authority on Attention Deficit Disorder, Lynn Weiss, Ph.D., was a practicing psychotherapist for thirty years and a radio talk show host and television commentator for a decade. She has written seven books on the topics of child development, emotional power, and ADD. The mother of an ADD son, she discovered as an adult that she, too, is ADD. Her firsthand experience contributes to her down-to-earth style of writing, which has made her a best-selling author on the subject of ADD in teens and adults.

Lynn says, "Life is my workshop as I strive to sharpen my self-awareness and live what I teach. Imparting what I've learned and observed is paramount to educate and change attitudes about behavior."

Her own children grown, her current mission is to pass on to the next generations what she's learned through writing, consulting, training, and living.

Lynn lives in central Texas.

Do I have ADD too?

If your teen has been diagnosed with ADD, you
may be wondering if you have ADD too.
After all, isn't ADD genetic?

If you're asking these kinds of questions, *Adult
ADD* can help. It identifies, explains, and dispels
the myths surrounding this disorder.
Adult ADD also examines the symptoms of ADD
and gives a reasonable method for diagnosis,
while emphasizing the importance of being professionally tested. And it explores a variety of treatment options and provides practical help for
overcoming ADD difficulties.

Written especially for adults who suffer from ADD,
this book works with the reader—providing
highlighted summaries and true stories to illustrate
the information. A valuable resource, *Adult ADD*
also brings a better understanding of adult ADD to
professional caregivers and the families, friends,
and coworkers of ADD sufferers.

***Adult ADD: A Reader-Friendly Guide to
Identifying, Understanding, and Treating
Adult Attention Deficit Disorder***
(Thomas A. Whiteman, PhD and
Michele Novotni, PhD)
Paperback / 0-89109-906-9